D1784346

Real Property, Real People, *un*Real Profits

Reno Kings
Geoff Doidge and Paul Eslick

Edited by Kerry Davies

Real Property Productions

RENO
KINGS

First published in 2004 by Real Property Productions Pty Ltd
PO Box 3141, Norman Park Qld 4170 Australia
Phone: 1300 550 656 Fax: 1300 137 073
email: info@renos.com.au
website: www.renos.com.au

Project Manager and Editor: Kerry Davies
Designer: Tim Bateman, Choice Creative
Cover Photographer: Heather Faulkner

Printed in Australia by Print Works, Brisbane

© Real Property Productions Pty Ltd 2004

All rights reserved. No part of this publication may be reproduced, stored in a retrieval system
or transmitted in any form or by any means without the prior written consent of the publisher.

National Library of Australia Cataloguing-in-Publication Data:

Reno Kings.
Real property, real people, unreal profits.

Bibliography.
Includes index.
ISBN 0 9756898 0 0.

1. Real property - Australia. 2. Real estate investment -
Australia. I. Doidge, Geoff. II. Eslick, Paul. III.
Davies, Kerry. IV. Title.

332.63240994

Disclaimer

The information, statements and opinions expressed in this publication are only intended as a guide
to some of the important considerations to be taken into account relating to property investment.
Although we believe that the statements are correct, they should not be taken to represent accounting,
taxation, legal or investment advice and you must obtain your own independent advice from an
appropriately qualified professional.

Neither the publisher nor any people or organisations involved in the preparation of this material give
any guarantees about its content or accept any liability for any loss, damage or other consequences
that may arise as a result of any person acting on or using the information and opinions contained
in this publication.

Contents

A pearl of wisdom

Life is a bit like a jigsaw. Everyone starts with more or less the same pieces. An education, perhaps a degree, then a job, a car, spouse, children, pets, a home (even if rented). Our jigsaw was complete, but then we entered the world of property investing. Lots of new pieces have been added – assets, cashflow, personal banker, solicitor, accountant, real estate agents, property managers, local councils, seminars, forums, gurus, books, books and more books, renovations, repairs, maintenance, areas, suburbs, cities, hundreds of points of view, more properties, larger numbers, bigger cashflow, equity and debt.

The puzzle grows as new pieces are added and the pace quickens, with more problems, more opportunities. Work on the problems and the solutions appear. Like a jigsaw, the larger it gets the more pieces can be added. We have some of the pieces that others do not have and they have some we do not have.

I like this world of investing and try to make intelligent decisions that open up more opportunities. A problem is often the doorway to an opportunity. Solving a problem leads to understanding, sharing information provides guidance and feedback, and allows us to determine if we're on the road to somewhere or the road to nowhere. Errors of judgement and failures happen but help show you where not to go. Don't get upset or disheartened; clear your mind, undo the error and get back on the path.

Hopefully you'll find eventual freedom from money problems and be able to live and do the things that will make life happier and more rewarding for you.

Les Irwin, property investor

Les and Brenda Irwin's story begins on page 65.

Foreword

When Paul and Geoff first approached me about writing the foreword for this book, at first I was a bit hesitant. Over the years I have been asked by so many people to have some level of "involvement" with them. I have always remained deliberately aloof from other property "experts", mainly because you can never be sure about their credentials. And, so far, this blanket policy has served me well, protecting me at those times when some of the more colourful characters have had their empires come crashing down around them.

But there has always been something about Geoff and Paul that I have really liked! Call it female intuition if you wish, but I have always just felt right being around them. They exude not only enthusiasm and a requisite amount of wit, but I feel they both possess a genuine desire to see people gain real benefit from their own experiences and advice. They are great educators and smart guys, and I think they really are members of the very small club of honest and down-to-earth people in this industry.

I love the stories they have chosen to share with you in these pages. Reading them motivated me all over again, and I don't usually need motivating! I immediately went out and bought three properties. What I like most about each and every one of these accounts is that they are about real people achieving real things. There is no smoke and mirrors. No complicated strategies that require you to take advantage of others and undertake risky or potentially illegal activities. No tax loopholes that may at some time in the future be closed. And certainly nothing underhanded.

Mel, Graham and Monique, Mark, Brenda and Les, Paul and Jenny, Elin, and Scott and Sandie all simply did what anyone can do, anytime – they took a big, deep breath and they took a chance – as did Paul and Geoff. They pushed the envelope just a little. They set goals for their future that they weren't assured of achieving, and look what happened – they all not only made it, but they ended up achieving more than they thought possible!

Getting ahead is about taking calculated risks. It's about having confidence in yourself and about wanting a better life than the average person gets. It's about hard work and determination. It has nothing to do with luck, good looks or unfair advantage, nor does it have to be about being unethical in any way.

Getting ahead is about starting today. Stop making excuses, take a leaf out of this book and follow the pathways set for you by these everyday, yet inspiring individuals, including Geoff and Paul, the Reno Kings. Work out what suits you best in terms of strategy and give it everything you have got. Aim for the stars and you just may hit the treetops!

And remember what I always say – another day you wait is another day you'll waste!

Margaret Lomas

Margaret Lomas is a financial advisor who has published several bestselling books about positive-cashflow property, all listed in the recommended reading list on pages 232–33. Margaret can be contacted through her website: www.edestiny.com.au

Preface

A few times a year we walk to the front of a workshop and in those first moments see the faces looking at us. We wonder what they are thinking. Some are obviously excited, eyes open wide and shining, keen to begin the journey. Some are torn between expectancy, anticipation and some doubt. Others are worried. They have saved long and hard just to be here. Will this work? Can I do this?

Then there are the "old dogs" who already have a number of properties. They do know the lifetime value of just one good idea. They see this as an investment. They will get their good idea, which they will twist and turn to suit their situation, and use and reuse for the rest of their investing lives.

All the people in this book have, at one time, been one of those faces.

Property has been so rewarding to us, we want to tell everyone that there is an alternative to selling your time to the false god Work. We found out many years ago that you can't work your way to wealth. For many people, life is a roof over their head, a car and a pension 40 years down the track.

Well let's shout it out. It doesn't have to be that way. All the "faces" have had their challenges, with disappointments, divorce, demotion and health scares aplenty. Some have been ripped off by smooth property marketers. They all have one thing in common. For things to change they've had to change.

They've all tried things out. If it worked, well, it may even have just been luck, but they're all now equipped with the lessons of others' mistakes and their own accumulated experience, and they have acquired both knowledge and skill. We are all privileged to receive the benefits of this knowledge and experience.

We, the people in this book, all have different strategies. We all have developed our niches. The exciting thing is that there is no one way to financial independence. There are many. This book reveals the individual people behind those faces. They are real people using real experience to build major property portfolios and make *un*real profits. As you read on, put yourself in their shoes and imagine yourself doing what they are doing and how maybe, just maybe, you could change your life to be what you want to be.

This book, *Real Property, Real People, unReal Profits*, is your property street directory, with a choice of "roads less travelled" by novice investors but well travelled by those who know the lie of the land.

The Reno Kings
Geoff Doidge and Paul Eslick

Acknowledgements

Geoff Doidge and Paul Eslick thank:

Our contributors, for sharing their strategies, skills and inspiration: Graham and Monique Bond, Scott and Sandie Elsom, Mark Galvin, Brenda and Les Irwin, Melanie MacDonald, Elin Power, and Paul and Jenny Roberts.

Also, for their support, Robyn Baranowskyj, and Steve Blaby of Real Property Productions Pty Ltd; for technical assistance, Richard Clarke of Horwath (Brisbane) and Margaret Lomas of Destiny Financial Solutions Pty Ltd; and our production team, Tim Bateman of Choice Creative and Kerry Davies of Kerry Davies Publishing Services.

We also thank the families of all those involved for their patience and understanding during the period in which this idea became a reality.

The publisher is pleased to advise that your investment in this book will help others to achieve. The Reno Kings and the contributors feel it is important that something from this project be given back to the community. So we've decided that not less than 10% of the net proceeds of the book will be donated to a worthy charitable organisation.

Brief versions of these stories were originally published in *Australian Property Investor* magazine (www.apimagazine.com.au). Republished here with permission.

No money down

Melanie MacDonald describes herself as "a bit of a capitalist hippy". She's made a million, lost it, and made it again. And her strategy? "Bite off more than you can chew and chew like crazy."

As a novice investor Melanie made all the mistakes we might expect of a 21-year-old setting out to buy her first property. But somehow, with a bit of luck, plenty of persistence and a tonne of guts, she turned error into strategy and became one of New Zealand's youngest property millionaires, only to lose the lot four years later.

But don't worry, it'd take more than the life-shattering loss of a fortune to keep young Melanie down. She made it all back again just a few years later, and has kept it this time.

This has got to be a lesson in how not to do things. Or maybe it's a lesson in the advantages of naivety, or the exuberance of youth, or maybe we're simply looking at the profile of a "natural investor". It seems Melanie has tried on just about every form of buying property with "no money down", without even knowing she was doing it.

Meet Melanie MacDonald

The seminar presenter Mel stumbled across could have been a wise financial adviser; he could have been an exceptional teacher and maker of fledgling millionaires. He could also have been a one-time real estate salesman and some-time insurance broker who had the gift of the gab and liked to make a bit on the side.

House #1, age 21: Just like in the seminar

Melanie saw the ad: "How to Make A MILLION $$ in *Real Estate* with NO MONEY DOWN!!!", attended the seminar and was blown away.

"He told us we could 'make a mint' by buying a large block with a rundown house, renovating the house, subdividing the block. I knew

I could do that and off I went to find the property," Melanie says. "I checked the real estate in the newspaper on the way home from the seminar and went to a local agent who had 'just the perfect place'. It was a big block and the house, he said, was a 'handyman's dream'. When I saw the property I was euphoric. It was just like in the seminar."

The daughter of teachers, Melanie had learned to trust those given the task of leading others. She was also too shy to ask questions, of either the seminar presenter or the selling agent, and expose her ignorance.

"Someone was living in the house and I didn't know I was allowed to look inside. The agent finally convinced me I was allowed to and I had a tentative look. I thought it had such potential – rotting carpet, no stove – and I said I'd take it."

The property had been on the market for a good while (and for good reason) and the surprised agent was only too willing to do the deal. Within an hour Mel was "stitched up" and the contract countersigned. Now it was time to pay up the 10% deposit, as per the contract.

"What deposit?" Mel innocently enquired. The agent patiently, though with rising alarm, explained the terms of the contract Mel had signed.

"I don't remember them saying that at the seminar," Mel thought, aghast at the fact that she had taken the seminar's "no money down" quite literally, and had absolutely no cash.

What do we do now?

The agent took some pity on her and agreed to amend the contract to allow for a $200 deposit only, but on the basis that the contract was made unconditional. She would have to buy the property regardless of whether the banks considered her worthy of a loan. Mel's job as an industrial chemist earned her $14,000 per annum, which wasn't bad for a first job in 1980s New Zealand, and she had no doubt that she'd succeed. That's what it was all about, surely: get a job, buy a house.

When the first bank told Mel they'd only loan her 80% of the purchase price Mel was shocked. "They obviously hadn't been to the seminar and didn't know about the 'no money down' concept," says Mel. At the next bank, when Mel ticked the box for Ms, as opposed to Mrs or Miss, on the application, she heard a loud, "Oh you're one of those are you? We don't lend to *those*." Rude shock number two. Well, it was the 1980s.

The third banker hadn't been to the seminar either, it seems, and also didn't know about "no money down", but they were willing to lend the money, though still only 80% of the purchase price, on the understanding that part of the block would be sold off and the house would be renovated to add value.

In fact, on Melanie's reckoning the bank shouldn't have given her a loan at all, as the repayments on the mortgage, with the interest rate at a whopping 23% (remember, 1980s New Zealand), actually exceeded her gross income, even taking into account the $150 a week rent she was planning on charging her future tenants. It seems some banks in the 1980s weren't particularly rigorous with their sums.

Scraping it together

The purchase price was $96,000. Mel needed $19,200 cash (double the $9,600 deposit that had just started to seem not entirely impossible) on top of the 80% bank loan. She rushed home to desperately try to raise the money. She applied for, and was granted, several credit cards (these were heady days), begged her parents, who were able to come up with $1000, as their daughter was "being responsible" for a change, but she was still $13,000 short.

At her wit's end Melanie turned to the seminar presenter. "I thought I must have been doing something wrong," says Mel. He was taken aback to say the least. "You did what? We don't expect you to go out and actually do what we say straight away! But, hey, for a person who didn't have a clue what she was doing, you've done really well."

Mel sat embarrassed and more than a little worried as he pointed out the legal implications of what she had done. "Where else can I get some money?" she pleaded. "I'm sure I've bought a great deal and I'll be able to pay it back when I sell off part of the block."

To the credit of the presenter, he didn't dump Mel. He introduced her to his solicitor, who willingly agreed to advance the shortfall on condition that the land would be subdivided and part of the block sold to repay the debt, plus interest of 27%.

"Whew," said Mel, "I'm saved. Now all I have to do is fix up the house, get some tenants, sell off the block and I'm on my way." Just a couple of things, and it was virtually no money down.

The nightmare begins

Eventually settlement day arrived and Melanie went to "fix up" the house, taking along the bunch of flowers the agent had given her. When you're excited about something, you often have to look at it for the second or third time before you see it in reality's harsh light. Well, Mel opened the door and her world fell in a heap.

"It was a pigsty, it was a hovel, it was a hole. I couldn't believe that I had just bought the place. It was my absolute worst nightmare come monstrously to life. I dropped the pathetic bunch of flowers and just crumpled."

A little later some of her friends came over to celebrate her new home. They were shocked to see the state of the property and one very distressed Melanie. "Come on Mel," they said. "Let's get started; there's a lot to do." They got stuck into cleaning out the muck. There were seven layers of wallpaper to be stripped, and half the carpet was rotten and stank to high heaven. Thank goodness for friends.

The psycho, the stripper and the bridesmaid

Melanie moved in and she and her mates started to clean up the place, but in the meantime Mel had to find two tenants to help pay the mortgage (she'd figured three people sharing the house was enough). The first instalment was due in six weeks. The house was still pretty much a hovel so she couldn't be too choosy in her tenant selection, or maybe it was just plain inexperience that she didn't do any background checks, barely even asked their surnames.

Tenant #1 was a quiet guy, a bit introspective, but Mel thought quiet was a plus, as long as he paid the rent. Tenant # 2, a woman about her own age, was a little more outgoing. Mel was pleased to be on her way at last. Then things went a little pear-shaped. Tenant #1 started to change, doing and saying strange things.

"It got quite scary," Mel says, even more so when she found out he had escaped from his last residence, the security section of the local psychiatric hospital. "As the medication wore off the 'mouse' became a 'lion', a total change of personality. Eventually the hospital tracked him down and he was taken away."

Tenant #2 kept Melanie entertained with stories of her ex-boyfriend, apparently a travelling male stripper. Whenever he performed in the local area the "outgoing" flatmate would turn up wearing what very closely resembled a taffeta bridesmaid's dress.

"Just a bit of harmless stalking," thought Mel, not about to lose her second tenant. She stayed through the renovation and beyond, then ran up a big international phone bill and skipped town a few months later.

Reno Kings Tip

Ah, the joys of being a lessor and minder of tenants. After Geoff experienced his first tenants (the bikies) he discovered that cutting corners on tenant selection is a disaster. You might save a couple of weeks rent by signing a less than satisfactory tenant but you will regret it as you spend 80% of your time trying to get the rent, cleaning up after them and listening to their tales of woe. You would happily pay back that money you saved to just get them out of your world. Careful tenant selection is the key to a peaceful life.

The $500 renovation

Back to the nitty-gritty of the real world, the renovations still had to be completed and were to be funded with the measly $500 remaining on Mel's brand-spanking-new credit cards. She and her mates would have to do it all themselves and do it "on the cheap".

"We hired a sander and sanded the floors ourselves. We painted the kitchen cupboards and fitted new knobs. The stove was basically stuffed, so I bought a similar one for $5 at auction and scavenged enough parts to make one working unit," says Mel.

An electrician friend checked the wiring, which was passable. No plumber was available so Melanie learned new skills in the kitchen, bathroom and laundry. The antique bath was a sad shadow of its former self and needed major restoration, which Mel couldn't afford. So she and her mates hauled it to the local panel beater, who repaired and professionally enamelled it for $20.

They polished the floors and they cleaned and scrubbed and painted everything in sight. Gradually the place started to gleam, even to show a little character.

The subdivision

Meanwhile Mel had approached the council to subdivide the block. She needed approval to subdivide within six weeks so that she could pay the first mortgage instalment with the proceeds, as well as repaying the solicitor his $13,000 plus interest. Bad news: subdivision would take at least six months, meaning Mel would be in default. She had no other way to repay that first hefty instalment.

Now here is a secret. When you hit the wall there is always another way; you just have to find it. You can go through it, you can go over it or you can go around it. Mel went around it.

Mel discovered a process called cross-leasing (only available in New Zealand), which is a little like strata titling on a unit complex. There is shared ownership over the whole block but each owner has exclusive use of their own portion. And, as it required a lesser degree of planning approval, it would only take four weeks.

Using this little-known strategy she received title for the separate block only two days before the mortgage was due. She had to sell and sell fast. She placed the block on the market with the estate agent and sold it for $25,000, immediately. Guess who bought it? The agent! He knew it was a bargain and snapped it up. She believes it was probably worth closer to $35,000 (though she was still so inexperienced she didn't even know what a valuation was) but she didn't care.

On to the next hurdle. To release the title of the new block and sell it to the agent she needed the bank to lift the mortgage on that portion of land. The bank said that selling the block would give less security and therefore they needed a $25,000 repayment or extra security for her loan.

Uh oh. Melanie had no spare cash and no other equity. Mel had to get creative (yet again). "I couldn't very well tell them I needed the cash to repay the mortgage, could I?" So she told them she needed it to do the renovations, even though they were now pretty much going to be completed for the $500 she'd set aside on credit. The bank agreed she could keep some of the sale price, writing it into her loan agreement, and Mel gave them $10,000 back.

The solicitor was happy to wait for the sale of the house for his repayment – at 27% interest he should have been happy. Eventually the bank insisted on revaluing the property. The "renovation" had increased the value of the property by $15,000, despite losing a third of the land, so it well and truly covered the bank loan and allowed her sufficient equity to do it all again. Whew!

The numbers

The last figure here, 80% of the revaluation, is in excess of the original loan of $76,800, which means the bank has sufficient security and Mel has enough money to repay the solicitor.

Wow, what a learning curve. We suggest no one does what Mel did, or in the way she did it, lurching from crisis to crisis. She did scramble out of the "black hole", but it was a close call and all so preventable, with just a bit of knowledge.

They say the journey of a lifetime starts with the first step. With the purchase of this property Melanie MacDonald had just begun the first step of what is one of the most amazing stories in property investment we have ever heard.

Here is how Mel managed this first property on "no money down".

Cash deposit (borrowed)	$200	
Parents (borrowed)	$1,000	
Credit cards (x 4)	$5,000	
Solicitor's loan	$13,000	at 27% interest
Bank loan	$76,800	at 21% interest
Purchase price	$96,000	
Renovations (credit card)	$500	at 27% interest
Land sold	$25,000	
Repay bank	$10,000	
Net	$15,000	
Revalue renovated property	$110,000	
80% of new value	$88,000	

It worked for me

After that first nightmare Melanie ended up buying a bunch more houses, mostly with no money down.

"It worked for me, so I just kept doing it," says Mel. I thought I'd invented the idea. I didn't go to another seminar for quite some time so I didn't realise that there were other people who bought property this way. About four years later I discovered that there were books and seminars about this stuff. Amazing."

Employer-supported buying: House #2, age 23

By 1989 Mel had married and the newlyweds moved to her home town in the North Island, Mel taking up a position with a pulp and paper mill there. The company was phasing out staff housing by selling its properties to staff members, and there was a lengthy waiting list.

"The job was fine, the marriage wasn't, and when we split up the housing officer took pity on me and moved me to the top of the buy-out list," says Mel. "The asking price was $7000 and it was financed totally out of my salary. The company even spent about $12,000 putting in aluminium windows and a new kitchen and bathroom, and completely refurbishing it before they sold it to me."

The house was revalued at $42,000 and when Mel left 18 months later it rented for $110 per week. That may not sound like much but it's a staggering 82% per annum return on the $7000 purchase cost and gave a 14% return on the new valuation, which produced a 500% capital gain.

The cancer scare (and houses #3 and 4)

Mel soon met the "perfect man" and fell in love. Life was a bed of roses. Then one day she felt unwell and went to her doctor. He did tests and called her back in.

"The doc told me I had cancer but not to worry, as 40% of people detected with this cancer at this stage survived for five years. What I heard was that 60% die within five years, so I went home to do just that. Some people are noble and heroic; I wasn't. I just cried."

Melanie called over her two best girlfriends and drank. She didn't go to work or get dressed ("Why bother?"), instead simply holding her own "wake". The mother of one of her friends dropped by to find out what was going on.

"I explained that as I was dying we were planning to drink till I went. 'Get up,' she said, throwing a few curly ones at me like 'Only the good die young,' and 'Don't you know you can't kill a weed?' So I did as I was told and, after treatment, was well again within 18 months."

This scare did not slow Mel down; in fact it had the opposite effect. She felt like she was in a hurry. In hindsight she says this was probably the best and most important thing that ever happened to her, as she realised life is short and not to be wasted.

Melanie's purchasing history.

Description	Date purch	Purchase price	Reno or subdivision costs	Total costs	Loan amount	Current value	Year sold	Sale price	Comment
#1 Mt Maunganui NZ 4 brm	1987	$96,000	$500	$96,500			1988	$135,000	Subdivision; house sold after market crash
#2 Tokoroa NZ 3 brm	1989	$7,000		$7,000			1996	$28,000	Employer funded
#3 Pahiatua NZ 3 brm	1989	$52,000		$52,000			1995	$35,000	Forced sale under value due to court settlement
#4 Palmerston North NZ 3 brm	1989	$81,000		$81,000			1995	$96,000	
#5 Palmerston North NZ 2 brm	1990	$84,000	$1,200	$85,200			1995	$95,000	Vendor financed; trsf to ex
#6 Pahiatua NZ 3 brm	1990	$38,000		$38,000			1995	$32,000	Forced sale under value to clear debt
#7 Palmerston North NZ 3 brm	1991	$90,000	$15,000	$105,000			1995	$110,000	Subdivision; trsf to ex
#8 Palmerston North NZ 3 brm	1992	$175,000	$1,500	$176,500			1993	$210,000	Rent to buy
#9 Nundah Brisbane 1 brm	Aug-99	$48,000		$48,000			2002	$75,000	Trsf to next ex
#10 Nundah Brisbane 2 brm	Feb-02	$140,000	$5,000	$145,000	$124,000	$280,000	held		
#11 Albion warehouse	Aug-02	$235,000	$7,000	$242,000	$195,000	$600,000	held		
Total		$1,046,000	$30,200	$1,076,200	$319,000	$880,000		$816,000	
LVR					36%				

Melanie took action. Over that year she bought houses #3 and #4, still with no money down, as it "seemed a good idea not to pay deposits".

Vendor finance: House #5, age 24

Then in late 1989 she discovered that a couple of workmates were desperate to sell their house. They'd renovated the place but gutted and not replaced the kitchen.

"Would you believe they wanted to wait so the new buyer could choose their own kitchen colours? Of course no one bought it as people don't have that much imagination and can't see past 'There is no kitchen in this house!' They couldn't sell and I didn't have much cash so I offered them an antique wardrobe, a fridge and my wrecked car as a deposit.

The car had been stolen and crashed and then returned with a cheque by the insurance company. The husband was a panel beater so he was pretty happy with that."

In addition to the deposit being comprised of goods and chattels (just one method of "no money down"), this was a prime example of vendor finance, not that Mel knew that's what she was negotiating at the time. She got her workmates (the vendors) to agree that $15,000 of the purchase price would not be payable for five years, which meant she only had to borrow 80% of the valuation from the bank and was within their lending criteria.

"Again, I thought I'd invented vendor finance at that point. I didn't know people had done it before."

Mel paid $86,000 in total (including goods) for the house and it was valued at $96,000 once the kitchen was installed, which was paid for by the vendor, with no money down. It rented for $180 per week. This is creative financing at its best. She created a $10,000 capital gain and a 10.9% rental return on a property bought with furniture and a written-off car! What an amazing use of deteriorating, non-income-producing items to purchase an income-producing house.

Rent to buy: House #8 age 26

Mel had bought a few more houses by 1991 (houses #6 and #7 were both bought for market value but were on large subdividable blocks), including one on a rent-to-buy basis. It was really outside her price range but Mel was keen to do something a little different.

"It seems I'd always bought hovels in not-so-great areas and I wanted to own a nice house in a nice area for a change," Mel explains.

She persuaded the vendors to give her an unconditional contract with no deposit and a 12-month settlement for $175,000. It was a lovely house in a nice area.

"It's amazing what asking can do!" says Mel. "I had to sell another house before I could buy it but I was happy to move in right away. Their house was empty so it suited them too."

Then she rented it from them for $300 per week for that year. She got flatmates in and did some basic renovations. All rent was credited toward the purchase price and Mel resold the house before her purchase of it was even settled (she had inserted a clause allowing her to bring settlement forward if need be).

"I made a quick 20%, $33,500 after the reno cost, and didn't actually have to part with any money," says Mel, though she did have to give up the "nice" house.

Over three years Mel had accumulated ten properties, including two additional blocks of land hived off from house #7 at a cost of $15,000. The net worth was about $1,040,000, or about $2.5 million in today's values, and most of these houses were bought on one form or other of "no money down".

Another brilliant career

Just before she bought house #8, in late 1991 Mel was telling her story to some friends in a restaurant and was overheard by someone who turned out to be on the committee of the New Zealand Property Investors Association (PIA). He was no doubt impressed, and asked her to tell the story at their annual conference.

"I was terrified of public speaking after being laughed off the stage as a 14-year-old in a school speech contest talking about birdwatching as a fascinating hobby. I decided I had to overcome my fear. At 25 I was now the laboratory manager in a dairy factory with 30 staff reporting to me and I couldn't even run a meeting."

Melanie dressed in a respectable cream sweatshirt and pink canvas skirt but had not thought about fronting up to a room full of middle-aged male "suits" (about 200 of them). All the other speakers wore black.

"All of a sudden I realised I couldn't do it and ran off to the ladies loo to throw up. White-faced and shaking, I told the organiser quite seriously, 'I'm sick and I'm going home.' He just said. 'Aaah, you'll be all right,' and headed to the stage to introduce me. I felt obliged to stay to save him embarrassment."

Mel clung to the lectern in utter terror as she spoke. Then something amazing happened. When she finished there was absolute silence.

"I got the first standing ovation of the day, followed by lots of backslapping and hugs from the audience, who had sat quiet and immobile though all the previous presentations. All I could think was, 'I didn't die after all.'"

Come hell or high water

Soon afterward Melanie was runner-up in the Business Woman of the Year awards as the youngest technical manager of a pharmaceutical company and the first woman in the position, as well as for her community contribution chairing the housing trust of a welfare group. Invitations to speak to various groups rolled in. She was also invited to speak again to the PIA the following year.

Then, literally, her roof caved in. She had no idea how things were about to change. On the way to deliver her speech she crashed her Jag XJ6 and, of course, she had forgotten to pay the insurance bill the previous week.

"It was the first of several examples of dropping the ball I displayed over the next few months. I drove the car off a 10 m cliff and landed leaving a head-shaped bulge in the car roof. All I could think of was that I'd be late for my seminar."

After climbing back up the cliff Mel hitchhiked to the seminar, did the talk with a shocking headache, then threw up.

"I had forgotten I'd given the talk and started telling friends I had crashed the car, obviously not seriously enough though. At the end of the day when I asked them for a lift, they didn't know why. When I told them the car was at the bottom of a cliff they were stunned. They thought I'd scratched the car, not crashed it.

"The hospital found I had a cracked skull and a bleeding brain (some say that explains a bit). After temporary memory loss and a strange loss of maths skills, thankfully also temporary, I recovered completely."

Melanie overcame her fears and enjoyed public speaking so much she decided to become a trainer. "In those days I didn't understand the difference, from the student's point of view, between being a presenter (wow, she is really clever) and a trainer (wow, I have learned a lot)." This was a conceptual difference that was to prove invaluable to Mel later.

We can't stress this enough

In 1992, at 26 years old, Mel was working in management, still in the manufacturing sector, and planned to retire at 30. She had $1 million in assets, the perfect man was still being perfect and she was on top of the world. But life was busy, very busy.

"I was working pretty much seven days a week, and really keeping the pressure on myself," says Mel. "I didn't even notice what was happening. Forgetting to pay bills and neglecting family and social responsibilities were sure indicators and I should have picked up on that. I realise now I was becoming a corporate lunatic. It was a classic case of burnout."

Corporate stress and unrealistic self-expectation led to relationship stress, which led to feelings of neglect, which led to him having an affair, which finally led to an explosion.

"I broke up with the 'perfect man' and we spent the next two years fighting in court. I lost almost everything. Out of the ten properties I owned there were just three left after the relationship break-up. Four went to him, three went to pay the lawyers and I was left with the rejects."

Even though only a couple of the houses were in joint names, Mel's former partner placed a caveat over all the properties, which meant that she couldn't buy, sell or negotiate. Her assets were frozen. When the caveat was lifted she was forced to sell properties at less than market value.

"This is what happens when emotions are running high," Mel understands now. "The only ones to gain are the lawyers."

Mel gave up public speaking after this. "I felt I had no credibility. No one liked a loser, least of all myself."

The depths: From $1 million to $100

In 1995 Mel had a gross worth of $100 ("on a good day," she adds. "No debts, no assets"). She realised her heart wasn't in her job and she began thinking again about starting her own training business.

"I got a real buzz out of motivating people and I also realised I was sick of the technical side of my work," says Mel. "I had come up through the ranks as an industrial chemist and was moved into management with an expectation that I'd be good at dealing with people and dealing with the responsibility of management."

In Mel's case that expectation was probably not far from the truth. Mel is good with people and she's certainly proved she can crunch the numbers. But she felt that there must be a hell of a lot of other good technicians, scientists and engineers out there who were being thrown into deep water as managers, without any real preparation. An idea was beginning to dawn.

"I got a job with an international training company so I could learn the business. This took me to Australia, which was terrific experience. The company had a Melbourne office and they sent me to do some consultancy work in Brisbane in July. The Brisbane winter was glorious, the people were relaxed and friendly – there were palm trees – I was determined to stay."

The company had other ideas, though, and weren't keen on Melanie basing in Brisbane. She accepted consultancy work with them all over Australia, from Brisbane to Perth, and lived like a gypsy in hotel rooms and friends' spare rooms, still considering Brisbane as her base.

"I was at a bit of a loose end one day and attended a property workshop being given by one of the Reno Kings. We shared stories and so started a very educational friendship."

Managing at a distance

Mel was working in Australia when she got a call from the bank asking why the mortgages on two of her three houses had not been paid for six months. It turned out one of her property managers had allegedly been pocketing the rent. The agency said it was not their problem as they didn't know what their now "former employee" was up to.

"I should have fought them but I was too far away and too tired of solicitors to sue, so I sold two houses to pay the loan arrears. I was then left with my last house but still getting no rent, even with a different agent." When Mel called them to ask why, they said they couldn't get a tenant, and she hit the roof.

"For six months? Are you people imbeciles?" She flew back to find a new manager and check out the situation personally. She arrived at her last remaining treasure to face metre-high lawns and vandalised windows. She talked to the neighbourhood children.

"The children said they lived next door with Daddy, who they explained was 'the President', and that 'the Headquarters' were in the house on the other side of mine. Looking at children and neighbourhood I suspected we were not talking Rotary."

Mel had discovered why the house was vacant. "They were prominent members of a well-known gang." Mel decided the house wouldn't rent and no one in their right mind would buy it, so there was only one thing to do.

"I knocked on the door and offered it to 'the President'. He bought the house from me for cash – literally, folding stuff, on the spot. It was just enough to cover what I still owed."

It was a real watershed. Melanie realised that her dream to retire at 30 was finished (she'd just turned 32). But more than that, she realised she needed her life back.

"I left a job that earned me $1200 per day consulting for one earning $12 per day teaching scuba diving in Vanuatu for three months. That's a 99% pay reduction, but you know I had infinitely less stress and more joy in the latter. I had discovered diving years earlier but hadn't given time to it in recent years. I absolutely love diving. What else can I say? I hope I die underwater when I am 100 years old. I've made a resolution to dive once per fortnight and have almost stuck to it. My happiest moments are diving, almost better than buying a house unconditionally without knowing how you will get the finance."

The Melbourne phase

The training company Mel worked for lured her back after her Pacific break, offering her a two-month stint in the United States. Again, terrific experience. Returning to Melbourne she met "perfect man number two". It was enough to shake off the Brisbane longing so she moved to Melbourne to work in the head office.

"I lasted about three minutes in the office environment, having enjoyed the freedom of consultancy work for three years."

Mel thought again about that idea of her own training company and resigned to set up the Line Management Institute of Training in mid-1998.

"With all of my clients in Brisbane, though, it meant a lot of commuting. The relationship started faltering and I eventually decided that some distance between us might help. I fled to Brisbane in mid-1999."

The ultimate home business: House #9

Melanie decided that this definitely felt like the right move. She bought a basic one-bedroom home unit in Nundah, a northern suburb of Brisbane that was starting to come good in the property market. This was home and office while the business was still young.

"I had gone through the Reno Kings to research the area and they said it was a future 'hotspot' and indicated it would be a steal under $50,000.

It obviously was, because the agent laughed at me when I made the offer," says Mel, "but after doing the negotiation 'dance' we settled at $48,000. That humble unit became the birthplace of the Line Management Institute of Training. I kept the copier on the stove. The office took up the living room and I lived happily in the bedroom."

Melanie says it wasn't easy to drum up business to start with. The fledgling company relied on individual students paying a one-off $350 fee for a one-day course or corporate clients paying $1200 per day.

"The mortgage was only $270 per month so I only had to sell one day of training per month to survive. But I was still afraid of getting into debt again, after being burned with my houses. I had been in the habit of catching taxis but disciplined myself to take public transport for the first 18 months (another Reno Kings tip!)"

The business started to pick up but the relationship stayed on a steady downhill slide. When she moved out of the unit she rented it out for $115 per week (12.4% yield) and recently sold it as part of a settlement to that same, now former, perfect man number two for $72,000 (more lessons).

Horns and hooters: The move to engineering

In late 2000 Mel's business was focusing on supervisory training work and she was doing some contract work in Melbourne for a medium-sized engineering manufacturing company with a turnover of about $30 million. Family feuding was forcing the company's sale.

"I was offered the opportunity to buy it but I felt it would be a conflict of interest so I declined." They kept asking so she eventually made "a silly offer" for one division.

"I offered $50,000 fully vendor financed, where they had wanted about $500,000 for that division alone. Another 'no money down' deal! I left it on the table and two days before their lease ran out they called and said, 'You can have it if you clear everything out of the factory by 5 pm Thursday.' This was 5 pm Tuesday."

Melanie ran around madly looking for factory space in Brisbane while the trucks were en route from Melbourne. She moved in the following Monday morning as the trucks rolled up.

"I gave myself tennis elbow trying to pull my weight unloading, followed by 16-hour days on the end of a screwdriver trying to catch up with $60,000 worth of orders that had come in unnoticed while the business was being packed up and sold. I have to admit, making industrial horns and hooters is something I hadn't seen coming, but the business became profitable again and I eventually transferred it to former perfect man number two to pay him out. (Note to self: More practice at judging perfect man needed; continue research.)"

Back into the house market: House #10

In December 2001 Mel decided to move into the Brisbane house market. It was one year into a boom.

"I saw a little fibro house in Nundah for $145,000 in the Saturday paper and went in to the agent at 10 am. It had already sold but the sale collapsed during the cooling-off period and the agent phoned me (always good to leave your number just in case).

"I paid $140,000 cash and spent one week and $7000 replacing the toilet, polishing floors (having removed carpets full of dog poo), painting the walls white and resurfacing the bathtub with a two-pot enamel treatment from the hardware store (this one didn't need a panel beater). I only used tradesmen for the new toilet and I did the rest with the help of friends. By 2004 it was worth about $270,000.

The warehouse: Property #11

In February 2002 Mel wanted new premises for the engineering business. She looked for about 12 months for something that could be a future warehouse conversion for residential development. She found one listed for sale by an "out of area" residential agent (she had previously been talking only to commercial agents).

She bought well, paying $235,000 for the empty building in Albion, just 4 km from the CBD, and spent $12,000 on the refurbishment. In 2004 it was valued at somewhere between $500,000 and $600,000 following changes to the city plan to allow residential development one year later. It is in the first street of light industry in a rapidly gentrifying near-city pocket. It's next to expensive residential property and opposite a park, so Mel is optimistic about future gain.

The upshot

Mel's training business now turns over more than $1 million, from zero seven years ago. She focuses on getting results for clients rather than profit-taking and spends most of the profit on growth. The business has moved premises three times as a result of underestimating growth and has now found premises to grow into, letting out part of it in the meantime.

The company has been commended by the Australian National Training Authority as one of the top providers of frontline management training in Australia and in 2004 made it into the top 400 Queensland companies.

This rollercoaster ride in property investment shows that even though you may start with nothing, investment success for all of us can be the result of finding and following your passion, mixed with knowledge, persistence and keeping the balance.

Here's how Melanie's properties compare.

Description	Case study #1 Mt Maunganui NZ, 4 brm	Case study #2 Tokoroa NZ, 3 brm	Case study #3 Pahiatua NZ, 3 brm	Case study #4 Palmerston North NZ, 3 brm	Case study #5 Palmerston North NZ, 2 brm	Case study #6 Pahiatua NZ, 3 brm	Case study #7 Palmerston North NZ, 3 brm	Case study #8 Palmerston North NZ, 3 brm
Date purchased	1987	1989	1989	1989	1990	1990	1991	1992
Purchase price	$96,000	$7,000	$52,000	$81,000	$84,000	$38,000	$90,000	$175,000
Reno or subdivision costs	$500	employer funded			$1,200		$15,000	$1,500
Total costs	$96,500	$7,000	$52,000	$81,000	$85,200	$38,000	$105,000	$176,500
Loan amount	$96,000	$7,000	$38,000	$65,000	$64,000	$32,000		
Rental pw at purchase	$150	$110	$120	$180			$180	$300
Yield at purchase	8.1%	81.7%	12.0%	11.6%			10.4%	8.9%
Rental pw at sale	$150	$120						$300
Yield at sale	8.1%	89.1%						8.8%
Year sold	1988	1996	1995	1995	1995	1995	1995	1993
Sale price	$135,000	$28,000	$35,000	$96,000	$95,000	$32,000	$110,000	$210,000
Capital gain	$39,000	$21,000	$(17,000)	$15,000	$11,000	$(6,000)	$20,000	$35,000

Yield at purchase=rent/purchase price   Yield at sale=rent/total cost   Capital gain=sale price-total cost

Description	Case study #9 Nundah unit, 1 brm	Case study #10 Nundah, 2 brm	Case study #11 Albion warehouse
Date purchased	Aug-99	Feb-02	Aug-02
Purchase price	$48,000	$140,000	$235,000
Reno or subdivision costs		$5,000	$7,000
Total costs	$48,000	$145,000	$242,000
Loan amount	$35,000	$124,000	$195,000
Rental pw at purchase	$110	$180	$646
Yield at purchase	11.9%	6.7%	14.3%
Rental pw at sale / current	$110	$185	$703
Yield at sale / current	11.9%	6.6%	15.1%
Year sold	2002	held	held
Sale price / current value	$75,000	$280,000	$600,000
Capital gain	$27,000	$140,000	$365,000

Yield at purchase=rent/purchase price   Yield at sale or current=rent/total cost
Capital gain=sale price or current value-total cost

The lessons

Mel has shown that you can blunder your way to success, but, take it from us, the better way is to get some training. Learn from others' mistakes. Above all, get started.

- *Look after your relationships as you would look after your business: divorce is a wealth destroyer.*

- *Invest in things to which you can add value.*

- *A successful business can be financially anchored by the assets of well-bought and value-added real estate.*

- *Mel's favourite: You don't have to use your own money.*

Reno Kings insights

What's your background

My parents were schoolteachers and I grew up in a small industrial town in New Zealand's North Island, to become an industrial chemist in my first incarnation.

Why did you get started?

I went to a seminar at age 21 and the "teacher" said it was possible.

What was your greatest fear?

Then, nothing. I was too ignorant to have any fears. Now, everything, including asking banks for money and not getting everything done in life that I want to fit in before I die.

Did your parents show you how to get started?

Not in business or property, as they had no experience; but definitely by raising me to love reading and to believe in my ability. Those two things can pretty much get you anywhere.

What was your greatest mistake?

Not paying attention to the little details. They get you every time. Taking too long to hire people to do the things I am not good at because I thought I couldn't afford to. In retrospect I couldn't afford not to.

What do you want to achieve?

I'm pretty ambitious I guess. I don't care about cars and things like that. It's about what I can do, not what I can have. I'm a bit of a capitalist hippy, if there is such a thing. I'm not a very materialistic person. I don't like shopping; my friends have to dress me. I think this whole marketing-driven culture we have, where to be successful and happy you have to buy more stuff and it has to have a label on it, is insane. I would much rather travel than buy stuff (except gadgets; I love gadgets).

To have my company in the Queensland 400 (did that in 2004) and to have my company in the BRW Fast 100 list of the fastest-growing private companies in Australia.

I'd love to have a talk show, and I want to be invited as the guest speaker at the end-of-year prizegiving at Tokoroa High School (after my final school report said, "It's such a shame about Melanie; she could have been successful if she had applied herself.")

And then to bugger off back to Vanuatu and scuba dive for the rest of my days.

How would you describe your strategy?

What strategy? Bite off more than you can chew and chew like crazy.

Any funny or bizarre experiences along the way?

My whole life! Apart from that, being stalked by my tenant, who turned out to be a Libyan terrorist and claimed to be in love with me; having a lawyer forget to settle on a property when I bought a unit in Brisbane and then tell me it wasn't his fault as the other lawyer should have called him to remind him; buying my first house with credit cards; having a shower in the dark in an open 400 sq m space because I'd installed the shower before the walls in the warehouse I'd bought for apartment conversion.

What's your best renovating and money-making tips?

Renovating tips

Polishing wooden floors is really easy if you are not looking for a perfect finish. If you are willing to do it yourself you can do an average house for under $200. Just use a nail punch to bang in any nails sticking up, hire a sander and try not to gouge the floors too badly with it, and after you've sanded tip a bucket or two of polyurethane upside down (in small doses) and mop the floor with a paint roller on a stick to spread it. Adds thousands to the value of the house.

You can make a bath look new for $45 by buying a two-pot enamel mix especially designed for baths, sanding the bath and applying it (instructions on the pack). It seriously looks new and it lasts really well.

There is a similar product to change the colour of bathroom tiles and refresh the whole room. Get a new toilet put in for a couple of hundred dollars and you have a whole new bathroom.

Money-making tips

Buy empty commercial buildings and get commercial tenants into them and have the place revalued. No renovating required and instant capital gain! You have to know a bit about what you're doing of course. Don't be like me and try this, just cause someone told you to, without learning how first.

Reno Kings Comment

Commercial buildings and leases are a whole new ball game. The "average" or inexperienced investor could get into serious trouble. Tenants are harder to get. They "go broke" more often. They may be harder to manage. When the economy recedes companies disappear. Research very carefully before entering this area. Yes, there are big profits for people who do commercial property well, but big risks for those who don't.

What would you do differently?

Learn to work with other people as partners. I see people who have successful alliances and they do so well. I know no woman is an island but I have never been brave enough to get into a business partnership with someone who is really switched on. I've had a couple of partners but they were there because I was in love with them at the time, not because they had any skills. I'd love to have a partner who was really smart. But I would probably drive them and myself nuts.

I love building businesses, but I plan to mix it in future with taking time off for diving, then come back and do the business thing again. Money to me is not the issue; I love the game and the buzz when you make a deal work.

How has your life changed since you began your property investment?

In every possible way. I was only a kid straight out of uni when I started, so I guess it would have changed anyway. But I have learned so much about myself, as well as the technical info. I wouldn't change it for anything. Although some days I might not say that. It has been the best and hardest thing I have ever done. I guess people who have kids probably say the same thing.

How do you picture yourself five years down the track?
Definitely still single (freedom to make my own decisions is so important to me). Responsible enough to get an indoor plant and keep it alive. Physically fitter than I am now. Either CEO of my own public company or diving in Vanuatu. Okay, so I'm a little conflicted about my goals. I don't do balance well.

> *Mel's current favourite quote: "If you are bitten by a dog three times, there is one thing that you can be sure of the third time. It ain't the dog's fault."*

Reno Kings Report

If you're thinking of buying commercial property contact the Reno Kings for our report, Tips and Traps of Commercial Property. See page 235 for details and how to order, or go to the website: www.renos.com.au

Finding a niche: Share housing

Graham and Monique Bond had dabbled in property for years but couldn't see their way clear to making any money, until they discovered their own investment niche providing affordable, quality share housing.

Finding your own niche in the property investment market is extremely important, even if it takes a while. It's about what works for you and your timeframe, and even how you feel, morally, about your investment.

One of the big lessons in investing in property is to understand, and then realise, the potential of your assets. Looking at what you've got and how you might improve it or change it can help to work out what your target should be and how you're going to reach it.

Some people fall into the property investment business almost by accident, so it can take a little longer to identify and reach that target. Something starts it off, perhaps an inheritance or a lucky chance, or even a niggling feeling that they should be buying property, but it's not quite enough, or thought through well enough, to really make a difference.

Meet Graham and Monique Bond

For Graham and Monique there had never been a grand plan for buying property. It was more something that happened to them along the way. By the late 1980s, then in their 40s, the Bonds had accumulated a modest property portfolio.

They had bought their own home at The Gap in Brisbane's inner west in 1977, on their return to Australia after seven years working in the UK. They also had a hobby farm in the hinterland of the Sunshine Coast, north of Brisbane, where they were gradually turning 4 ha of groundsel and lantana into a small plantation of eventually saleable cabinet and timber trees. In 1985 they purchased a block of two flats on the coast. The intention was to eventually retire to one flat and rent out the other for a little cashflow. It seemed like a reasonable plan for this energetic couple.

A recent addition had been a three-bedroom house in Fairfield, a southern suburb of Brisbane. Nearly a decade earlier they'd bought a tenanted house in Milton, close to the city, for just $20,000 and doubled their money four years later when they sold it (ah, the wonder of 1980s property prices). Perhaps they could repeat the exercise, they thought. Still, there was something troubling Graham in all of this. Was it enough to ensure their future?

"I had virtually no superannuation. People didn't think about super so much and employer payments weren't compulsory back then. We spent all our money on living, visiting family in Europe and educating the kids. I think we both suddenly realised that we weren't getting any younger," says Graham.

"Although we had these properties we weren't sure how we could generate a reasonable income for our retirement. We didn't really want to be relying on the pension. A chance dinner conversation with a work colleague in 1991 marked a turning point. He referred to Monique and I as 'asset rich', but said we weren't using our assets properly. We weren't using the right concepts."

Monique continues: "He told us we should be borrowing against our assets to get leverage. I think we were both pretty scared at the prospect of borrowing, especially at our age."

But this conversation planted the seed; it might be possible for the Bonds to use their assets not just as security but to actually create wealth. About this time the Bonds sold their home at The Gap and with the proceeds bought again in the older inner suburb of Highgate Hill.

"We established an equity credit loan, which was then a very new concept, to allow for further investment. Those flexible loans were very, very helpful for enabling investment without tying money to certain properties," explains Graham.

Reno Kings Tip

Anyone who has been knocked back for a loan in the past should check out the current loan situation. It has changed dramatically. There are so many loan products it's like a smorgasbord of finance. Check it out!

The Bonds' purchasing history.

Description	Year purchased	Purchase price	Reno or conversion costs	Furniture/ consumables	Total costs	Year sold	Sale price / current value
1. The Gap, land	1967	$3,000			$4,967	1976	$30,000
2. The Gap, 4 brm (PPOR)	1977	$35,000	$5,000		$41,977	1991	$165,000
3. Milton, 2/3 brm	1980	$20,000			$21,980	1984	$40,000
4. Sunshine Coast, land (house built 1999)	1984	$27,000	$160,000		$188,984	held	$250,000
5. Sunshine Beach, 2 flats	1985	$100,000	$10,000		$111,985	1995	$330,000
6. Fairfield, 3 brm	1989	$92,000	$6,000		$99,989	2001	$180,000
7. Highgate Hill, 3 brm (PPOR, addn 2 brm teenage retreat)	1991	$177,000	$255,000		$433,991	held	$700,000
8. Highgate Hill, 4 brm (conv to 9 brm)	1996	$191,000	$45,000	$12,000	$249,996	held	$500,000
9. Highgate Hill, 3 brm	1996	$227,000	$12,000		$240,996	held	$550,000
10. South Brisbane, 5 flatettes (conv 6 brm; addn 6 brm house built)	1998	$230,000	$220,000	$30,000	$481,998	held	$900,000
11. Yeronga, 5 brm (Conv 2 units, 9 brm; 6 addn units, 4 brm each; total 33 brm)	2001	$350,000	$1,800,000	$100,000	$2,252,001	held	$2,800,000
Total		$1,452,000	$2,513,000	$142,000	$4,128,864		$6,445,000

Which way to go?

The Bonds dabbled in a few things, trying to find the best way ahead. Graham had worked for years for an IT company that had employee shares.

"We bought shares in it from loyalty," says Monique. "We also hoped it would be a good investment, but felt it was dangerous to tie up most of our money in the company in case it developed problems. As it turned out the company was sold at about the time Graham retired and we did very well out of it, especially as quite a lot of it was from before the 1985 capital gains tax changes."

The next thing the Bonds tried was multi-level marketing, first in a weight-loss company and then a cleaning products company.

"We hated it," says Monique. "There was way too much marketing and it implied a way of shopping that was so alien to us that we simply couldn't promote it to others. Then we decided to put a toe into shares, but that didn't feel right for us either. We consulted an 'ethical investment financial planner' to ensure we didn't invest in things we were morally against, such as BHP mines, bombs, exploitative companies, and also to research the links between companies. There's such a network it's easy to accidentally invest in something you're absolutely against.

"But it was hard to find ethical companies that were also making money. New companies doing things such as water purification, solar energy, stormwater sieving or mine waste rehabilitation take years to become profitable and about 70% go bust. Not really a good prospect. Still, we did manage to find acceptable companies and started a modest share portfolio, which has been pretty positive."

Shared housing: There's an idea

At this time Monique was teaching English as a second language (ESL) to overseas students living in Brisbane. She was aware of a pressing need for good-quality share housing. She and Graham had also seen at first hand the dramas faced by their own children, as young adults, living in share houses – many of them dingy dumps with multiple bond payments and dodgy facilities.

Monique had met local property entrepreneur, architect and town-planner Paul Hey through a business colleague and found herself chatting about the need for purpose-run student accommodation in Brisbane. Paul's Property Search P/L specialised in "adding value" to property and he didn't need much convincing. Pretty soon he started experimenting with niche student accommodation and proved its potential.

A combination of Monique and Graham's growing interest in share housing, their relationship with Paul Hey and Monique's participation in Geoff Doidge's workshop in 1995 gave them confidence to take the plunge.

"I now felt we had the tools we needed to take this next step," says Monique. "First we'd established a rapport with Paul Hey. He said he'd help us to find the right property and we booked him to manage the conversion once we had it. And at the workshop I picked up a lot of good information. The manual was clear and gave step-by-step instructions for getting a loan, buying and renovating. There was no hidden agenda."

Monique says the message that she took from the workshop was clear: "It's possible to invest in property and enjoy yourself; make some money and have fun at the same time. I needed more confidence in how to approach banks for finance and how to analyse property with the aim of making some money. We'd always thought the tax system would never allow anyone who wasn't dodging it to get ahead. That's where all this new information set us straight. It's about active management, where we take control of our own fortune."

Case study #1: The house next door

In 1996 the house next door to Monique and Graham was up for sale. They talked with Paul Hey about the possibilities of converting it to student accommodation.

"Paul was adamant that it was only worth $160,000 but our neighbour wanted $190,000 and felt very strongly about it. She got an offer but it fell through, so we then offered $191,000. Our neighbour was feeling quite upset and we felt it would make her happy to offer the extra $1000."

After refinancing the Sunshine Coast units and farm, they signed up and appointed Paul Hey to project manage the renovation, setting aside $50,000 for the reno costs. Four bedrooms became nine bedrooms, with two kitchens, three bathrooms, two living areas and a covered patio. This property was a going concern in the student housing market.

"We finished just before Christmas and were very keen to get tenants. The first tenancy was short term, through the rental agency Paul Hey had set up. It was a group of schoolchildren from Asia, who particularly enjoyed bouncing on the doubledecker bunks we'd bought for them.

"We'd worked out that our market was keen on new and shiny rather than old and picturesque, so the important thing was to make everything look as new as possible. We focused on modern-looking furniture and buildings rather than my own taste for Queenslanders."

Tenants were offered accommodation on a room-for-rent basis. The general living areas and eating and washing facilities were shared, and Monique and Graham took care of utilities (electricity and gas) and the regular cleaning of the common areas.

"We wanted overseas students especially to be able to rent clean, high-standard houses and pay a single bond with minimal fuss," Monique explains. "I thought it would be great if students from different language backgrounds could share accommodation, practising their English and giving each other support at the same time."

Monique's vision has in fact been realised. "They particularly enjoy the back patio and the lawn. They like to sit out chatting in the evenings and do far too much sunbaking. I have to restrain myself from going round and talking to them about melanomas."

This property was a winner and started to make money from day one, but Monique warns that anyone wanting to enter this market should go in with their eyes wide open.

Watch your costs

"This share accommodation takes a lot of time and money to maintain," says Monique. "Don't worry, we don't make their beds or anything, but the running costs are around 40% of the rental income. It costs more in agent's fees, because of the number of individual tenancies, and we rent the property out furnished, both the individual rooms and the common areas, on top of paying for the utilities, consumables such as cleaning products, and cleaners to maintain the bathrooms, kitchens and living rooms. We furnished and equipped this first one for around $12,000."

Another drawback to share housing, particularly student housing, is that occupancy rates do fluctuate, something Monique warns the potential developer to be constantly aware of.

"This can really break you if you're not ready for it," she says. "There are the usual vacancies over the Christmas break but sometimes there's also a cyclical effect, with an increase in demand in the first semester, followed by a decrease in the second. We only ever count on a 48-week occupancy over a year, but it can be even lower."

> **Reno Kings Tip**
>
> *Try to get leases that terminate in January. This is the peak letting period of the year. You will slash your vacancies and your costs.*

Case study #2: Oops, Monique did it again

At the property workshop that Monique had attended we had run a mock auction, taught a number of bidding strategies and discussed how to buy a bargain at auction. Monique learned how to judge if a property was undervalued and how to bid. It must have made an impression. On her way home from a guitar lesson Monique saw an auction sign two streets from their house and popped in to satisfy her curiosity. Imagine Graham's surprise when Monique told him that she had bought another house.

Here are the numbers for the Bonds' last four investment properties.

	Case study #1	Case study #2	Case study #3	Case study #4
Description	Highgate Hill, 4 brm conv to 9 brm	Highgate Hill, 3 brm	South Brisbane, 5 flats conv to 6 brm+addn 6 brm	Yeronga, 2 dwellings+addn 3, total 33 brm
Year purchased	1996	1996	1998	2001
Purchase price	$191,000	$227,000	$230,000	$350,000
Reno or conversion costs	$45,000	$12,000	$220,000	$1,800,000
Furniture/consumables	$12,000		$30,000	$100,000
Total costs	$248,000	$239,000	$480,000	$2,250,000
Rent pa at purchase		$10,400		
Yield at purchase	0.0%	4.6%	0.0%	0.0%
Rent pa current*	$47,520	$14,040	$72,000	$182,160
Current yield	19.2%	5.9%	15.0%	8.1%
Current value	$500,000	$550,000	$900,000	$3,000,000
Capital gain	$252,000	$311,000	$420,000	$750,000

* Rent for #s 1,3,4 at 48 weeks per annum
Yield at purchase=rent/purchase price
Current yield=rent/total cost
Capital gain=current value-total cost

"We were not really looking for another property but the top bid was definitely below what I thought the property must be worth," explains Monique. "I hadn't even walked through it but I had a good idea of the value of land and views in Highgate Hill. So I made a bid."

Having made the highest bid, though still below the reserve price, Monique was able to negotiate with the seller, who was anxious to pay for a trendy apartment in Teneriffe, a near-city suburb taking off.

"The auctioneer was her cousin so, unlike many agents, he was really doing his best for her," explains Monique. "We discovered that a retaining wall in the front had a bow in it and were able to use this to shave something off the price."

It is a very pretty house, with two-street access and city views, and came with ready-made tenants, who were local postgraduate students.

When they are ready to move on they just pass the lease for the house on to their friends, which means low vacancy rates and low tenancy costs.

"They're excellent tenants, always keep the house clean and look after the garden, which has made up for the fact that the rent doesn't cover the interest payments," says Graham.

"Despite that, we did give it a bit of a scrub-up, replacing door handles, fixing shower leaks, stormwater pipes and window locks, enough to make it decent. We have just recently painted the outside at the tenants' request," says Monique. "Eventually the rent crept up to increase the yield but it is the increasing value of the property that is attractive here."

"We decided to let this one sit," Graham adds. "The tenants were good (still are), and it has more than doubled in value in the time we've had it. We call it our 'sleeping investment'."

Case study #3: Building on experience

At the end of 1998 Paul Hey alerted the Bonds to another opportunity, a Queenslander split into five flatettes on a big block of land in South Brisbane that looked perfect for subdivision. Having completed one successful conversion to share housing, Graham and Monique were ready to do it again on a grander scale. This property was big enough to build a new dwelling for share housing, as well as converting the original house.

"The owners were elderly and found the flats too hard to manage. We were prepared to pay a realistic price but were also quite willing to point out things that needed doing, says Monique."

The Bonds always commission a property inspection with a written report, so that they can point out any serious problems. Even though this is after the contract has been signed, producing the report before the contract goes unconditional gives some opportunity for a little jigging of the final amount. Monique also emphasises the importance of finding a lender who understands your vision.

"Purpose-built share housing was an incredibly new concept in 1998 and we needed a lender who was open to our successful history and client-worthiness. Some banks were not even prepared to consider the kind of thing we were proposing. Our contact at the bank was very helpful. He'd do anything for us, whether it was depositing a cheque at the counter or arranging a better deal on our loan."

Monique recommends shopping around till you find someone helpful and then "cling to them like grim death". A few years after this purchase the Bonds lost their treasured loan manager and it took a couple of years to find someone reasonable at another bank.

"It was important enough to make us change banks," says Monique. "Think about the advantage in being able to phone someone and say, 'Hi Bruce, it's Monique. We've got something interesting coming up and may want to borrow another $200k–$300k. What sort of deal can you offer?' When we go in with all the details, he is already primed and wanting to lend us money."

It sure beats having to go through the whole rigmarole of establishing your financial standing from scratch. It gives you some power in the equation so you're not being given the run around, which is as good for your self-confidence as it is for your prospects of success.

"There are many useless people in banks who make difficulties and don't do their homework, and don't try to do a deal with you. They seem more interested in covering their backs and finding petty rules."

The conversion

In this case, with treasured loan manager still on board, the Bonds refinanced the two Highgate Hill share houses to pay for the conversion of the existing Queenslander at South Brisbane and then refinanced the Queenslander to pay for a new house at the back.

Monique and Graham were more confident this time about the kind of share housing they could develop and kept to the principle of developing accommodation they'd be happy to live in. They cleaned up the existing house, turning it into a six-bedroom share house instead of five flats. They polished floors, put in a new kitchen, spruced up the two bathrooms and put in a third toilet, and made some interesting bedroom/study combinations.

"Some rooms now are very large; others are smaller but have part of the sleepout as a study. It is a very friendly house and the students like it," says Monique. "The covered patio at the back makes it easy for them to socialise with the students in the new building as well."

The new house is also a six-bedroom dwelling, and was based on a successful development of Paul Hey's. They used the same architect, with the plans being modified through experience.

┌─ Reno Kings Tip ─────────────────────────

Redevelopment of a site to achieve its full potential can be extremely profitable but requires careful planning of key aspects. Some of the more important aspects are:

Correct zoning. *Employ other professionals, eg, townplanners, to ensure the zoning of your property permits the type of project you have in mind.*

Size of land. *Most councils have laid down a minimum size of land (and frontage) that can be developed.*

Flooding. *If you are in a designated flood area you will have difficulties getting approval to develop.*

Services. *The ability to establish or connect to services, ie, water, sewerage, power and telephone, will have to be proven.*

Drainage. *Stormwater is always an issue. Land sloping to approved stormwater carriages, ie, kerbs and channels, solves a lot of problems.*

The council changed the rules!

Another thing to be wary of with developments such as share housing is that regulations can (and frequently do) change.

"Back then six bedrooms was the maximum the council allowed without registration as a boarding house," says Monique. "This has now changed to five, which has had expensive consequences for us in terms of fire regulations, registration and general bureaucracy."

This really highlights the importance of research for anyone starting out now, especially in share housing.

Graham says, "We wanted this project to be attractive but simple and environmentally friendly. We chose our fittings and fixtures for their functionality, durability and energy efficiency. So we installed things like water-saving showers and solar hot-water systems. Even though these can be more expensive initially, they take a hell of a lot of beating before you have to replace them, and when you're the one forking out for gas and electricity their efficiency is definitely worthwhile."

Midway through the construction Graham and Monique took off for a six-week camping trip to the remote Kimberley region of Western Australia, which is probably just a tad risky. This is where a trusty banker can really make a difference.

"We left our unfortunate daughter with power of attorney to sign cheques but our darling banker just advanced the money anyway without bothering her and looked after everything beautifully," says Monique. "This was especially appreciated when we had the unexpected expense of building a new sewer, for about $22,000, the cost of which we had to bear ourselves, even though the property adjoining ours benefited. This was something we hadn't realised when we first did our planning."

Reno Kings Tip

Watch out for combined sewer drains! Always get a trunk sewer plan, stormwater plans and detailed drainage plans. De-combining a sewer line could cost you $10k to $50k or more. Get the advice of an hydraulics engineer and experienced town planner. There won't necessarily be an easement over the drain. Bridging an existing large drain can cost you heaps too.

Meanwhile, down on the farm

Monique and Graham were able to put their experience here to good use as they were about to embark on planting a house on their hobby farm. Up to this point they'd made do with their Ford transit campervan, upgrading to a converted bus with no motor, when they stayed on the farm. Now they were about to get serious about building a comfortable and energy-efficient house for themselves.

They bought a good, simple loft-design kit house and sat down with the designers to adapt it to the site and improve its overall design. They added wide, covered decks, including a 5 x 4 m deck facing south-east to the prevailing breezes and a deck on the west to shelter the house from the afternoon sun.

"Banks of louvres were designed to keep the house cool in summer, with an efficient woodburning stove in the middle of the house to keep it toasty warm in winter," explains Monique.

As well as solar hot water, they installed PV (photovoltaic) cells on the roof, which generate 1.5 kW of electricity, plenty of insulation in the ceiling and walls, a composting toilet and water-saving taps, and they only needed water for washing and cooking.

"Now we can sit on the deck and watch the wallabies and birds carrying on around the house and the clouds chasing each other across the sky," says Monique. "Bliss." Or they can sit around thinking about how their investments are going.

Monique was keen to learn more about property investment and kept in contact with other investors she'd met through the Reno Kings advanced workshops. Talking to them she realised that she and Graham were paying too much to the managers of their rental properties.

"While the properties do require more work from the property managers than standard rentals, we were paying 3% above the norm. With a little renegotiation we brought that down to 1.5% above the norm and were ready to go again."

Case study #4: The Yeronga development

In 2001 the Bonds stuck their necks out again. This time it was a large block of land, approximately 1440 sq m, with a beautiful big 1930s Queenslander opposite the Yeronga Railway Station, and just across the river from the University of Queensland. The property was accessible to a number of educational institutions, on foot or by public transport, and it was a bike ride to the ferry for the university, though too far to walk.

"We'd developed a bit of a passion for the share housing concept by then," Monique says. "We wanted to develop a style of accommodation that looked good, and that allowed people from mixed backgrounds to live together with privacy, as well as having a communal feel."

"And the market isn't just students," Graham continues. "The property is very close to several major hospitals, with visiting relatives, hospital staff and ancillary workers looking for accommodation in the area."

There is also a substantial market for furnished, share accommodation among short-term contractors, people new to the city, who appreciate the social support, and low-paid workers who want to share housing costs.

"The market is definitely there but a medium to market to these people has not yet been developed," argues Graham. "These are people who would have lodged in private houses 40 years ago but have higher expectations now and don't want to look at grotty, run-down old houses."

From one house to 33 bedrooms!

For the Yeronga development the Bonds "slid" the existing Queenslander to a better position and completely rebuilt it on the block. They then renovated it so that it became two flats, a five-bedroom unit upstairs and a brand new four-bedroom unit downstairs, with a two-car carport. They then constructed three new buildings, purpose-built for sharing.

> ### ┌─ Reno Kings Tip
>
> *Raising* a house can create cheap space. Lifting and building under is far more cost-effective than extending or new constructions but there can be some problems. Ensure you can comply with any height and set-back restrictions, ie, distance from neighbouring properties. If you build upward and block a neighbour's "amenity" (light or air) you may have to set it back. Always check these restrictions by using a surveyor to peg out your boundaries.
>
> *Sliding* is a fantastic system suitable for moving timber houses. These houses (sliders) are often stuck smack bang in the middle of a large block. You can engage a company to just pick them up and slide them to the most appropriate position on the block. Be aware of any set-back restrictions. Sliding can create a whole new block available for redevelopment and you still have the original house, which can be renovated and built under to create even more value. A triple-whammy way to instant equity.

This is some project! Each building has two units of four bedrooms each. Three buildings of two units each by four bedrooms per unit equals twenty-four bedrooms, plus the nine bedrooms of the original house. That's a total of thirty-three bedrooms.

Each bedroom has its own phone line and cable internet available, as well as its own vanity unit, with shared shower and toilet for each two bedrooms. Cooking and living areas are shared and there are substantial covered outdoor areas for each unit, including balconies and patios.

"The whole point was to build units that were thoughtfully designed, attractive and affordable," says Graham. "They were built to take advantage of the breeze, with cross-ventilation, a substantial covered deck and views that range from spectacular to reasonable. And they all have good sound insulation, which is important for share housing."

Monique and Graham have done extremely well in the design stakes; so well, in fact, that when council officials inspected the development they brought their planners back again to check it out.

"They were particularly impressed with the way we had hidden the ten parking spaces so that five of them are grassed, and two function also as extensions to the patios. They also liked the way we had designed the required privacy screens on the windows, extending them at the sides and bottom, thus serving as security screens as well. The vanity basins for each room, with dual access showers and toilets shared between two, also struck a chord, balancing personal privacy with cost-efficiency.

Still, the Bonds are not certain that this is their property niche after all. Perhaps the Yeronga development was just a little too big (though perfectly formed), for their comfort zone.

"I'm still not quite sure why we decided to go ahead with a $2 million housing project that took two years from our lives to complete," Graham says. "If we'd just hung on to the land for a couple of years and done nothing, we could have cleared about half a million. Mind you, we wouldn't have received any of the rent from the new development."

Rules and more rules

Shared housing can be a great investment, but setting it all up isn't always plain sailing. Governments have become pretty strong on safety issues for houses with multiple independent residents, especially since a fatal backpackers hostel fire a few years ago. One of the main concerns is protecting the elderly from boarding-house fires. According to Graham, with student housing the path isn't always clear.

"The rules do seem to change a bit, in terms of the regulations and who they apply to. At first we were told that fire safety legislation applied to housing catering for more than six unrelated people. Then it was six people and more. For a while there they were talking about share houses with four or more people being classed as boarding houses. It seems the rules were getting caught up with accommodation for elderly and incapacitated people."

After much discussion with relevant government departments and a very good report on student accommodation commissioned by the Queensland Residential Tenancies Authority, in May 2004 state government legislation was passed that exempted predominantly student housing from Residential Services Accreditation regulations. However, they are, of course, still covered by the fire regulations. Even so, Graham recommends that would-be investors check with both state and local government authorities to find out their legal obligations and that developers build to the highest standards of fire and safety legislation.

Monique says that sometimes the problem can be that the regulations don't differentiate between multi-unit dwellings and share housing.

"The regulations are not framed for a situation where not every tenant needs a car space for instance," she says. "However, it is possible to negotiate on this. In one nine-bedroom house we only have two car spaces but five bicycle spaces. In Yeronga we ended up with one car park per unit and two visitor spaces, which seems to be adequate."

"A good townplanner and building certifier should be able to help," says Graham. "Even if they don't have all the information, they can often tell you the best government departments to talk to."

Statutes and by-laws tend to change without much notice though, so be careful to get your advice in writing and find out where to get updates. In particular, real estate agents who do not specialise in share housing are very unlikely to even know about much of the relevant legislation.

We did it our way

What is so impressive about the Bonds' story is that they did it their own way. As with many property success stories, it wasn't just about money.

"If you only looked at our gross rental income for these investment properties," Monique says, "a lot of people would say it's 'money for jam', a profit way above a straight return. But actually up to 40% of our income goes on maintenance costs – management fees, utilities, cleaning – and then there's the interest to meet. But it's important to us that we provide high-quality accommodation at an affordable price."

Graham takes up the theme. "That's right. We feel we've helped to meet an obvious need, and at the same time improved our financial status. And we've held on to our values. To us it's a win-win situation."

The Bonds did compromise in some areas. "We had wanted to break new ground by generating at least some of the needed electricity on the properties by using photovoltaic cells but, in 1992, the government subsidies were only available to owner-occupiers so it was not really viable for investors who wanted to rent out at affordable rates.

"The same was true for solar hot-water systems. The subsidies were only available to owner-occupiers. I believe solar hot-water systems should be mandatory unless there is a reason they're not suitable. That would make the market much bigger and really bring the prices down. The same with rainwater tanks. There have been many changes in this area so it is always wise to check out the position as you do your planning.

"The conclusion we've come to ourselves", says Monique, "is that we want to contribute something positive in our bid to create 'an earner' for ourselves. We're interested in making money for our retirement but we're not into empire building, or giving financial security to the whole family. Our kids need to fend for themselves; though we would certainly help them if they were in trouble. We don't need wealth beyond that which we can use in our own lifetime and in contributing to worthwhile causes."

"Contrary to the rumours, we are not builders, or even renovators," adds Graham. "That's for other people. We don't mind paying experts to do it."

The upshot

Currently Graham and Monique own six properties. Of these they own their own home and the farm outright. The other four properties currently have 57 rooms under lease and only one property is negatively geared. The remaining three bring in around $25,000 per month, or $300,000 per annum, before costs and interest.

After Monique and Graham's estimated 40% costs and around $144,000 interest that's an annual income of about $36,000. Then there are the "add-backs" from building allowance, depreciation on fixtures and fittings and other tax deductions, such as fees and interest. In all they provide good accommodation to some 60 people from many countries. Not bad for a couple of reluctant investors in only a few years.

Reno Kings insights

What's your background?

Graham: I'm a boy from the bush, from Wondai in Queensland's South Burnett region. I got a scholarship to Churchie in the 1950s. I enjoyed the sporting facilities and became a gymnast, representing Australia at three Olympics. I studied mining engineering at uni and then politics, philosophy and economics at Oxford. I got into computing in the very early days and have worked in the IT industry ever since.

Monique: My mother was Dutch and my father French and I was born in Algeria. My parents' marriage broke up and I was eventually brought up by my mother and a British stepfather in Italy and England, only being reunited with my father, brother and sister in my teens. I was accepted to read history at Oxford, where I met Graham visiting a mutual friend. We married in England and settled in Australia. We had a daughter in Brisbane, a son in Sydney and another daughter in Melbourne before returning to Europe, in case we moved to Adelaide and Perth and produced children there too! We returned to Australia in 1977, having driven our campervan from London to Bombay with the three children.

Why did you get started?

Monique: We couldn't see what we would live on Graham's retirement. There wasn't much super and we wanted something other than a pension.

What was your greatest fear?

Monique: Getting into a financial venture that failed and becoming bankrupt.

Did your parents show you how to get started?

Graham: My parents were financially independent but with limited means. They didn't see how this could change so settled with what they had.

Monique: My parents worked very, very hard to become relatively well-off. I'm sure they expected their children to be well off too but we never really discussed it. They didn't tell us how to be successful in business. They did show me how to run a cheque account and put me on a budget when I went to university in the UK, an annual lump sum. From this I had to pay my fees, travel home (Italy and France) and buy clothes. I did pick up the importance of saving and investing. When we were first married, with a young baby and living on Graham's scholarship, money was very tight, but I insisted that we save something each month, however small.

What was your greatest mistake?

Graham: We assumed that we couldn't live as we wanted to – comfortably – and still accumulate wealth in an ethical way.

Monique: Yes, we thought that investing successfully to make money was totally incompatible with our values.

Graham: But our experience has proved that we can do it.

What would you identify as some pitfalls?

Graham: I think, like a lot of people our age, we were too busy with the present to think about our future and what we might need in retirement.

Monique: We also held on to some old beliefs: beliefs that we now think were wrong. For example, we felt that the taxation system made it impossible to accumulate wealth. We now know this isn't true.

Graham: I don't think we placed enough value on understanding how wealth creation can work. We didn't see how using our assets, with a sensible proportion of debt, could build up our capital and our income. We understood about living fairly frugally, not buying flash cars or expensive holidays but we didn't know how to increase our assets.

Monique: We were also pretty much all over the place, unfocused. I went to stock exchange courses to learn about shares but it all seemed too hard, too illogical, and so much based on making money only when someone lost it because they sold when shares were going up, so we gave up.

What do you want to achieve?

Graham: To have enough money for a comfortable, not lavish, retirement.

Monique: We'd also like to have enough spare money to substantially contribute to worthwhile environmental and social projects.

Graham: As far as the properties go, I think we have a clearer goal now than a few years ago. It's basically to provide good-quality, affordable share accommodation for anyone who wants it, not just students.

How would you describe your strategy?

Monique: We didn't have one at first. Our financial planner would ask, "What do you want to achieve?" and I'd say, "Five million by 2005 sounds nice." It was just a figure conjured out of the air because he wanted a figure.

Graham: We tried to buy good property, turn it into student housing that we could rent at a reasonable price and still make a fair income.

Monique: We tried to investigate ways of doing what we wanted to do, while keeping some balance and safety.

Any memorable experiences along the way?

Monique: We discovered the new Residential Services legislation would affect our share housing, even though our tenants were not the kind the legislation was aimed at. We wanted the government to acknowledge this and make some changes. Most people thought it would be impossible for us to have the need for change sufficiently understood for there to be any action but we thought it was worth trying. After considerable effort writing submissions and talking to politicians and bureaucrats, a workable solution was arrived at and the necessary legislation passed. This is probably the only time in our lives we will have directly influenced Queensland legislation.

Graham: Before we started investing in share housing Monique had discussed it with Paul Hey but didn't know how to implement the ideas. A few years later we met Paul again. He'd worked out how to run share housing efficiently and had set up a property management company. That enabled us to get started. Without that we would never have done it.

What's your best renovating tip?

Graham: Stop thinking you're going to live there. Tell your suppliers you want durable, energy-saving equipment with a five-year life, preferably ten.

Any other tips for investors?

Graham: Try to stay focused on your project. Our biggest problem is losing focus. We buy a property and start plans, and then something else comes up and we do that as well and find ourselves losing focus on the first project.

Monique: Still, I think you have to play the game the way it suits you and your lifestyle. We have lost focus sometimes but we're still doing okay.

Graham: Find someone who's good at property management and pay them to manage. It's good to spread the money around. You might even want two property managers for several properties. All offices have their ups and downs, and it might give you an option if one of the companies is having personnel problems, which is fairly common in this business.

What would you do differently?

Monique: Learn to enjoy the decision-making process, instead of getting stressed and frazzled about making the best decision. And remain focused on the current project and not go camping in the Kimberley, or go away to visit family, or volunteer to work at the Olympics in the middle of it all. Both are probably impossible with our current personalities.

How has your life changed since you began investing in property?

Monique: We feel more positive about our finances but we also spend more time thinking about them. I sometimes wake up at night wondering if we have made the right decisions.

Graham: It's good to have extra financial assets and be able to see our grand-children overseas. It's also good to be able to finance worthwhile projects.

Monique: It's given us confidence to realise we can make money. We've also enjoyed meeting builders, plumbers, chippies and many of our tenants.

Graham: At the moment our lives are much busier than we'd like because of our latest big project at Yeronga. It's turned out to be much bigger than we realised and it's taken more time and energy than we want to give it.

How do you picture yourselves five years down the track?

Graham: We'll be spending as little time as possible on our investments and concentrating more on doing the things we like to do.

Monique: We might also be looking at how to allocate our assets, such as setting up a charitable trust before we die, to leave money to existing charities or causes we believe in.

The Bonds' keys to successful share housing

1. Provide secure, spacious bedroom and study areas.
2. Ask for only one bond per person to minimise problems on leaving.
3. Pay gas and electrical utilities to stop hassles of who used what (cover this in rent charged).
4. Establish good house rules for residents and guests (covering such things as noise and privacy, cleaning, smoking and other inflammables) so that everyone can enjoy the place.
5. Provide sensitive, efficient management.
6. Take responsibility for cleaning public areas (no washing up).
7. Provide housing close to transport, shops, educational facilities.
8. Provide good maintenance of contents and building.
9. Assist tenants wishing to move to a different house if relations with other housemates deteriorate, especially in their love life.
10. For overseas students, encourage a mix of language backgrounds.

Reno Kings Report

There are all sorts of ideas for niche markets, and they can really give you an edge in property investment. If you'd like to know more contact the Reno Kings for our report, Niche Market Opportunities. See page 235 for details and how to order, or go to the website: www.renos.com.au

Big gains on a small income

Mark Galvin is a young bloke with a bright future in property investment, thanks to his longing for a Ferrari. He's even added share trading to his portfolio.

We often get asked by budding investors attending a workshop, "I only earn $600 a week. How can I possibly afford a property?" The sorry truth is that some people on $150,000 a year struggle just living week to week. Their spending always expands to meet (or exceed) their income.

Here is a major financial tip: It's what you do with what you earn, not what you earn, that determines your financial future.

How could someone on a low income of $30,000 per year at age 31 make it big as a property investor? It's not easy, but people on a low income can still build a substantial property portfolio. It's about establishing a saving pattern; always putting aside something from what you earn and then making that money work for you.

It's amazing how we receive formal school education for 10 or 12 years or more but never get a practical financial education. That might have been fine in the days when your bank was as familiar and as trustworthy as the corner grocer. But things have changed and you can no longer rely on your friendly bank manager to look after your interests – the branch was probably closed years ago anyway and the staff "downsized".

If you're interested in getting into property you really need to familiarise yourself with a few finance basics. There is a golden rule that you should always save 10% of what you earn, no matter how much that is. It's worth remembering, and doing. Simply put, take control of your own finances and pay yourself first.

Of course, then you need to use what you've saved to its best effect, by purchasing assets that either gain in value or bring in cashflow or, even better, both. Once you apply that first financial principle, just about anything's possible, but you still have to know what you're doing.

Meet Galvo

Mark Galvin (Galvo to his mates) was born in the small Victorian town of Birregurra, grew up in nearby Geelong and went to school at Corio Tech. He couldn't wait to leave school.

"I was in the half of the class that made the other half look good. I had the attitude that, if you don't get paid, why go?" He left at age 16 with no real qualifications or ambitions and got a job at an electrical wholesalers.

Mark was a pretty typical young bloke, hankering after cars, a good social life. Still living at home, his expenses weren't over the top and by 1991 his savings allowed him to buy a car, a 1976 Torana that was his pride and joy. He paid just $8000 for it. It was a regular street car but cut it pretty well on the drag strip as well.

Over the next eight years Mark poured another $20,000 into it, even though he sold it for only $11,500. To some of us that might seem an incredible amount of money to spend on a car, but this was a serious passion. Then Mark saw the '78 Kingswood, a bargain at $1500, and he had to have that as well.

The problem here was that, while the cars gave him some enjoyment on the drag strip, as well as personal satisfaction in working on them, they were not doing anything much for Mark's future.

This was Mark's sad financial position at age 26 in 1998.

Asset	Value	Loan	Income from assets
Car #1 1976 Holden Torana	$11,500	nil	nil
Car #2 The '78 Kingswood	$2,000	nil	nil
Furniture	$2,000	nil	nil
Cash	$537	nil	nil
less	$(1,500)	credit card	
Total	$14,537		nil

Twenty-six years on this earth and 10 years in the workforce and Galvo had measly assets worth just $14,537. Note: His cars were a rapidly depreciating asset, even a liability. They cost money, produced zero income and would eventually be worth nothing.

Then Mark saw the young bloke in the Ferrari.

"I want one of those," was his immediate reaction. "And I want a better lifestyle." It was enough incentive to wake him up to the fact that he was going nowhere fast. He'd heard that 90% of wealthy people had made their money through either shares or property, so he started reading books on property investment and a plan began to emerge.

He realised that if he was to get ahead he would have to make some changes. He left Geelong to work seven days a week in the mines at Mount Isa to save the deposit for an investment property. This was to be the beginning of his quest for what he didn't get at school, a practical financial education.

Mark decided to take control of his own future. He investigated property investment and renovation strategies and techniques. That was the beginning. For the first time Mark learned how to research a property deal, how and where to get the best finance, how to negotiate to buy and how to add serious value through renovation.

Baby steps

Mark's first investment property, purchased in March 1999 on a brief trip home from The Isa, was a three-bedroom house in Corio, a lower-income suburb of Geelong. It was a bit of a bargain at $72,000 and he had no problem getting finance, as his earning and saving capacity was now proven.

"The place had been in the paper for ages. When I first spotted it they were still asking $84,000," says Mark. "I made an offer and it pretty much fell into my lap."

The house was fairly neat and Mark rented it out as it stood for $140 per week. Three years later, having picked up a few Reno Kings tips, he decided it could do with a little spruce up. His mum had just replaced the carpet at home, even though it was still in good nick, which gave him a bright idea. He tore up the old carpet, replacing it with his mum's pre-loved deep pile, and did a little retiling in the kitchen and bathroom.

The whole lot took all of two weeks and cost a pittance of around $1500, which could be claimed against his tax. His rental income increased to $165 a week, an increase of $1300 per year, and the value of the property increased as well. This is a good result: spend $1500, get back $1300 per annum rent and claim the $1500 on tax.

Good as new

Soon after he bought the Corio house Mark was called in to work at the Mount Isa company's head office in Brisbane. He was there for a few months, so he had a look around for property, as you do.

"I was still very new in the property game and, being on a fairly high income, I was looking for ways to bring my tax down through depreciation, as well as decreasing maintenance costs. Being inexperienced I thought new was the only way to go," he says.

Mark ended up buying a two-bedroom townhouse in Enoggera, an older suburb of Brisbane that was getting an upward boost in the property stakes. The townhouse was so new Mark had left Brisbane even before the finishing touches were completed. He's never, in fact, seen it finished, proving the point that you don't have to be emotionally involved with your purchases. Sometimes, the greater the distance, in this case physical as well as emotional, the more chance you have of succeeding.

The good thing about buying houses built after 1985 is that you can take advantage of the building allowance. This is a type of depreciation on the value of the structure itself (as opposed to land value and fixtures and fittings), which you can write off against tax. The value of the structure should be given in the quantity surveyor's report, or equates to the original costs of the construction, if available.

Using Mark's townhouse as an example, the purchase price of $135,000 would include fairly low land value, possibly as low as $20,000. The value of the land component of any property you buy will depend on many things, including the type of dwelling and local land values. Once the value of the land has been deducted off your purchase price, the remaining amount represents the value of both the building and its fixtures, fittings and furniture.

Properties built between 18 July 1985 and 15 September 1987 will have a building depreciation allowance (based on the assessed original cost of the building) of 4% every year for 25 years, and you may claim the balance of this, depending on the age. Properties built after this qualify for a building allowance of 2.5% for 40 years. In addition to this, all fixtures, fittings and furniture inside the property will qualify for depreciation allowances of beween 3% and 40% for their effective lives, depending on the item.

The quickest and easiest way to determine what you might be allowed to claim is to engage the services of a quantity surveyor who, for around $400–$600 plus, will provide you with a report that will last the life of your investment and allow you to maximise your tax deductions.

A bit of sound advice

Mark had been an avid reader of *Australian Property Investor* for a while by now and had read articles about some of the people who'd done the Reno Kings workshops. He was still keen to learn more so he booked in.

"The advice seemed really sound. The workshop showed me how to do things in order to turn a good profit," says Mark. "And it was a good laugh too. Using Mum's old carpet was a tip I'd picked up from the workshop."

Being able to examine the cost-effectiveness of a particular strategy, whether it's financing the deal or recarpeting the lounge, is one of the Reno Kings' key points.

> **Reno Kings Tip**
>
> *Don't spend a dollar to make a dollar. You are just wasting time. Try to get $3 to $5 back for every $1 spent. More bang for your buck.*

Case study: Investment property #3

The finance

By the end of 2002, just 10 months later, Mark was ready to leap in again, even though he'd returned to Geelong and was now earning substantially less than the Mount Isa gig. His first step was to get finance for another property. He rang a mortgage broker, as suggested by the Reno Kings.

"Because of the equity I'd built up from the first two properties I got pre-approval for the next loan so I knew how much I could spend on an investment property. This allowed me to get into the market."

"I was approved for $180,000 so I started looking around for a house around $120,000 to $150,000 to leave 'wriggle room' for renovation costs and purchase costs."

The research

Mark started the research process, checking prices on a few of Geelong's surrounding suburbs.

"I could've made heaps if I'd had just another $50,000 to play with, as the returns were proportionally higher, but the houses were out of my price range."

Two months down the track and after some serious searching, he was looking in a real estate agency window, one of more than 15 he regularly checked after work.

"One day there it was, a 1920s, two-bedroom, chamferboard bungalow in a little pocket just across the road from Geelong West, a very good suburb. It was advertised for $140,000. I reckoned I could get it for a bargain $125,000. I rang up the agent and went for an inspection. When I arrived there were a couple of people already looking at it."

Mark's reaction to the state of the house wasn't unreasonable; as a negotiating tactic it can also sometimes help.

"What a dump! I went through and bagged the s*** out of it hoping to turn the other people off. Then the agent agreed with me, and I thought they were supposed to be acting for the seller, not the buyer. But the place really was a dump."

The negotiation

Mark did some more research on values in the area and offered $125,000 the next day. The agent rang back to say someone else had put in an offer.

"Don't they always?" says Mark. "They told me I was the first to offer so they'd let me counter offer." Mark increased his offer to $135,000. In two minds, he rang his dad, whose advice was: "If you want the bloody thing, just buy it."

"Little did he know," says Mark, "that he was going to help me fix it up." Mark rang the agent back 10 minutes later and said, "Okay, I'll take it for $140,000," which was the asking price. Done deal.

After work, he went down to sign the papers. The agent asked for a substantial deposit and was somewhat taken aback when Mark said, "Sorry, I only have $100. That's all I'm putting down." In fact, Mark was well within his rights here to offer a low holding deposit. The usual 10% deposit isn't in fact required till a couple of weeks later (or whatever is negotiated in the contract).

The agent said the other buyer had also made a full-price offer. That buyer had rung back just 15 minutes after Mark did. "It pays when you see

---

> ┌─ **Reno Kings Tip** ─────────────────────────────
> *Always try to negotiate a deposit not greater than the agent's commission,*
> *say 3%. You will be amazed how often this is accepted.*

---

a bargain in a 'hot' market to just take it off the market before someone else snaps it up," he says.

That was on a Tuesday. It was advertised for sale in Saturday's paper as the agent had forgotten to cancel the ad. On the following Tuesday Mark got a call from the agent: "I've had about 50 phone calls about the house and one Melbourne buyer really wants it."

The property had been in the Melbourne buyer's family soon after it was built and he was willing to offer $155,000, a $15,000 equity gain. Not bad for a week's work. Mark's response? "No, but hey buddy, it's his for $300,000 if he really wants it."

Mark wisely negotiated a longer than usual 120-day settlement, which allowed him to plan the reno work during the contract period, with agreement from the vendor that he could have access to the property in that time. This also held the property for him at the agreed price and yet he didn't have to lay out any cash apart from the deposit. Taking into account the rising values over that period he basically got his deposit back in the increased equity.

Back to bricks and mortar, though. Once he had everything in place, it was time to get his hands dirty.

The renovation

He booked the restumpers for the day after settlement as "the house was not real straight", then got to work stripping the place. There was a lot to do.

"I threw out everything that was no good. The house wasn't that good but I couldn't fit it in the mini-skip!"

Mark started on the kitchen and bathroom, as they needed the most attention. The bathroom was a nightmare, needing new fittings and work on the walls and floors. He ripped down the badly cracked plaster, then started fixing the rear of the house, where the toilet and laundry were.

"I moved the toilet into the bathroom and moved the laundry across about 3 m. This made room for a new bedroom, which I figured would generate some extra cashflow, as I now I had a three-bedroom house."

> **Reno Kings Tip**
>
> *Extra bedrooms created under an existing roof are inexpensive, easy to do and bring in more rental dollars.*

He hung the plaster himself and got a plasterer to finish it off. Though Mark was pretty new to tiling, he was ready to have a go at anything. "We tiled the bathroom, kitchen and laundry and had cupboards and a new kitchen installed."

Once that was done Mark started on the original two bedrooms and the lounge. Just one bedroom needed replastering and, while he replastered inside, he had a painter work on the outside, having already replaced many rotten weatherboards.

Here's what the reno of house #3 cost.

Restumping	$5,500
Tree removal	$250
Fencing	$1,397
Rubbish removal	$238
Plumbing	$1,784
Tiles	$1,736
Carpet	$1,714
Stove	$848
Plaster	$1,882
Electrical	$1,200
Paint	$1,135
Timber	$3,712
Painter	$2,000
Kitchen and cupboards	$3,250
Nails, brushes, locks	$1,500
Total costs	$28,145

Back to the kitchen, the existing stove now looked totally out of place with the new kitchen. It was in very poor condition and impossible to clean, so he replaced it with a new one at a cost of $848. After a weekend of painting, he had finished all the rooms inside and hired professionals to lay the carpet. The inside was pretty well done. Outside, for street appeal, he cleaned up the yards.

"The jungle was so bad, you couldn't see the house." He dug in a little garden, built a classic picket fence out the front and he was finished. The reno work took all Mark's spare time, after work every evening and every weekend, over four months. It also took every cent of spare cash.

"I even used my credit card and interest-free offers from the larger stores, which are quite useful when you're renovating on a low income, as long as you know you can pay up when the first bill comes in," Mark says. "Don't get stuck in the credit trap."

"I didn't have much of a social life then, but mate, it was so worth it," he says. "It'd be worth it for the learning experience alone but the value it's added is phenomenal and it's getting me a reasonable rental yield as well. I had tenants knocking on the door to move in more than a month before it was ready."

Yield on Mark's properties.

Asset	Original yield	Current yield
#1 House Corio	10.1%	11.7%
#2 Townhouse Brisbane	7.9%	8.1%
#3 House Geelong	0.0%	5.9%

Current yield includes reno costs

The numbers

Mark's experience here is a classic example of how successful renovations can catapult you to the next deal. Mark's reno cost just over $28,000 and created an equity gain of $110,000. A gain of this size allows you to draw down approximately 80% as a line of credit. Here's how it works:

80% of $110,000 = $88,000

You can use this as a 20% deposit to buy property worth five times $88,000, which equals $440,000 (subject to serviceability). This is a "fast track" to a major portfolio. Mark spent $28,000 to create $110,000, or almost $4 for every $1 spent. That's instant equity.

Mark's 2004 asset position.

Asset	Date purchased	Purchase price	Loan	Current value	Income pa
#1 House Corio	Mar-99	$72,000	$60,000	$160,000	$8,580
#2 Townhouse Brisbane	Jul-99	$135,000	$135,000	$230,000	$10,920
#3 House Geelong*	Nov-02	$140,000	$175,000	$250,000	$9,880
Shares (covered call)	Jan-04	$50,000	$50,000	$70,000	$40,000
Total		$397,000	$420,000	$710,000	$69,380
LVR			59.2%		

*Loan for #3 includes reno cost
LVR = original loans/current value
Mark's loan to value ratio (LVR) = $420k/$710k = 59.2% geared

> ┌─ **Reno Kings Tip** ─────────────────────────────────
> *When you first start investing your LVR may be high, say 80–90%. If it is over 80% you will generally have to pay lenders mortgage insurance (LMI). You can add value through renos or other means, and the property value will rise over time. As the value goes up your LVR will drop. Once it is below 80% you generally have "available equity" and no LMI. You can borrow against this equity for the next deal. The power of this strategy is that you don't put any of your hard-earned after-tax dollars in; you just use the available equity. And, if the property value rises within a year, you can have it revalued and apply for a 50% refund on your LMI.*

Congratulations to Mark for taking action and starting on the bumpy path of property investment. Many people are surprised to discover that only 13% of investors own more than one investment property. Mark has already become a member of an exclusive group.

Laying the ground work

Mark has set a goal to have 10 properties in the next 10 years. He has made a great start so far and is still actively looking for more. Although over the last couple of years he found some great property deals, he became very frustrated in his search for finance.

His challenge was to convince financiers he could afford the repayments on another property. The bankers said he was "too rent reliant". A good response to that, we've found, is that the bankers are "too job reliant". Twenty years on you might well still own your original properties, and many more, and they may have doubled or tripled in value, while many of your former bankers will have been made redundant.

Mark uses a property manager for all three of his properties, and the 7% of his rental income that it takes is claimable on tax. He also has cash reserves to fall back on in case of any major repairs that might spring up.

"That's really important, to make sure you don't come a cropper," Mark says. "With the rental return on all three properties, it costs me less than $70 a week to service the repayments and maintain the properties, and I only need to spend an hour a month on them, compared with the 45 to 50 hours a week I'm at my job. And my social life is back on top."

Mark has started bringing in extra cashflow through shares now as well, using what is known as a "covered call" option. This is a share-trading strategy built on an option to buy.

"If I've got 5000 shares that are worth say $10 each, I write a call option for $10.50 in lots of 1000 shares, so each of the five parcels is worth $10,500," explains Mark. "Each person who takes up the option is granted the right to buy a parcel of my shares at a certain time in the future if they reach that price, should they choose to."

The options are for a limited time of a month or two but for that right to buy the purchaser pays Mark a premium of around 20 cents per share each month, whether or not the shares reach that price in that time. That's an earning of $200 per month for each parcel or $1000 for the lot.

"This has got to be one of the best low-risk share-trading strategies around," says Mark. "It really helps my cashflow."

The future

Mark is just about ready to sell the Corio property, as its value has pretty much levelled out. That will give him the deposit for two more houses, which he hopes to have in the next year.

"House prices started going up after 2002 and the rental yields weren't matching them, so I'm waiting till interest rates go up and will hopefully find a bargain or two," he says.

Mark has also found a finance broker, who has struck the right balance for what he needs and broken his finance problems.

"It's marvellous what the right wording on your loan application can do for your prospects. And it's amazing how much the experts don't tell you. Even your own accountant can forget to pass on basic tax-saving tips. It seems you've got to learn a lot on your own, and find out the right questions to ask."

Mark still lives with his parents, an arrangement they're all happy with, but he is getting ready to perhaps buy or build for himself next time.

"I'm taking my time so I get it right, but when I do go down that road it's going to be big first time," he says. You know, I look at my mates and they're still where we all were five years ago – they've really got nothing. Thank God for that kid in the Ferrari."

> ┌─ **Reno Kings Tip** ──────────────────────────────
> *You need to get enough training to "know the questions you need to ask to get the answers you need to know".*

The upshot

Successful property investment and renovation is not easy. You need sound strategies for research, property selection, negotiation, renovation and property management. And you can't do it all yourself.

You need a team: a solicitor for legals, accountants for tax and business planning, quantity surveyors for depreciation, a broker and financier for your loan. And, don't forget, you need to know the right questions to ask. Then there are the tradespeople and the project management skills you need yourself, as well as a property manager once you've done the deal. All this can be difficult, but the rewards are substantial when you get it right. Mark, among many others, can certainly attest to this.

Reno Kings insights

What's your background?

I worked in electrical wholesale for about eight years, but couldn't save a cent. I decided to work up in the mines so I could get a deposit for a house. I was lucky to land a job that paid three times what I was used to. I also sold the Torana to help. Within eight months I had bought two properties.

> ┌─ **Reno Kings Tip** ─
> *Sometimes you need to "sell the flash to get the cash". A car costing you money can be sold to finance investments that make you money. It can turn your whole life around.*

Why did you get started?

The reason I got started is that I didn't want to work for the rest of my life. I had read about some people who had done well financially. I started to investigate and found that most people had become wealthy through property or shares, so I started buying property.

What was your greatest fear?

My greatest fear was not being able to make the repayments on the loan. I was worried about getting tenants and if they would pay on time. As it has turned out I have had no trouble with tenants except for one midnight flit, and their bond paid for that.

Did your parents show you how to get ahead?

My parents were from the old school: "Work hard, pay off your mortgage then retire on your super and, when it runs out, the pension."

What was your greatest mistake?

My greatest mistake was not starting soon enough. If only I knew then what I know now, but I think you have to live a little, then you realise that you have to take a risk in order to get anywhere. Anything is achievable if you put your mind to it.

What do you want to achieve?

My goal is to own 10 houses and not have to work any more.

How would you describe your strategy?

Research your area so you know a deal when you see it. You make your money when you buy. Add value to increase your equity. Draw down any added equity and do it again. Try to get as close to cash positive as you can.

Any memorable experiences along the way?

My most memorable experience has taught me not to trust old houses when they are falling apart. Always make sure there are no live power wires around when you are pulling off old boards. I was using an axe and chopped through a live wire – 240 volts up my arm. Didn't I jump.

> **Reno Kings Tip**
>
> *Always get an electrical safety switch fitted first thing. The cost is only $200 and it could save your life, or someone else's.*

Were there any funny things that happened?

I was taking some old tin off the roof when the beam broke and my legs were dangling through the ceiling. Hey, it needed plastering anyway. And my old man went through the verandah floorboards. But we had a lot of fun working together. Dad was always good at fixing things at home but it was especially good for us to work together on the renovation.

What is your best renovating tip?

My best tip is to replace something with new if it is too bad to repair. One instance was in pulling off wallpaper. It took me two weeks to do two rooms, but if I'd looked closer I would have seen that the plaster needed replacing anyway. I found it quicker and cheaper to replaster as it only took two days a room to hang.

What would you do differently?

For any future major renovations I would organise my tradespeople before settlement and make sure they know I work to a schedule. I'd also go through the house one room at a time before settlement and write down everything that needs to be done. I didn't start to rebuild the back of the Geelong house until eight weeks into the reno. Getting tradespeople organised was a nightmare as it was five days before Christmas.

Galvo's six top tips for getting started in property

1. **Give it a go.** It's a good idea to get some training before you jump into the deep end. It can save you making major mistakes.

2. **Do your research**. Research the area that you are looking to buy in – know your market.

3. **Look for median-priced houses.** Don't buy top dollar, as you won't get the rental return.

4. **Work on your cashflow.** Try to get as close to cashflow positive as possible (not always easy).

5. **Remember, it's a business.** Treat your houses as a business and your tenants as clients and you should have no worries about vacancies.

6. **Get your finance right.** It's critical to have the right loan in the right names and in the right structure.

Reno Kings Product

Find out from the Reno Kings how you can find a property-wise accountant. See page 235 for details and how to order our free report, or go to the website: www.renos.com.au

Some women buy shoes ...
I buy houses

Les and Brenda Irwin have done what some experts would say is impossible, creating a multi-million-dollar portfolio in six years, much of it in just 18 months. They don't call Brenda the Cashflow Queen for nothing.

What an extraordinary story this is. The Reno Kings have been privileged to meet a number of high-achieving investors over the past 10 years. None are more extraordinary than Brenda Irwin and husband Les.

Just try to absorb the power of what Brenda has achieved. She bought 20 cashflow-positive houses in 18 months and now has a total portfolio of 24 houses worth more than $3 million, churning out rent of $168,220 per annum. And she has zero non-deductible debt. All investment debts are principal and interest (P&I) and the properties are still cash positive after all expenses.

Her debt per house is steadily decreasing, her equity is increasing and the cashflow is increasing. This is a powerful combination: debt down, cashflow and equity up. This means her serviceability increases every time she buys a house.

Let's look at how it works. Brenda buys a "fully borrowed" cash-positive house. Her cashflow increases, which increases her serviceability and allows her to buy another cashflow-positive house. This again increases her cashflow, and on and on and on. The result is a cycle of property accumulation and endless cashflow. She has more money in her pocket *after* she buys than *before* she buys.

Brenda says: "To calculate whether an investment property will be cashflow positive there are a number of factors to consider. On the outgoings side of the equation are interest payments, council rates, insurance, renovation and maintenance costs, and on the other side of the ledger (income) there are rents and tax deductions."

"For a quick and easy estimate of returns, I just calculate the gross yield by setting rental per week times 5200 (being 52 weeks in a year by 100 to get a percentage) and dividing by the purchase price, eg:

$125 per week x 5200 / $125,000 = 5.2% gross yield.

Reno Kings Tip

It takes about 2.5–3% of your gross yield to pay outgoings. If your interest rate is 7% then you need a gross yield of 7% + 3% = 10% to guarantee a cashflow-neutral return (before tax). The age, condition and type of property can vary this because of tax deductions, eg, depreciation and capital allowance. It's important to contact a "property- wise" accountant to understand how non-cash deductions can affect your cashflow.

"For me these non-cash deductions, ie, depreciation allowances, can offset some of the profits in the short term, so less tax is due on profits. This has the effect of increasing my cashflow, indirectly, and gives me a better chance of building a profitable portfolio for the future. However, these deductions are not indefinite. Eventually they run out and you have to pay tax on your rental income profits."

Meet Les and Brenda Irwin

Brenda and Les were both raised on farms, near Wondai and Goomeri respectively, in south-east Queensland's South Burnett region, which is about 300 km north-west of Brisbane. They married in 1990 and lived in Tara, about the same distance to Brisbane's west. They were a single-income couple and Les's job as a country town bank teller, like most people's, was never totally secure.

"We worried at the lack of assets and income we had to rely on if he lost his job."

With no savings at the time, they couldn't afford to buy a house, but they were able to borrow to buy a block of land. In 1991 they purchased an acre for $10,000 in Brenda's home town. They planned to repay the loan over time and then reborrow to build a house that they would rent out until they could move there. It seemed the sensible thing to do.

By 1994 they had been blessed with two sons. They also had enough equity in the land, $4000, to buy another acre block of land in a prestige area of Kingaroy, a larger rural centre 30 km from Wondai. Land sales had seen very good growth there and they thought that they could resell in a few years to make a tidy profit.

"At the time the newspapers were scaring people into thinking there was going to be a shortage of good building blocks in the near future so now was the time to buy. Sound familiar? They are still telling the same story 10 years later."

So much for the hype. Three years later they sold the land in Kingaroy for exactly the same amount they'd paid for it, $39,000. In fact, both land purchases were really a bit of a mistake. While much of their spare cash was going into repayments and earning them some equity, there was no income from the vacant blocks and little capital gain.

"It seems we had bought at the height of the boom and values hadn't moved since."

Reno Kings Tip

All investments have two factors: capital gain and income. Vacant land may, repeat may, have capital gain but it usually doesn't generate income. This has a major drawback. The interest on any loan for non-income-producing vacant land is not tax deductible. If the market takes a dive you will also find it hard to sell but you still have to keep forking out for rates, weed clearing, etc. Money out, no capital gain, no tax deduction for the interest and no money in can turn your "dream" block into an investment nightmare.

House #1: Well, it's negatively geared but it's a start

In late 1997 the family took a beach holiday at Burrum Heads a small beachside town (Town A) near Hervey Bay. They loved the place and the local people, and vowed to return some day. Les went one better and asked, "Why don't we buy our future retirement house here now?"

They were figuring that the rental income would cover the expenses so they spent the rest of their holiday annoying the real estate agent and looking for a retirement house. Finding a property with the right prospects was not as easy as first thought.

"Beachfront was out of the question. No way did we have enough equity or wages to pay for it, so we looked everywhere else instead. We found a nice, fairly new timber house in the town. It was only a few streets back from the beach and had three large bedrooms. It was also fully fenced and had a huge shed, suitable for a future boat purchase. We got a contract for $125,000. Now for the tricky part, finance. We still had $4000 equity in our first block of land, and Les cashed in his life insurance policy for around $15,000. We borrowed on a P&I loan and took 'honeymoon rates' at first to get the cheapest interest rates possible."

Reno Kings Tip

Do not mix emotion with buying an investment property. If the numbers don't work don't do it, especially while you are on holiday. The facts are:

1. *You will want to use it when everyone else is on holidays. That's the peak rent period. Don't do it.*
2. *You will probably grow sick of the same holiday in the same place year after year.*
3. *The off-peak period is a very low-rent, high-vacancy period and should be considered when you do your calculations of the return.*
4. *Distance management is expensive, eg, a leaky tap may need a new 50-cent washer but will probably cost you a plumber at $40–$70 per hour, and more on weekends.*

So in January 1998 the Irwins had their first investment house, which rented out at $125 per week, a gross yield of 5.2%. Unfortunately, it was not cashflow positive, though the building depreciation allowance write-off was a help with their tax.

This is what is called a non-cash deduction. It is a depreciation allowance provided by the tax department on building structures, fixtures and fittings of an income-producing investment property. Losses from investment properties (negative cashflow) rather than profits (positive cashflow) can be used to reduce your taxable income, perhaps even producing a tax rebate. During the honeymoon period of the loan they paid as much as they possibly could to get the loan amount down, leaving little for anything else.

"I remember shopping trips when the entire floor and boot of our little Corolla hatch was full of no-name, cut-price and on-special groceries, mostly canned for a long storage life. We bought very few new clothes, no new shoes (except my trusty Masseur sandals) and there were no more beach holidays. We budgeted absolutely ruthlessly during this time and managed to pay off a fair amount of the loan, which also gave us more equity," says Brenda.

House #2: Discovering cashflow

Brenda's sister was living in a unit in Kingaroy and wanted to move into a house instead. They looked around for a cheap but livable house and found a two-bedroom, rundown but adequate house in nearby Murgon (Town B) and bought it for $27,000.

"My parents, my sister and Les and I got to work and for a few thousand dollars did the little house up into a home. Most of the expense was to install a new bathroom, a second toilet upstairs and some built-in wardrobes. The rest was just scrubbing, painting and evicting the resident fleas. My sister rented the house from us for $100 per week. This produced an impressive gross yield of 17.3% from the purchase price plus $3000 for renovations. The house was then revalued at $38,000. This second purchase really helped our loan serviceability and, hey, we had discovered the joy of a cashflow-positive investment."

House #3: Home, sweet home

Meanwhile, Les had been transferred to Lowood, a bit closer to Brisbane, and they moved into another rental house. Little boys, though, are not gentle on houses and the constant, "Don't touch that wall; you can't do that in a rental house; you can't hang that there," was getting them down.

They bought their own home in 1999 for $70,000 in Lowood (Town C). It was a high-set, 100-year-old Queenslander on a big 3600 sq m block with subdivision potential.

"The advertised price was $85,000 but we thought we'd be smarties and offer $68,000," says Brenda. "Imagine our surprise when the agent turned up on our doorstep with a contract and said if we were willing to pay $70,000 we had ourselves a house. It needed a lot of fixing up but the 'bones' of the house were good and it already had a brand new roof."

Brenda recalls someone saying to her, "Ah, a Queenslander. You'll spend the rest of your life renovating." But she and Les plan to be around for quite a few years yet, so they're pacing themselves slowly on the reno.

"What we really fell in love with was the huge 200-year-old Moreton Bay fig tree in the back yard. It attracts every bird from miles around."

House #4: Now we're getting there

In 2000 the trend was to buy in Brisbane to get capital growth so they decided to have a look.

"We couldn't afford anything right in the city and any bargains that did turn up there were quickly snapped up. We did manage to buy a reasonable house on a busy road in Upper Mt Gravatt on Brisbane's southside though for $105,000."

This house also has a story. When Les and Brenda drove past for a second look it was one of the hottest summer days in history.

"The owners were trying to trim the trees in the front garden and tempers were getting pretty frayed. Although the house was listed for sale at $120,000, we offered $105,000. The owner had paid $110,000 for it in 1992. They just wanted a sale, as they had already built themselves a brand new home in another suburb and were keen to move in, so our offer was accepted."

⌐ Reno Kings Tip

Some people will tell you that property always goes up in value. They are wrong, and right! It just doesn't go up evenly and some areas go up when others do nothing. The increases are like an uneven set of steps so there is an advantage if you know when to sell and when to buy. The profit or loss through mistiming can be enormous. In the above case, the sellers waited in vain for eight long years for a profit and got a $10k loss. A financial disaster. Compare this to a home Geoff bought in 1992 for $220k. It was worth $400k in 2000, a capital gain of $180k (82%) over the same period. The difference? Timing, the right property in the right area at the right price.

Les and Brenda were starting to get into the swing of this property investment business. To obtain access to their equity, they got their three houses and the block of land revalued.

"We were pretty shocked when our own home was devalued by $10,000. Our equity should have been around $100,000 but now we were a bit short. We had to borrow very close to the purchase price, which meant we had to take out LMI (lenders mortgage insurance), costing $2400. We didn't want to lose our latest bargain so we borrowed the extra money needed to cover the insurance from our families."

The house rented for $170 per week so the gross yield was 8.4%.

House #5: A nice little earner

By this stage the Irwins realised they needed to get a little more serious if property investment was going to be their future.

"Our investing bargains were kind of a one step forward, one back, affair and we needed some sort of training. In 2001 Les and I had finally saved enough money to attend a renovation course with the Reno Kings. We had no trade skills and very little income to do renovations, but the course taught us that it didn't matter. What did matter was that we could do something, even if it was just mowing the lawns and washing down the walls. This gave us confidence to get out there in the market and look at all potential properties, no matter how filthy or overgrown they were."

"Some properties we've looked at had cavernous holes in the floors, chest-high grass, leaking plumbing and fleas that jumped onto our legs as soon as we walked in the door! We've passed on the cavernous holes and the flea pits but we have bought a few with leaky toilets and jungle gardens. We stuck to the Reno Kings tips and only bought properties with a good building structure."

Reno Kings Tip

Some people don't buy "dumps" because they think, "I couldn't live there". Hey, remember you won't be living there. Many "dumps" can be quickly made over into perfectly satisfactory rentals for very little cost and effort.

The search for cashflow-positive properties continued. They decided the Brisbane market was not really their cup of tea, but nearby Ipswich was looking good, even though capital growth had been very slow there since 1992. Employment was good in the area, wages were stable and rents were cashflow positive from day one.

"It was also closer for us than Brisbane and our children were learning the chime of 'Not house-hunting again'. We found a nice three-bedroom, high-set timber house in Ipswich that didn't need renovation and bought it for $55,000. It rented for $135 per week for a gross yield of 12.7%, nicely positive cashflow.

"Meanwhile, we realised we were never likely to build on our land in Wondai and we'd gotten sick and tired of mowing it, so we sold it for $14,000. We had made a gross profit of $4000 in a ridiculous 10 years."

Reno Kings Tip

Geoff did the same thing when he was a novice investor. Vacant land: no income, all outgo, and the interest is not tax deductible. This is a cashflow disaster if you don't put a house on it.

House #6: When all else fails, do it yourself

In February 2002 the real estate market in Ipswich was finally starting to show capital growth and Brisbane was already rising in leaps and bounds.

"We used the proceeds from our land sale as a deposit and bought our first serious renovator in Town C, close to home, for $50,000. It was a two-bedroom, timber house on a fenced quarter acre (1012 sq m). The overgrown garden was hard work but I managed. I completely repainted inside and ripped up the pet-stained carpet from the hardwood floors."

> **Reno Kings Tip**
>
> *Leave your carpets down as drop sheets while you paint. Store them for future use and they may be a tax deduction. Ask your accountant.*

Then disaster struck. All the professional floor sanders were booked up for the next six weeks and Brenda couldn't hire a sanding machine in town. She decided to get creative.

"I bought myself a belt-sander, hooking it up to our own dust extractor, and started to sand the floors myself. This was the hottest few days in the whole summer and I burned out the belt-sander. They were on special for $100, so I bought another one. All day, every day, for two weeks I sanded all the floors in the entire house and then applied a polyurethane sealer myself. The floors came up as good as a professional job and I got the place tenanted immediately for $135 per week."

Taking into account the $1000 worth of renovations, the gross yield was 13.8%. The house was revalued at $65,000, an increase of $15,000 (that's a huge 30% equity gain), and the value on their own home had also increased by $15,000, to $75,000.

"We had equity and positive cashflow so off we went shopping again. The market was still going up, albeit slowly, and there were still a few 'cheapies" for sale in Ipswich that could give us more positive cashflow."

Houses #7, 8 and 9: Now we're really talking

In June 2002, armed with their new-found equity, they hit the market. Three frantic weeks later they had bought three more houses in Ipswich suburbs. House #7 they got by accident.

"At the Reno Kings course we attended in 2001 one of the tips was to put in lots of low offers. And we believed them! We offered $35,000 on a 'renovators delight' in Ipswich and the vendors accepted. To accept such a low offer was quite unusual as it was a three-bedroom 'miners cottage', which are usually in demand and can fetch quite a good price."

Brenda went into hard labour mode again, mowing, washing and painting. This one needed a new toilet installed as the old one was cracked.

"There were two rats living there also. One rat drowned in the old toilet just before the plumber arrived. He removed the body for free and installed a new toilet for around $350. The other rat moved out of it's own accord and I quickly bogged up all the entry holes in the floors so it couldn't get back in. Another thing to get fixed was the hot-water system as it was inside on a timber floor and leaking like a sieve. We got a 'new', secondhand one installed on the outside of the house and fixed the floor for a few hundred dollars. We added a garage door to make it lockable, and a new mailbox for $55. The painting was tedious as the walls and ceiling were tongue and groove and had never been gap filled, ever."

> **Reno Kings Tip**
> *Putting in a new toilet is a small expense but it is always well received by renters and buyers.*

One of the delights of renovating Queenslanders is filling the gaps in VJ (vertical joint) boards. Over time the house may move slightly or the timber boards (tongue and groove) will expand and contract, opening up the vee, and you get ugly vertical gaps of varying width. These are then filled with the appropriate gap filler, which is easier to paint and gives a cleaner, well-maintained and well-built look.

"I gave Les a gap gun and asked him to help me. I nearly had heart failure when he asked how it worked, but 75 tubes of gap filler later he was truly an expert. I did all the painting with a brush, as the roller kept missing the grooves, but it looked great when finished. We rented immediately for $125 per week and with the $4000 worth of renovations included we got a gross yield of 16.7%. The house was revalued at $80,000 so we had gained more than $40,000 in equity. From $35,000 to $80,000 less $4000 reno costs gives 117% equity gain and a $10 return for every $1 spent! Happy days!"

> **Reno Kings Tip**
> *Due to the movement in VJ boards only certain gap fillers are designed for sealing. Always read the label to see if the product is suitable.*

House #8 was a three-bedroom, post-war timber home that needed nothing done. At $58,500 Les and Brenda wondered why it was so cheap.

"Crook neighbours, we found out later, was why it was cheap. After a lot of hassles, which included the neighbour grazing his guinea pigs near the back door of our rental house and doing burnouts with his car on our back lawn, our property manager complained to the owner of the house. Eventually the tenants were evicted so the problem was solved. We got tenants in ours for $140 per week, producing a gross yield of 12.4%."

Reno Kings Tip

When you buy a house you get the neighbours too. Check them out. Ask the one next to them what they are like. They will normally share with you. You really do need to know if the local drug dealer/rock band/bikie leader is nearby. It could affect your future capital gain and rental. Don't believe me? Read Melanie MacDonald's story again.

House #9 was a high-set, three-bedroom Queenslander and came full of furniture. They hired a quantity surveyor to assess the depreciation.

"He had a field day with it and got us lots of tax depreciation dollars ($11,000 worth). We bought it for $64,000 and rented it for $145 per week, giving a gross yield of 11.7%."

Buying in bulk

"We also found there were reduced costs when you bought multiple properties. The bank only charged one search fee, for example, and there was only one application fee. (We now pay no application fee because we pay an annual professional investor's fee of around $400 per year).

Significant savings can be had with this method if you are an active investor. The properties must settle on the same date though or they might freeze your accounts between differing settlement dates.

"We had this happen once. It was really frightening to live off 'fresh air' for a week, between settlement dates, with no money."

Houses #10, 11 and 12: On the up

Brenda's research, checking newspapers and running up a large phone bill to real estate agents, showed Brisbane property prices were rising quickly. Ipswich had risen by between $5000 and $10,000 and it didn't look like it was going to stop there. The 'wave' of capital growth was spreading out from Brisbane city, through its suburbs and affecting Ipswich. With the rising prices, the revaluations on their previous purchases were also increasing, creating even more equity.

"We still looked for the cashflow-positive bargains and bought another three houses, all typical three-bedroom timber types, in Ipswich for $65,000 each. Two were side by side and rented for $135 per week each. The other I renovated by painting the interior and Les fixed a few holes in the walls. This reno was quite a challenge. Les would drop me and the children at the house before he went to work and collect us on his way home. The children were home-schooled so I had to supervise their work while renovating, on top of bottle-feeding a tiny premature puppy every two hours. My own housework took a nose-dive for a few weeks."

This one rented for $145 per week and was revalued at $80,000.

House #13: Staying ahead of the ripple

The Ipswich market by the end of 2002 was getting a bit expensive for Brenda's liking so they had another look at Town B, where they'd bought four years earlier. They figured the price rises would soon begin to ripple out from Brisbane and Ipswich, and it was worth looking further afield. By then Brenda had also developed a good business relationship with the property manager looking after their first purchase in the town.

"This next house only cost $36,000, which was below median price for the area at the time, but the vendor was a fellow investor who wanted his money as quickly as possible to invest closer to the city."

The three-bedroom, post-war timber house needed no work and came with an existing tenant paying $90 per week, giving 13% yield.

> ### Reno Kings Tip
> *Brenda is now creating instant equity, 23% equity gain in a few weeks, by adding value.*

House #14: Room to move

They still searched for property in Ipswich but by now there were very few houses for sale under $100,000 and "Brisbane prices were crazy". One morning while checking out the real estate in the local paper, they noticed that the property beside houses 10 and 11, the two neighbouring houses they'd bought in Ipswich, was for sale. Brenda thought that three 1000 sq m properties side by side could be very promising for future development opportunities.

"The open house was to be held that Saturday afternoon, but we didn't want anyone else looking at it so we were on the agency's doorstep when it opened."

They asked to inspect the house immediately and said that if it was what they were looking for they were quite prepared to make an immediate offer. The agent took them to inspect the house, a fine, high-set, three-bedroom Queenslander.

"Les started the negotiations himself, direct with the owner, he wanted it so badly. The agent was left to just stand around with me while they went at it."

They signed it up for $92,500. Only after settlement did they reveal to the agent that they also owned the two houses beside it. The house rented for $160 per week for a gross yield of 8.9%. This was lower than their preferred 9%-plus yield but it had development potential.

They have since asked a draftsman to inspect the three blocks. He agreed the slope is perfect for drainage, the transformer on the footpath is ideal for electricity and even the driveways are perfectly situated for a future development.

⌐ Reno Kings Tip ─────────────────────

One of the keys to a development site is removal of stormwater. If your land is sloping to the street this is ideal. We recommend you use a townplanner or development consultant to do your due diligence.

Halfway there

At this point, at the end of 2002, it had been five years since Les and Brenda bought their "retirement" beachhouse, and only two years since they'd started getting serious about investing in property. Most extraordinary though is that in just the previous six months they'd bought eight houses. By now their portfolio was worth more than $2 million and was bringing in around $90,000 per annum in rent.

But they certainly didn't stop there. In fact, they were starting to get this property investment business down pat.

"Les and I work as a team. I am the ferret for finding, renovating and running the properties. Les is the whiz at getting the finance and repaying the loans," says Brenda.

The Irwins' current portfolio.

#	Town	Purchased	Purchase cost	Loan balance	Repayment per month	Rent per week	Current value	Sale price	Capital gain	Yield (rent/cost)
*1	Town A	Jan-98	$125,000					$185,000	$60,000	0.0%
2	Town B	Dec-98	$27,000			$110	$80,000		$53,000	21.2%
**3	Town C	Dec-99	$70,000				$165,000		$95,000	0.0%
*4	Brisbane	Nov-00	$105,000					$220,000	$115,000	0.0%
5	Ipswich	Aug-01	$55,000			$150	$170,000		$115,000	14.2%
6	Town C	Feb-02	$50,000			$150	$130,000		$80,000	15.6%
*7	Ipswich	Jun-02	$35,000					$80,000	$45,000	0.0%
8	Ipswich	Jun-02	$58,500	$55,102	$415	$150	$160,000		$101,500	13.3%
9	Ipswich	Jun-02	$64,000	$65,367	$487	$150	$165,000		$101,000	12.2%
10	Ipswich	Oct-02	$65,000	$70,607	$428	$150	$165,000		$100,000	12.0%
11	Ipswich	Oct-02	$65,000	$67,530	$410	$150	$160,000		$95,000	12.0%
12	Ipswich	Oct-02	$65,000	$67,530	$410	$145	$165,000		$100,000	11.6%
13	Town B	Nov-02	$36,000	$39,179	$238	$105	$85,000		$49,000	15.2%
14	Ipswich	Dec-02	$92,500	$95,330	$577	$160	$190,000		$97,500	9.0%
15	Town B	Jan-03	$52,000	$53,260	$327	$130	$105,000		$53,000	13.0%
16	Town B	Jan-03	$52,000	$54,739	$327	$130	$87,000		$35,000	13.0%
17	Town B	Jan-03	$38,000	$39,945	$239	$115	$75,000		$37,000	15.7%
18	Town B	Mar-03	$30,000			$105	$75,000		$45,000	18.2%
19	Ipswich	Mar-03	$122,000	$130,979	$790	$195	$240,000		$118,000	8.3%
20	Ipswich	Mar-03	$100,000	$102,154	$618	$175	$190,000		$90,000	9.1%
21	Ipswich	Apr-03	$105,000	$112,584	$683	$190	$210,000		$105,000	9.4%
22	Town B	Jul-03	$53,000	$47,962	$313	$120	$83,000		$30,000	11.8%
23	Town B	Jul-03	$52,000	$46,551	$304	$120	$75,000		$23,000	12.0%
24	Town B	Jul-03	$52,000	$46,551	$304	$125	$105,000		$53,000	12.5%
25	Town B	Nov-03	$67,000	$69,464	$416	$125	$87,000		$20,000	9.7%
26	Town B	Nov-03	$69,000	$66,839	$416	$125	$95,000		$26,000	9.4%
27	Ipswich	May-04	$145,000	$151,000	$948	$160	$165,000		$20,000	5.7%
			TOTAL COST	TOTAL LOANS	TOTAL REPAYMENT	TOTAL RENT	CURRENT VALUE	TOTAL SALES	CAPITAL GAIN	AVERAGE YIELD
	Total		$1,585,000	$1,382,672	$8,650	$3,235	$3,227,000	$485,000	$1,862,000	10.6%
	per annum		*excl houses sold		$103,800	$168,220				**incl PPOR
	Current LVR			42.8%						

Notes:
*#1 sold $185k May 2003
*#4 sold $220k August 2003
*#7 sold $80K July 2003
**#3 PPOR
(principal place of residence)

Index	type	population
Town A	coastal SEQld	800+ off season
Town B	rural SEQld	3000+
Town C	rural SEQld	3000+
Ipswich	city SEQld	127,000

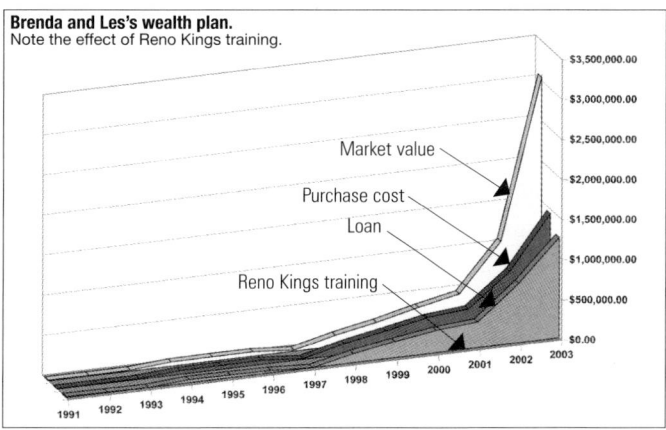

Brenda and Les's wealth plan.
Note the effect of Reno Kings training.

Houses #15, 16 and 17: Back to Town B

In January 2003 Brenda and Les decided to revisit Town B and give Ipswich a rest, buying three more houses there for a total of $142,000.

House #15, a three-bedroom, high-set Queenslander, had already been renovated by the previous owners and there was no work to be done. Lovely! The purchase price was $52,000.

"Being newly renovated, when the quantity surveyor assessed all the new capital improvements to the house, we were entitled to claim an extra $5350 capital works deductions (the modern ATO term for special building write-off) on our tax return. Funnily, although the house was three hours drive away from us, the vendors turned out to have moved to our town in the next street."

The other two, #16 and #17, both low-set houses with three bedrooms, were $52,000 and $38,000 respectively. They both also had existing tenants so there were no letting fees. House #17 had an existing safety switch, saving $300 (in some states these are compulsory to install when you buy a property). All houses were on 1012 sq m blocks. Rents totalled $365 per week ($125+$125+$115) for a gross yield of 13.3%.

> ┌─ **Reno Kings Tip** ─────────────────────────────
> *Install an electrical safety switch in every property. It may save you from being sued but, more importantly, it may save a life. Just do it!*

House #18: Oh for a carport!

In March 2003 it was time to buy again. They bought another "cheapie" on 1012 sq m in Town B for $30,000.

"The only reason it was cheap, as far as I could see," says Brenda, "was that there was no car accommodation. We got a carport professionally erected for $2000 and the house rented out for $100 per week, giving a gross yield of 17.3%.

"This buy was an absolute beauty. A quantity surveyor's report revealed that the house had been moved to the block in 1988, after changes to ATO rulings on depreciation write-offs. This meant building write-offs on restumping, rewiring, replumbing and a new front fence. This, together with several items of furniture, fixtures and fittings (including an antique lamp), meant that the value of the house and land left after depreciation came to only $5,627."

Houses #19, 20 and 21: The turnaround

As the previous four houses, with gross yields up to 17.3%, were generating substantial surplus cashflow Les and Brenda decided to vary their plan. They returned to the Ipswich market for some quality houses.

"In March and April 2003 we bought three more for between $100,000 and $122,000 each."

House #19, a two-storey, three-bedroom brick home, was "only off-contract for 10 minutes" before Brenda and Les snapped it up. It cost $122,000 and the dining room was converted to a bedroom for $1000. This allowed them to increase the rent from $165 to $185 per week. It's now worth $240,000. That's 98%, capital gain in under two years.

House #20, a three-bedroom high-set, was put under contract for $100,000 without even going inside. The tenant had denied them entry without the required notice. It has since almost doubled in value.

House #21 was a building society repossession. There was a hole in the ceiling from roof damage ($1000 repair). The pool was green. The house was filthy. The total clean-up and repair cost close to $5000.

"Les took eight loads of rubbish to the tip and I hired four professional cleaners for three days non-stop to fix the mess. That cost me $1000!"

While they were excellent buys and great for capital growth, these purchases proved to be their undoing. The combined yield on the three new properties at the time was just 8.3%.

"Our positive cashflow had dwindled and the bank was not prepared to finance any further lending."

Unless they changed direction, their plans for buying more property were finished. They pored over their portfolio looking for a strategy that would get them back into the market. At last they worked it out!

The four-step restructure strategy

It was time for Brenda and Les to take drastic action. They decided to restructure their portfolio in four steps:

1. Sell all non-performing (low-yield) or "problem" properties.
2. Pay off any non-deductible debt (their home loan).
3. Reduce debt on sufficient houses to create surplus cashflow.
4. Purchase more high-yield, cashflow-positive houses.

Step 1: Selling up

House #1 was sold. They sold the beachhouse for $185,000. On current values it was yielding only 3.9%.

"The beachhouse was negatively geared and after owning it for five years it was still negative and looked like it was going to stay that way for the next twelve years," says Les. "A capital profit of $60,000 in five years, with rent receipts of $36,347 less $49,292 in expenses, is hardly anything to write home about. We were simply casting out a poor performer to enable us to use the capital gain to pay out the loan on our own home."

House #7 was sold. They sold their $35,000 "renovators delight" in Ipswich for $80,000. The house was in a reactive "black soil" area and needed major relevelling and landscaping.

"Our main reasons for selling were the constant threat of termite invasion from neighbouring properties and the need for professional restumping, which was now becoming urgent. It was also next to a noisy panel beater (he was quiet when we bought). This upset prospective tenants and forced us to lower the rent."

House #4 was sold. In the 2003–04 financial year, they sold their $105,000 house in Upper Mt Gravatt for $220,000. The yield (on the market value at the time) was only 4% and there was a road caveat on the property for an extra few lanes of traffic to be taken from the front yard in the near future. They decided to take the profit on this potentially "problem" property to complete their restructure and increase cashflow through purchasing small-town properties.

"The sale of the 'high land value' property in Brisbane and the purchase of 'low land value' in small towns also reduced our exposure to land tax," says Brenda. "Land tax in Queensland is based on the unimproved value of land held above a certain threshold."

Step 2: Paying off

With the proceeds from the sales of houses 1, 4 and 7 they paid out the $67,000 loan on their own home. This "killed off" their only non-tax-deductible loan to create major discretionary cashflow.

Step 3: Reducing debt

They paid out $160,000 to clear the loans on four of their investment houses, two in Town B, and one each in Town C and Ipswich, which were all in the lower end of the market but with high yields. They now had their own home with no debt and four investment houses with no debt, which were also pouring in high rent returns.

This strategy immediately added to their serviceability and their ability to borrow. They were now ready to hit the market again.

Step 4: Buying up houses #22, 23 and 24

With the improved cashflow created by the debt-reduction steps 2 and 3 Les and Brenda "went shopping for cashflow properties" in Town B. They bought another three houses in July 2003 for a total of $157,000.

House #22 had been totally renovated and capital depreciation on the renovations were tax deductible at $12,830. An extra bonus.

House #23 was a three-bedroom dwelling on 809 sq m. It had two massive trees that were attacking the external paintwork and guttering. They cost $1200 to remove.

"The street appeal of the house once the imposing trees were gone was impressive," says Brenda. "You could now see the house for the trees!"

House #24, a four-bedroom Queenslander on a large 1839 sq m block, was only $52,000.

"We figured this was a bargain as we had been considering a similar house on the same size block for $85,000, but it had gone under contract to someone else. We didn't mess around with this one and signed the contract right away."

Total rents are $345 per week for a gross yield of 11.4%. Net positive cashflow from the new properties was $4097 per annum and savings on interest repayments was worth $12,147 per annum. Total cashflow from the restructure is: $12,417 pa + $4097 pa = $16,514 pa or $318 pw. The result of Step 4 is more positive cashflow. "We love cashflow!"

Houses #25 and 26: Reaping the rewards

In November 2003 Brenda and Les were on the prowl again. They bought another two houses in Town B for a total of $136,000. Both were three-bedroom, high-set on 1012 sq m each. Rents totalled $240 per week for a gross yield of 8.8%. They were good-quality houses and "cashflow neutral", as interest rates had just risen by 0.5%, remembering you need at least 2.5% to cover other expenses. (A year later, with rent increases, they were over 9% gross yield and were cashflow positive.)

Effective property management

Brenda and Les have two property managers (PMs), one in Town B and one in Ipswich, to manage their properties. Their management fees are between 8% and 9% of the rent charged, though some can be as low as 5% or as high as 12%.

"Our two PMs are both great; friendly, but tough on any defaulters. Occasionally we'll use the original manager when we make a purchase. We transferred one property to our preferred manager on settlement as I was not comfortable with the fat file of defaults the previous manager had with the tenant. Tenant eviction was also stressed within that contract, so we got our preferred PM and new tenants for that property."

Property managers can also be a great help to out-of-town buyers.

"You can ask them to do a rental appraisal before you sign any contracts if you wish, though they may charge for this service. Never take a real estate agent's word for what a suitable rental amount would be for a certain property as they may only sell real estate. Always consult a PM to get accurate rental information."

Brenda uses their guidance whenever she's on the hunt for new houses in those towns. If the property manager says, "I wouldn't buy that house. There is a major problem with the neighbours and in fact I won't manage it if you do buy it," then she stays well away.

> **┌─ Reno Kings Tip**
>
> *From bitter experience it is bad enough to handle your own unruly tenant let alone a neighbour from hell next door. Tenant after tenant will leave, your cashflow will be destroyed and there is not a lot you can do about it. Best to stay right away from those areas. The advice of an informed local is invaluable.*

House #27: The new addition

Les and Brenda bought their latest addition in May 2004, back in Ipswich, and down the street from another of their Ipswich houses. At a cost of $145,000 it required no immediate work and had an existing tenant paying $160 per week rent, giving a yield of 5.7%.

"Not only was this house $20,000 undervalued when we bought it," says Brenda, "it is sitting on a lovely, sloping 809 sq m block suitable for units. Before signing the contract, I checked to see when the tenancy lease was to expire. It had only one month to go, so as part of the settlement contract I specified the rent was to increase to $170 per week.

This would produce a better gross yield of 6.3% from day one. It is still negatively geared against our current interest rates but this should improve within the next three years also, as the rents increase in line with inflation. It really sets us up for when we move into the development phase of our strategy."

Risk management

Some in the industry would say it is just not possible to assemble a multi-million-dollar portfolio in just six years (most bought in just 18 months). Well Brenda and Les have done just that. Now they have to hold on to it. Let's look at some of the risks they might face.

Interest rate rise. See Les's advice on "reference rate" mechanisms. Brenda also says that if interest rates rise then the surplus set aside to fix tenants' non-urgent maintenance requests would be diverted to pay the higher interest rates.

Regional downturn. Half the properties are in the one small town, so if there is any risk it may be here. This could be the case if, for instance, a major regional employer went under. However, many of the tenants are "government employees", ie, they are on social security or pension payments, or are public schoolteachers or council workers. This means that their income is basically guaranteed, as opposed to the risk of a large private employer possibly going under. However, diversifying into other areas is the key.

┌─ **Reno Kings Tip** ─────────────────────────────

Basically there are no future guarantees in a very small town. You trade off the higher rental return for higher risk. Any major loss of employment will slowly kill the town as the parents stay and get older, the kids get bored and maybe disruptive or grow up and leave for job prospects elsewhere. The result is a gradual decrease in income to the town, a slow degrading of services and at worst a ghost town. Small mining towns are a good example. They are totally run by the economics of the mine. The mine loses money, the mine shuts, the town dies. End of story. You can get some risk protection by diversifying into larger regional towns as Brenda has.

Vacancies. As there is plenty of diversification through the number of properties held they would be unlikely to have more than one or two properties vacant for long. In fact, Brenda says they have tenants waiting.

Redundancy, injury or illness. There is only one salary but because Les has been in his job for so long there would be a substantial payout in the case of redundancy. This would go to reducing the debt and creating more cashflow. Superannuation and lots of accrued long-service leave provide an extra buffer. At worst Brenda says she has a couple of properties that have doubled in price and would sell easily, even in a slow market. In the case of serious illness or injury Les has income replacement insurance, which should go some way to helping.

Divorce or death. Divorce is unlikely. Brenda and Les have never been happier and work as a team. They love what they do and have the time to do it well. As the properties are jointly owned, if one party dies the other immediately gets control of all with no stamp duty or capital gains tax.

The upshot

Whew! This has been quite a journey, and it is certainly quite a portfolio, especially when you consider that during the peak of their investing some 20 houses were bought during an 18-month period. Very busy investors indeed. More like a feeding frenzy than steady accumulation.

With their portfolio now worth close to $3.25 million and their current loan to value ratio (LVR as current loan balance to current valuation) at 42.8%, Les and Brenda are again in a very powerful position. The average yield, with rental income of $168,220 per year, is a cashflow-positive 10.6% and the capital gain, including the proceeds from property sales (aside from the early vacant blocks) is $1,862,000. Debt repayments are $103,800 per year on loans of $1,382,672, leaving surplus cash of $64,420 per year (before $51,916 for rates, insurance and agent fees). Maintenance costs vary greatly and come from the surplus income.

That's a net income of $12,504 per annum (before tax). This net income will increase as the debt is repaid and more cash-positive properties are bought.

In reality this remarkable couple do not have to do much more. The portfolio is built. It is almost sufficient to support them. Debt is going down. Values are going up. The portfolio is cash positive. There is no non-deductible debt. Their tax rate is extremely low due to the depreciation. They are on track to the "promised land" of all investors: financial independence.

Reno Kings insights

What's your background?

Les: I've been an employee of one of the major banks for 28 years, since I left high school.

Brenda: I'm a retired dental assistant, jillaroo and meatworker. I retired to become a full-time wife to Les and mother to two sons, Michael and John-Luke.

Why did you get started?

Brenda: I didn't want us to retire late in life to a government pension.

Les: We had a toehold in the property market, initially with our dream home on the coast to retire to and then as a way to build up our cashflow first and asset base second.

What was your greatest fear?

Brenda: That Les might lose his wages before our portfolio could make capital growth.

Les: We would end up with bad tenants and lots of debt and no one would help us. This didn't happen, almost the opposite.

Did your parents show you how to get started and get ahead?

Les: Yes I think so. Though not directly involved, they were always encouraging and probably just as worried about us getting in too far. A good upbringing and understanding, honesty and integrity in all matters is more important than any final outcome.

Brenda: My parents have never bought a rental investment. They were nervous about borrowing money to invest and used all their income to raise a family. Their children were their investment and they passed on to me the importance of family. We try to include our kids in all our purchases and in running the properties and try to educate them that Dad's ATM can't keep giving out money for them to spend if there's no money in the account.

What was your greatest mistake?

Brenda: Buying land instead of cashflow-positive property.

Les: Buying two blocks of vacant land and then a rental property at the beach. We sold both blocks and later on the beachhouse. By then we understood the lesson of cashflow, cashflow, cashflow.

What do you want to achieve?

Brenda: Financial independence with an ongoing passive income. Les likes a pyramid of 10 on the bottom, then 9, 8 and so on, which totals 55. I like 100, then sell 50 and retire on the rest. We are both in our early 40s and reckon we'd better make up for lost time. Who wants to suffer severe budgeting for more than 10–12 years? Better to have a big "do without" now than wait too long and perhaps not want to do the hard yards at all.

Les: A lot more than we thought was possible. We have always tried to keep as many options open as possible. We are careful to not lock ourselves into a position where we would be left with only one option, such as to sell.

How would you describe your strategy?

Brenda: A careful balance between capital growth, for equity, and positive cashflow, for debt serviceability. Our strategy is to build up the cashflow with increasing median rents then, with a good solid base, go for the more speculative ventures. All properties are jointly owned. Land tax is not yet applicable as the cut-off amount is per person in joint situations, and that is now almost $276k each in Queensland. Be careful though, as the land tax laws differ in every state; check your own legislation.

Les: To get returns as high as possible while buying the best properties we could find. Most of these were leftovers or "don't wanters" but only required some basic renovation to make rentable. We left a lot of good capital growth properties for people with more income than we had. The capital growth we experienced mainly happened with the property boom and not as a direct strategy. We relied on initial renovations for small amounts of capital growth. Also, we only spent money on essentials for ourselves, such as food, phone and power bills, putting petrol in the car. All remaining income went into the property purchases.

Any memorable experiences that happened along the way?

Brenda: The devaluation of our own home was not something I'd expected at all. On the funny side, one of our sons, at around 10 years old, started building "investment houses" out of bit and pieces in our back yard and selling them to his dad for a few dollars. When Les accidentally bumped one with the lawnmower our son repaired it "for free", saying "It's okay, Dad, your insurance will pay for it."

Les: Standing underneath a house negotiating a price with the owner while the agent looked on was pretty memorable. And looking through the front door of our half-renovated pride and joy and seeing two great rats jumping over each other and having the time of their life. Having people walk in and want to rent the property while we renovated was impressive also.

Where do you find your deals?

Brenda: We keep annoying our real estate agency and we keep in touch with the property managers too. Sometimes other investors who have properties managed by them are willing to sell a bit cheaper "in-house" for a quick sale. We check out real estate websites. Go to the Reno Kings site *www.renos.com.au.* They have more than 40 sites to surf there. We call councils, visit areas, talk to locals and shopkeepers (hardware shops are my favourite). If you find a particular area that looks promising, then run up a phone bill and speak to the property managers in the area. They are a wealth of knowledge and you might find a good one that way. The *Australian Property Investor* magazine has stats and rents as a guide for most areas in Queensland. I have some properties I have never seen but they bring good cashflow. I just bought them on the property manager's recommendations, the building and pest reports, and the numbers.

What's your best renovating tip?

Brenda: Keep it quick, clean and simple. Do a cosmetic reno. Any major structural renovations will slow you down. Initially I did the labour jobs myself as money was tight, but now I use tradesmen as they are tax deductible and you get a professional job.

Les: We discovered you don't have to spend a fortune on renos. A basic good scrub-up and paint can really add value. Add a fence and a carport, replace that leaking toilet, fix the holes in the walls and you can add spectacular dollars in the form of revalued equity and increased rental return. So, instead of shying away from the grubby, overgrown garden, leaking toilet deals, we found these "dumps" very negotiable and it opened up a whole new facet of the market. Essentials for that: sugar soap, gap gun, Solvers brand linseed oil undercoat, and then paint. (Very few brands of undercoat include linseed oil. It can be extremely important when painting over newly puttied windows as the undercoat will bond to the putty.)

What's your best money-making tip?

Brenda: Make sure you have an excellent property manager. Poor rental yields and long vacancies can break you.

Les: Buy well and stay away from major structural problems.

Any other tips for other investors?

Les: We always sign subject to building and pest inspections and finance approval.

Brenda: We engage a quantity surveyor (QS) after settlement to estimate building write-off. The building inspection should give you a rough "guesstimate". If it's an old house with no building write-off, I'd guess there'd be from $6k to $8k for regular fixtures and fittings (F&F) depreciation. It's not a lot but every little bit helps. We recently bought a property with an above-ground pool and found it was depreciable at 15% per annum as opposed to 2.5% capital write-off for an in-ground pool. But be aware that from July 2004 there are new classifications to depreciation rules. Always check the latest version before putting in a tax return, as the rules may have changed. I use a QS on all properties regardless of building age, as I have to prepare a purchase summary of all new purchases each tax year. The F&F items the QS unearths are deducted from the full purchase price to find the basic house and land amount. The QS report keeps the tax agent happy.

What's your advice to people getting started in property?

Brenda: The first thing your lender will ask is, "How much have you saved?" They want to know if you have the budgeting know-how to be able to repay loans. If an expensive property scares you then look for a cheapie. Once you start investing it's like the battery bunny on TV, you just keep going and going.

Les: Don't buy the expensive car. The number of people who load themselves up with a huge car loan and then want to make money investing is unreal.

What would you do differently?

Brenda: We were very busy in buying as much as our budget could take so I doubt we could have bought any more than we did. I wouldn't have bought three capital-growth investment properties at once though. We really needed a balance of cashflow-positive ones in between them.

Les: I think perhaps later on we realised we were part of a team and not a two-man band. More initial attention to team building would have made building the portfolio easier.

How has your life changed since you began investing in property?

Brenda: Mine hasn't changed much at all. I'm still a housewife and mother. Now I have this extra "interest" and it's nice to be able to talk about investing, rather than just how the children are growing, or what's the best floor cleaner nowadays. I do now have retirement security and peace of mind, which, indirectly, has got to be a help to a better, less stressful, state of being.

Les: Property investing is a great pastime. Lifestyle-wise little has changed apart from having better cashflow and being able to buy better quality rather than always buying the cheapest. My world is certainly bigger, with lots of new friends and going places I would never have dreamed about.

Some further tips from the Cashflow Queen

Brenda and Les got to where they are now by learning through experience and strong research, and they're now often asked how they did it. Here they share some of their wisdom.

Capital or cashflow?

My definition of positive cashflow is simply when the income is greater than the expenses. Some people use tax deductions in their calculations but, as this is subject to ATO approval of their returns and may not be a sure thing, I don't take it into account to calculate cashflow. Capital depreciations able to be claimed in tax can add as much as 1% to a net yield, but I look on these more as a bonus than a reason to buy an investment property.

On the question of capital appreciation versus positive cashflow, the answer is that it depends on what you do with the profits.

With capital appreciation you can only use that money by either refinancing or selling the property. If you wish to replace your wage with a regular amount of money coming in, then positive cashflow is best. Cashflow-positive properties are not dependent upon rising values of real estate to make their value felt. The value comes in the steady and constant rent returns.

Another common question is whether it is possible to buy cashflow properties today. Yes, it is possible, but they may be in areas where there is very little prospect of any capital appreciation, and you really need to be wary of rental vacancies. No rent = no income. Research any area carefully to assess the risks. You need some of both cashflow and capital appreciation to continue borrowing and buying.

Remember: Not all properties will achieve positive cashflow by themselves in a reasonable amount of time (three to five years is my preference). Not all properties will achieve fantastic capital growth in a reasonable amount of time (seven to ten years).

Capital appreciation is relatively easy; positive cashflow can be more tricky. You need a good balance of both.

Brenda's tips on turning negative into positive

How can a negatively geared property be turned into a cashflow positive property?

1. Time. Wait for natural inflation to raise the rents until you show a profit. Wages increase over time, as do rents. If you have the income to hold the negative geared asset the rental returns will eventually grow enough to cover your expenses. It may just take a little while.

2. Refinance to interest-only repayments. The repayments may be less than the rental income, thereby achieving positive cashflow. If you are worried about interest rate rises in the future, you could investigate fixing the interest rate for a term. Always consult your financial advisor or financier to check all your options.

3. Pay in a large deposit. Borrowing less makes the loan smaller and therefore the loan repayments are also smaller.

4. Try honeymoon rates. On our very first property we took cheap "honeymoon" interest rates for the first six months. We invested every spare dollar we had during that time to reduce the loan amount so that when the honeymoon rate expired and we went to variable interest rates we had paid a substantial amount off the loan already and were ahead in our loan repayments.

5. Take a long loan. With a 30-year P&I loan the repayments will be smaller than on a 20-year loan. We still have two 20-year P&I loans at present but will be getting those extended to 30 years in the near future as it does affect our cashflow.

Reno Kings Comment

The use of P&I is a totally different strategy to the interest-only method used by most professional investors. It works where you are getting positive cashflow in lower growth areas and it creates equity by debt reduction. If used for negative cashflow properties you will very quickly run out of loan serviceability and that means no more loans.

6. Buy two properties instead of one. When the values double with time, sell one property and pay out the loan on the other. Compound the idea and buy lots more, selling some and paying out the ones left. I do not have a "never, never sell" strategy. I like to sell one when it has achieved good capital growth and use the profits to reduce the debt on the rest of the portfolio, thereby saving on interest and increasing cashflow. I do a lot of calculations on our own financial situation to weigh the pros and cons of selling and buying more.

7. "Find" an extra bedroom. This will increase the rental return. Formal dining rooms in older houses quite often easily convert to an extra bedroom. All you have to add is a wall and a door. Easy. A three-bedroom house commands a far better rent than a two-bedder. The value of your house might even increase with an extra bedroom.

8. Do a cosmetic makeover. The effect of a good scrubdown and paint can be dramatic. Just putting in new handles on kitchen cupboards can dress the kitchen up. You don't have to spend heaps of money, but enough to attract a tenant who'll be happy to pay a higher rent.

9. Try share housing. Turn the property into furnished, student accommodation and bring in higher rental yield. This is a potentially huge market, so if you have a property near a university and there is public transport available you may be able to pursue this niche market. Always check any by-laws with your local council. (And check out Monique and Graham Bond's story.)

10. Subdivide a large block. Keep your house on one side (or move it there) and sell off the spare block to pay down the debt on the house. Tenants mostly hate mowing an overly large block. Some subdivisions are not too expensive to do, but check relevant fees with local councils. If you are short of cash to fund anything like this, there may be people around who are interested in investing in the subdivision with you and claiming some of the profit upon the sale of the new block. These are called joint ventures. (Read the story on joint ventures later in the book.)

11. Strata title a block of units. You can sell a few off to pay down the debt on those left. Again, you need to check with the local council to see if it is possible. There are niche market investors who specialise in buying blocks of units and strata titling them for a profit.

12. Raise a low-set house. A high-set house gives the tenant extra room under the house for storage and you may even find the improved views from a high-set house. Both should command a better rent return. If you can achieve city views or water views the value of your property could increase dramatically.

13. Put in a fence and allow pets. Tenants with a dog will often pay a higher rent for the privilege. Make sure the rental lease specifies any pet damage to your property is the responsibility of the tenant. Tenants with pets do tend to stay put in a rental property, so you have no vacancy rate problems there either.

14. Get a quantity surveyor's report. Always get a QS report done on any property to claim any depreciation through taxation. The government wants you to provide accommodation and will reward you well through your tax return. There are a whole stack of tax deductions associated with rental properties and you are entitled to claim them. Consult with a tax accountant, preferably one who has rental properties of their own, to learn what they all are.

15. Give it three to five years. This is how long I would give a negatively geared property to get itself into a positive situation in a fast-track strategy. If it isn't looking better by then, I'd cut it loose and sell. Be aware of what the current market is doing when you assess the negative gearing situation. You don't want to sell one cheaply if there is likely to be a sharp rise in property values in another year's time. After you sell can you get back into the market with a better buy? You may not want to hold something that is going to be negatively geared for the next 15 years or more and no capital growth for 10 years either. There are exceptions. A house on the shores of Sydney Harbour may be well worth hanging on to, despite negative gearing.

Les's tips on interest rates

Les also has some advice to offer, on interest rates. Owing more than $1million, he is often asked how he sleeps at night. His answer?

Brenda and I use the "reference rate" mechanism. Debt of $1.38 million over 14 separate loans would usually be a cause for concern in a rising interest rate market. To allow us the "sleep at night" factor our bank uses a mechanism to limit repayment rises to an agreed formula. The mechanism works in the following manner, simplified here.

   With a variable rate the interest rate fluctuates up and down. When you negotiate each loan you can select a "reference rate", which can be below or equal to the interest rate of the day. The reference rate remains fixed for the life of the loan and the difference between the reference rate and the interest rate determines the rate of increase in repayments during the annual repayment review.

   If the reference and interest rates are equal then there will be no advantage. However, if the reference rate is more than the interest rate when rates fall, the term is shortened but there is no increase (or decrease, unless requested) in repayments. If rates rise then repayments will increase by the difference between the reference rate and the interest rate at the annual review.

If the reference rate is 6% and the interest rate is 9%, the repayment increases by 3% per year / per year. This indexation allows for more gradual repayment increases when interest rates rise more sharply and allows time for rentals and wages to rise in order to increase serviceability. Incremental rises produce ever-increasing repayments over time and the loan should always be cleared within the term.

For example, with a repayment of $1000 per month indexed at 3% per year / per year, the monthly repayment in year one is $1000, in year two $1030, in year three $1061, in year four $1,093, and so on. The increase is linked to the difference between the reference rate and the interest rate at the annual review and increases cease only when the interest rate is again equal to or less than the reference rate.

This is a much better idea than having repayments increase by say 50% if rates went from say 6% to 9% in the case of an interest-only loan. With the reference rate giving a gradual increase over several years, the loan may initially go backward before repayments eventually overcome the rate rise.

The reference rate mechanism is a product offered by some banks. Check with your own financial advisor for more information.

> **Reno Kings Tip**
>
> *Interest rate rises in some past periods have caused a 50% increase in repayments. Meeting these repayments can be very stressful and potentially fatal financially. Fixing your interest rate and keeping a buffer reserve is the solution in this case. Keep your eye on the future direction of interest rates and be prepared to bite the bullet and fix if you get nervous. You can't go broke by being careful.*

Reno Kings Report

Brenda has answered many more questions on our website. If you'd like more of an insight into Les and Brenda's story or want to ask your own questions, ask for Brenda's Q&A report. See page 235 for details on how to order, or go to our website: www.renos.com.au

Duplexes: The power of two

Paul and Jenny Roberts are two gutsy individuals turning their dream of financial independence into reality – and they're ahead of schedule.

After a shaky start in the property investment game this Gold Coast couple have written their own success story. Their focus has been on the humble and vastly underestimated duplex, believing, "If one is good, surely two is better!"

They have based their investment strategy on the idea that property (or shelter) is "one of the basics of life", as compared with shares, for instance, which are "strictly investor driven". So property has a strong sustained demand, no matter the financial climate.

"Land is the main ingredient of any property investment, so it's logical to maximise the returns from that single commodity," they explain. "If a vacant block of land has high holding charges, and of course there's no rental income, then it makes sense that two dwellings on that same block of land will significantly reduce the impact of your holding charges. And why accept one rental income, one building depreciation and a single dwelling valuation when you can have two?"

Meet Paul and Jenny Roberts

Let's start at the beginning. In 1996 Paul and Jenny decided to follow their dream of early retirement through investing in property. As Paul explains it, their goal has never been so much about money.

"It's all about time. We're buying time, to spend with each other and to enjoy our lives. We set a goal to be financially independent and working part-time by our mid-40s and to be financially free to retire by 50."

To kick-start this goal, they bought a negatively geared property in outer Brisbane through two-tiered marketing, which stitches up all aspects of the deal with the marketer's own financial provider, solicitor, and so on. In the end this simply increases the purchase price, way over market price, on the basis that they are handling "all the worry". Paul admits they were gullible.

"Of course, we were ripped off!" he says. "Too high a price, too poor a return. These days there are efforts to at least force these outfits to include a cooling-off period, but it's still largely 'buyer beware'. Unfortunately we were naive and believed the 'salesman'. He told us that it would only cost $25 per week, and with capital gain he reckoned we'd make a killing."

Someone made "a killing" all right and it wasn't Paul or Jen!

The power of positive thinking
Investment property #1

This first investment property turned out to be a dud, remaining negatively geared and gaining very little by way of capital growth. But even though they lost money Paul and Jenny didn't seem to know the meaning of failure. According to them everything in life has a positive side. This was the beginning of a learning curve that sees them today close to reaching their financial and lifestyle goals, years ahead of schedule. This setback (experience) taught them a couple of valuable lessons, the principal one being the importance of doing their homework.

"How stupid were we? We should have confirmed the valuations, looked at recent sales, looked at future supply, looked at rents and vacancy rates and much, much more."

Then a serious health scare shook the couple to a new reality and motivated them to re-evaluate their situation. They looked again at their long-term goals and their bid to create more time for each other.

"We sold the first property, wiped the slate clean and looked at the options. We could have gone on the dole and escaped to the country or we could get ourselves financially independent."

The Roberts have a philosophy, a formula: Good luck = knowledge + opportunity. They set about acquiring knowledge about property investment, as well as actively looking for investment opportunities.

"I attended as many free introductory seminars I could find, including one given by Geoff Doidge," says Paul. "I also read profusely – books, magazines, anything I could lay my hands on."

Then Paul signed up for the Reno Kings workshops, later also doing the renovation workshop.

"One of the themes that really struck a chord with me was the need to 'add value'. It's something we strongly believe in."

Case study #1: What a shocker!
Investment property #2

Paul and Jenny did their research and in 1999 came up with an area on the Gold Coast that looked promising. Paul and Jenny had escaped to the Gold Coast from New Zealand in the late 1980s and love its carefree lifestyle, so they decided to keep their investments there as well.

The area they had their sights on was close to the beach, a sleeper suburb when others next to it had started growing and being gentrified. They familiarised themselves with the area and local prices. An agent showed them a vacant house.

"This was a very sad-looking home," Paul says. "The yard was a nightmare and the whole place needed a lot of TLC, but the land was duplex zoned."

Jenny was also shocked at the state of the property: "The grass was waist-high, with junk everywhere. Old bike tyres and even a set of iron gates were buried under the rubbish. And it was painted a trashy pink inside!"

Structurally there were heaps of potential problems, as Paul elaborates: "The place had apparently been rented out to drug dealers who had taken a circular saw to the bedroom floor to make a space to hide their stuff. Of course, this completely wrecked the hoop pine floors. There were also termites in the back shed and in the walls."

Time for some of that positive thinking! Paul and Jenny remembered the transformed "dumps" they'd examined in the Reno Kings workshops and realised that the layers of muck and mess were hiding a great opportunity.

"It was next to a council laneway that led to a beautiful park. This gave the property extra space and an impression of size. It was well priced and in a great location within walking distance to all local amenities."

Paul's brother, still in New Zealand, specialises in building townhouses, so Paul's thinking went toward the duplex idea as a great way to add value. The plan was to renovate the old house at the front and build a townhouse at the rear of the property.

So with just a $7500 deposit (and a little fear) the Roberts bought their first duplex development for $155,000. This was at 95% LVR (loan to value ratio), a little higher than the 80% the Roberts (and the banks) tend to favour, and so required mortgage insurance, but they saw the potential to make some serious money.

Blood, sweat and tears

Now came the hard part. There was a price to pay in time and effort to get this project done. Paul and Jenny were both working at full-time jobs, Paul as a paramedic and Jenny as a medical receptionist. For the next three months they spent every spare waking hour renovating the house, doing a lot of the work like painting, fixing fences and the floors themselves. They used their lunch hours and time after work to oversee the building of the townhouse at the back of the block and contact "tradies".

"We flogged ourselves," Paul laughs. "And at the end we organised our own 'backyard blitz'. We got a whole lot of mates over for a couple of days and landscaped the lot. The day after the whole thing was finished, Jenny and I jumped on a plane for Singapore for a couple of days R&R."

The numbers

The Roberts bought the property (a house on duplex-zoned land) for $155,000. The cost of renovating the older house on the front of the property and building the new townhouse at the back was $182,000, giving them a total buy and build cost of $337,000.

After strata titling, which Paul did himself, saving close on a couple of thousand, the bank valuation came in at $510,000. They had turned their capital of $7500 into equity of $153,000. Their rental income was $455 per week, or $1970 per month, with interest payments of $1685 per month.

This was a very sweet deal. The bank loaned against the end value or "built value" of the finished project, including estimated rental returns, the total package. This is a construction loan. The money is loaned in stages as the project is built.

The result was an outstanding 2040% "cash on cash" or 20.4 times the original deposit of $7500. The capital created was $173,000 in a period of nine months. Great result! The house and the townhouse were sold separately for a total of $525,000.

"The money for the new building was all, and I mean *all*, borrowed," Paul says. "You get a 'to be built' valuation and the bank loans against that valuation, with no other capital tipped in. It's very simple financing."

In other words, they have created massive value simply from an idea and a drawing!

Case study #1 return on a project basis.

Sale price	$525,000
Less buy and build cost	$(337,000)
Gross profit	$188,000
Gross return	$188,000/$337,000
Percentage return	56%

Lessons learned

So what did the Roberts learn from their first duplex experience?

"We learned about CPP – communication, preparation and planning are the keys to any successful project," says Paul. "You need to talk to your tradies and builders, and build up a relationship with them."

"We've also learned not to accept anything at face value," Jenny adds. "We learned that the hard way from the first investment house. You have to do the research and planning yourself."

Paul strongly recommends having a structured plan in order to leave your mind free to deal with problems as they arise.

"A good day is when you have six or less problems to solve! You also have to strictly control the project, particularly when it comes to time. Once time blows out, so do holding costs like interest charges, rates and insurances. These are significant expenses and can build up quickly."

This first duplex also taught the Roberts another valuable lesson about their long-term goal of creating wealth and a lifestyle. They sold the new townhouse to pay out their own home loan. Their overall strategy is never to sell, but "bad debt is the enemy and needs to be eliminated, never to be seen again". The sale of the new duplex realised $275,000, less the loan of $182,000, allowing them to pay out their PPOR loan.

"It was an easy plan that, once implemented, paid our home off in less than a year – much better than 30 years. But we should have stopped there and kept the reno at the front," Paul now realises. "But before long someone waved a cheque in front of us for the house, and after a couple of glasses of wine, we accepted their offer. The short-term gain wasn't worth it. There was no logical reason to sell. Most successful investors in real estate don't sell – holding on to properties is the only way to accumulate capital."

Of course, it's always easy to be wise in hindsight, but the important thing in this business is to learn from your mistakes.

"Can you believe we sold an appreciating, self-sustaining asset and ended up with a capital gains tax bill?"

Two heads are better than one

Jenny and Paul both agree that their success so far is partly the result of their exceptional partnership.

"We're very close," says Jenny. "We talk well together and we've both learned to compromise. For example, I love to spend money, and Paul keeps me on budget!"

According to Jenny, Paul's positive, "can do" attitude is a huge plus, but Jenny contributes her own strengths to the partnership.

"Paul is tenacious – he never lets go. Between us we reckon there's always a way to make things work. Paul's more practical than I am. He does the number crunching. But I'm more intuitive. I can walk into a place and see in my mind's eye just what could be done – move a wall here, add some windows there. We're definitely a team."

Duplexes made easy
Investment properties #3 and 4

Paul and Jenny are passionate about their duplex investments, though after the hard yakka of the first development they were able to take a break from serious renovating and building. They were still on the hunt, however, when they found a complete pair of duplex units in 2001. They were both three-bedroom units in a high-growth area of the Gold Coast.

This was a case of "don't assume anything".

"This single duplex had been sitting on the market for ages. It had multiple agents and still no sold sign. It was in a prime position and we assumed (wrongly) that it must be overpriced. Our normal valuation of it would have been $300,000. After driving past many times the same question about price kept nagging us until we just had to find out the exorbitant price."

Here is Paul and Jenny's purchasing history.

IP	Description	Purch date	Purchase price	Reno / build costs	Total costs	Loan amount	Current value	Year sold	Sale price
#1	Calamvale 3 brm	1996	$165,000		$165,000			1999	$170,000
#2	Gold Coast hse, duplex block	1999	$155,000	$15,000	$170,000			2001	$250,000
	New townhouse	2000		$167,000	$167,000			2001	$275,000
#3	3 brm in duplex	Dec-01	$246,000	$1,500	$247,500	$197,000	$430,000	held	
#4	3 brm in duplex	Feb-02	$260,000		$260,000	$208,000	$430,000	held	
#5	House, duplex block	Nov-02	$340,000		$340,000	$272,000		held	
	New duplex	Nov-03		$519,000	$519,000	$519,000	$1,060,000	held	
	PPOR, line of credit					$20,000	$400,000	held	
	Total		$1,166,000	$702,500	$1,868,500	$1,216,000	$2,320,000		$695,000
	LVR					52.4%			

LVR=original loan/current value

They were stunned to find it was in fact $250,000, way under the current market.

"The tenants were also paying below market rent and their level of care for the place showed it. But beneath the grime was a gem. We negotiated a contract (the agent was still lax even with a contract in his hand) and purchased it for $246,000 using the equity from the sale of our previous duplexes. The reno on this was ludicrously easy."

Paul and Jenny spent around $1500 on smartening it up, and the rent went from $180 per week up to $250, with a bank valuation of $290,000. It's currently at $310 per week.

"We loved the place so much, we bought next door for $260,000 and it needed no work whatsoever. The twist to this is that the original vendors had purchased through a two-tiered marketing scheme and just wanted out. Being overseas vendors with poor agent representation, we got it at a discount again."

This was purchased in 2001, just a couple of months after its sister. It was initially renting for $230 per week and now returns $290, not a great yield at 5.8%, but with these properties the capital gain is looking good. At the end of 2003 the bank valuation was $430,000 for each of them.

"The area was red hot and these were ripe for the picking. Good luck is knowledge meeting opportunity yet again."

> ┌─ **Reno Kings Tip** ─────────────────────────────
> *My favourite: a "no reno" reno! Perfect for the handyperson-impaired. Spend a couple of weeks and $1500 to get $3640 per annum (39%) rent increase and increase your equity by $44,000. Nothing more demonstrates the fabulous leverage of well-bought and value-added property. Access 80% of that equity as a 20% deposit and buy five times more property. Here's how it works:*
> *80% x $44,000 = $36,000 drawn as line of credit (LOC)*
> *Use LOC as 20% deposit to buy property worth 5 x $36k = $180k*
> *So hasn't your $1500 reno created assets worth $180,000? What makes this even sweeter is when the original $1500 was borrowed from the bank. How sweet it is!*

Case study #2: Building on the goal
Investment property #5

By the end of 2002 Jenny and Paul weren't slowing down. They were fired up to get closer to financial independence, and having more time.

"To us money is a concept. We believe in the Kyosaki and Burley approach that money is an idea. Through what you project, how you see a situation and then what you can conceptualise it doing for you, it swells into a reality. To achieve you have to conceive and believe. We see 'bargains' and opportunities everywhere, because we believe and accept that they are out there. Once an opportunity is found then we strongly assess projects based on their 'cash on cash' returns. If we invest anything – time, money, equity – what we need to know is how soon we get it back."

The next project demonstrates this. In this case the house found them.

> ┌─ **Reno Kings Tip** ─────────────────────────────
> *Average investors say, "I can't find a bargain." Advanced investors say, "I don't have enough money to buy the bargains I find. They are everywhere."*

The research

"We were working on one of our properties and an agent we knew pulled up, asking, 'Are you in the market?' 'Not really,' I said, "What have you got?' Next thing we were leaning on the bonnet signing a contract."

It was an older property on duplex-zoned land with a waterview. ("You could smell the salt air!") They placed a contract on it with a due diligence clause. This took it off the market and gave them the opportunity to explore all the options and relevant government regulations.

The negotiation

They then set about working out how this project would work, from the price of the block to the contracts, supply of materials and council approvals. All of it needs a strong element of negotiation.

"It's *not* about grinding them all down. It's about getting the best value from your input, be it time, money or ideas. We believe in frugality – getting the best 'bang for your buck', as the Reno Kings often put it."

With this property Jenny and Paul paid the asking price of $340,000.

"Some people think you *have* to place an offer, but if you're looking at a good buy, why blow it for a few bucks? It comes back to knowing value in your local area. We have even gone above list price to get a property."

The development

The cost of demolishing the place and building a brand-spanking-new duplex was $451,000. The bank valuation was $1.06 million for the two on completion. But first it was time to get "the dirt under the nails".

"This was a simple build with multiple hiccups, but only minor stuff. The communication, planning and preparation were all being ironed out. This is Jenny's forte, and the planning and organisation always gets easier as you do more."

The whole development took 12 months from beginning to end.

The numbers

Paul and Jenny used "no money down" for this investment, ie, no cash input. By now they were able to use the equity from their holdings to get the result they were after.

"Our equity input to the loan was only $68,000 and the return was $1.06 million less $791,000 costs, giving us $269,000 capital gain. We refinanced at the project's end and our original equity was returned to us."

The beauty of the duplex strategy

It seems that the "two is better than one" plan is working for them. The duplex has become their "cookie cutter" method of making money. So exactly what is it about this particular type of property that makes it such a great strategy for them?

Here are the numbers on Paul and Jenny's two duplex developments.

	Case study 1		Case study 2
Description	Investment property #2. House reno, duplex block	New townhouse built 2000	Investment property #5. House demolished, new duplex built 2003
Year purchased	1999		2002
Purchase price	$155,000		$340,000
Reno / build costs	$15,000	$167,000	$451,000
Total costs	$170,000	$167,000	$791,000
Loan amount	$147,500	$182,000	$791,000
Rent pw at sale / current	$200	$255	$900
Yield at sale / current	6.1%	7.9%	5.9%
Year sold	2001	2001	held
Sale price / current value	$250,000	$275,000	$1,060,000
Capital gain	$80,000	$108,000	$269,000

loan covers reno and build
Yield at sale or current=rent/total cost
Capital gain=current value-total cost

Paul says it's a matter of supply and demand, with a limited supply of duplexes as most residential blocks are developed for single dwellings.

"They're not what I would call rare but you need to ask your agent to look specifically for them. They are in less supply than residential housing lots, and more than multi-unit sites."

"There are a lot of people fighting for this precious commodity. There's strong demand from builders and developers who want to maximise their returns by building and selling two residences. And in the established areas duplex blocks are usually in prime positions. Councils recognise that medium- to high-density living needs to be closer to facilities. As you get closer to the beach or CBD, zoning density increases. People want this for lifestyle, regardless of zoning. This creates strong demand for duplex living.

"We believe that duplexes are the future for people of many ages and types. They appeal to the baby boomers wanting low-maintenance property close to schools, shops, water, transport. First homebuyers with limited purchasing power want a place with some yard for the dog and capital growth. And there's the cafe society profile – these are people who again want low maintenance with easy access to amenities."

The upshot

The Roberts bought five investment properties over eight years, four of which they still retain. Once they'd cleaned the slate after the first blunder they have only used $7500 cash, using only equity ever since.

Total rental returns are currently $78,000. They've also built in a line of credit of $20,000 against their own home, as a utilities fund. That frees up other income for them, which they call their "toy fund".

"We use this for all sorts of good things, like travel, a caravan, stereo and other 'toys'. Now we live off our capital."

Paul and Jenny are now in their early 40s and work part time, a goal they achieved two years earlier than they had set for themselves.

"Most people define time in terms of a number of years – 'In five years I will have achieved X, Y or Z' – and we used to be like that too. But five years just slips by and nothing's achieved, so we set our goals by linking them with my age and that's worked for us."

As a reward for all their hard work they've also given themselves a year off from real estate investing.

"We've been 'head down, bum up' for a good three years. Many people don't realise how much work is involved in all of this, particularly during the building phase of a project, but it's also the research side current market prices and demand, legislation and council by-laws, builders and tradies, estate agents. There's a heck of a lot of preparatory work."

They also now know that their "superannuation" is covered.

"Our next step is to complete our own journey, and to make our son and grandkids (hurry up son!) financially independent."

This story shows the power of two. Two inspired, gutsy and focused individuals using the "power of two" property strategy (duplexes) to achieve their common goal of financial independence.

Reno Kings insights

What's your background?

Paul: I'm a paramedic, Jenny is a medical receptionist, both now part time. We have given ourselves 2004 "off" real estate and will re-enter in 2005. We aimed to be part time by age 45 (2006) but achieved this in 2004. This allows us the freedom to pursue more real estate and camping.

Why did you get started?

Paul: To get more time. Money is irrelevant; it is only an idea used to attain freedom and time to be with each other, our family, and pursue our hearts' desire, not someone else's. We were jump-started by a health scare and realised that time is the most precious thing. Time for "the love of my life", family, dogs, all the things that bring happiness. I'm happy without Ferraris, large houses and the mega-excessive materialistic stuff. Give me time with my wife, a sunset while camping, my dogs and I'm as happy as can be. Money is just the catalyst allowing us to stop working for wages.

Jenny: We wanted the lifestyle we saw others enjoying, to travel, spend more time together, and most of all not to work for anyone but ourselves.

What was your greatest fear?

Paul: Not having time.

Jenny: I don't consider us successful, after the hard lesson of our first property (two-tiered marketing), the fear of making the wrong decisions and ending up with another white elephant, another mess to extract ourselves from. We were, in a sense, flying into the first duplex development blind. We were "green" and tackling not just one project, but two at the same time with no previous experience of this sort of thing (renovating one house and building a new one behind it). We were unsure of the exact cost of the build. We knew we had to budget for more than we expected, but what about the unexpected costs? We had very limited funds available – could we finish it or would it sit empty, unfinished and not rented or sold while we scraped together more funds?

Did your parents show you how to get ahead?

Paul: They taught me the values, drive and tenacity necessary to succeed.

Jenny: Although my parents spent most of their lives in business, I was the last of a large brood. By the time I was able and *willing* to understand they had retired and lost touch with financial practices. They did teach me how to budget, pay back loans. They generally taught me the value of money.

What was your greatest mistake?

Paul: Hard to pinpoint our greatest lesson (mistake), there are so many. In general, not being educated enough, not enough research, not learning enough.

Jenny: Buying the Calamvale property. Looking back it could also have been the best thing. It made us more careful, more prudent and taught us some hard lessons first up. One of them was never to take things at face value. Look, research and pull everything to bits before jumping in.

How would you describe your strategy?

Paul: We stick to a couple of principles: add value, preferably with a double twist, duplexes and double blocks. We use the ReBATES idea from the Reno Kings – Research, Buy well, Add value, Time manage, Expenses down, and Sell or keep. We look for cashflow-positive properties with high capital growth. We use another Reno Kings favourite, the KISS principle (keep it simple, stupid).

Jenny: To date that's been the duplex market. Different types of duplexes appeal to a range of people. The contemporary style appeals to the baby boomers, minus children, settling into a relaxed way of life, with the money to spend and the will to spend it to achieve their lifestyle. The older duplex type appeals to single-parent families and singles with tighter budgets looking for a foothold in the market. And there's the middle of the range type – for them, duplexes make great rental properties – double the rent for one piece of land.

What do you want to achieve?

Paul: To be working part time (done), and have financial independence by the time I'm 45, and financial freedom by 50.

Jenny: A happy balance of work, lifestyle and social interaction without financial restraints. To build an asset base that will give us the freedom to go on to buy, sell, build and renovate when the deals appear, without being restrained by having to acquire loans. To build a portfolio that will give our son and any future family he has financial security (and our puppies a good lifestyle with plenty of Schmackos).

What's your best renovating tip?

Paul: Paint is great, talk to tradies – they've seen and done more than you. Buy them lots of beer and have one with them!

Jenny: Keep the costs down, but with maximum impact. Be inventive, creative and think laterally. Don't think that if it hasn't been done before it can't be done now. Keep the "builders bog" close – it fixes just about anything!

Any other tips for investors?

Paul: "Screw it, just do it," as Richard Branson says. Have a contingency plan.

Jenny: Be positive – anything is possible. Write down your goals and post them where you will see them every day. Don't quit. If you hit a wall, find a way around it, or over it, or through it. There is *always* a way. Look at every angle. Have a plan for things going wrong. If a property doesn't sell, you could rent it out and still come out ahead. Surround yourself with a good team, people you connect with. Be prepared to work "hard and long" when needed. Some days never seem to end, but the results are worth it. The most successful teams are involved up to their armpits in the dirty work.

Any memorable experiences along the way?

Paul: Removing a wall while doing a reno and finding a termite nest filling the entire wall. Luckily the house was framed out of Cypress pine (termite resistant) and the damage was small.

Jenny: Climbing onto a roof for the first time and being accepted as "one of the boys". The builders began calling me the TA (trade assistant).

What's your best money-making tip?

Paul: Understand and assess your "cash on cash" returns. Yields and all else is baloney. Supply and demand rule – no ifs, buts or maybes!

Jenny: Buy well, preferably below market value. Look for the 'X' factor that makes a property popular, eg, waterviews, cafe society.

What's your advice to people getting started in property?

Paul: Education, education, education. 'Location, location, location' is for the masses. Smart, successful people continuously educate themselves.

Jenny: Educate yourself: books, seminars, and talk to people who know more than you. And don't get a manicure before building a fence.

How has your life changed since you began your property investment?

Paul: There's been a major paradigm shift. We have more time to focus on things other than wages or work, eg, environment issues, family.

How do you picture yourself five years down the track?

Paul: We will be further toward our goals. We will never retire in the classical sense but working for wages will be a hobby and a social event.

Reno Kings Report

If you'd like to know more about duplex strategies contact the Reno Kings for a free report. See page 235 for details for more information and details on how to order, or visit our website: www.renos.com.au

Feel the fear and do it anyway

Elin Power turned adversity into achievement in just a few short years, taking on the financiers as a single mum, and winning.

The last person you are likely to think of as a successful property investor is a sole parent of small children, let alone one who achieved that success fast on the heels of finding herself with that status, and with only a part-time job to boot. Adversity, though, can sometimes be the catalyst that produces great achievement. Fear can stop you from doing a lot, but facing your fears can also be a great motivator.

The Reno Kings know about FEAR: False Expectations Appearing Real. Fear can paralyse you. When you are nervous or scared of something, especially the unknown, it is far easier to do nothing. Why take a risk if you don't have to? The hidden risk in doing nothing is that nothing will change.

Whenever you do something for the first time, of course you will be a little nervous and scared of making a mistake. But imagine yourself as a child learning to crawl. You fall down. If you said, "No way that I'm doing that again. I could get hurt," you would miss learning to walk, learning to run, learning to jump and maybe even to fly. All because of FEAR.

Start to see mistakes as "learning experiences" and the whole concept of doing new things changes. Life takes a new meaning, challenges become fun and you open up a whole new chapter of your life. Elin's story demonstrates this ably, from divorce to development, single mum to project manager, finding the funds for groceries to financing a major development. She has gone from buying "home brand" to building homes.

Meet Elin Power

In 1997 Elin Power found herself divorced and six months pregnant with her second child. Elin had been an executive in local government but was then required to take a lesser-paid part-time role. As she puts it, "Divorce left me with half a house, half a boat, half a job and half a pregnancy – half a life really." Yet, in only a couple of years this self-confessed "over-achiever and eternal optimist" turned her life around and the future is looking great for her and her kids.

"For that first six months, though, I couldn't even bring myself to tell anyone outside my immediate family about the break-up (including my bank manager), and it was a year before I told anyone at work. I felt so insecure. I felt a failure," explains Elin.

At first, also, the lifestyle changes were enormous. Gone were the designer-brand makeup and clothes, and Vegemite sandwiches became Elin's regular take-to-work lunch.

"Eventually I realised I was suffering postnatal depression, paralysed by the drop in my self-esteem and complicated by a chronic back condition. I needed to do something to turn it around and prove I could fly solo."

Elin was now determined to rise above it all, rather than sink further into the pit of despair or slide into single-parent poverty. The marriage settlement left Elin with $110,000 after splitting the proceeds from the sale of the family home.

Now eight months pregnant, Elin's "nesting instinct" was also getting stronger and she had to steel herself to find somewhere she and her two babies could live. She then set herself some strict criteria for a replacement. The new home would have to offer strong capital growth and be within 15 minutes commuting time from the CBD, where she worked.

"This was pre-internet days for me," says Elin, "so the search was frustrating. How did everyone do it back then? I ended up relying on concrete anecdotal recommendations that led me to Brisbane's inner north-west."

After hours of research and inspecting more than 50 houses, Elin bought a house in Ashgrove for $235,000, which was $30,000 over her limit. For the next couple of years Elin struggled, battling the stresses of being a sole parent to two kids under four, bouts of postnatal depression and a financial situation that was outside her control to a great degree.

What are you going to do about it, kiddo?

To Elin, though, these difficulties were simply a call to arms. She explains her philosophy: "We're all the authors of our own destiny. I accept full responsibility for the position in which I found myself. But, if you don't want to be in your current situation, you have to ask yourself, 'What are you going to do about it kiddo?'"

Determined to regain control of her life, Elin read everything she could lay her hands on about investing, particularly about passive income. She decided to tackle on-line share trading. Capital growth on the house had enabled her to increase her borrowings to give her a float of around $60,000. Some early success increased her equity by $10,000. She bought computer software and heaps of resource material, and embarked on some expensive training programs, outlaying about $7000, to learn the ins and outs of technical trading.

"Despite much training and research, my endeavours left me about $20,000 down on my personal equity over two years," Elin says. "Thank goodness for tax write-offs. This reduced the pain by about half."

It was just before the dotcom tech stocks crash and by 2001 Elin saw the writing on the wall and sold every share she owned, except for the one that gave her shopping discounts.

"I bailed out in just one weekend – that's one benefit of shares. I licked my wounds for about three months, considering my options, then decided it must be property's turn for a run."

Investment property #1: A personal milestone

In July 2001 Elin signed a contract on her first investment property, having again set strict criteria for a renovatable character house close to the city and transport.

"Leading up to the purchase I inspected and researched about a hundred properties within a 6 km radius of the CBD, and loved every minute of it, even though I was also really nervous. Let's face it, shopping is fun, and this was retail therapy on a grand scale. I inspected this property in Windsor, an inner Brisbane suburb, at 5.30 pm and had a contract at $275,500 by 8 pm that evening. There were two offers on the table but evidently I had bid the highest."

Although it was on a small 400 sq m lot, the property had a lot going for it – fantastic street appeal. It was a Federation-style Queenslander raised to legal height for building underneath, making it a good renovation or resale prospect, with polished timber floors and a pleasant elevated view from the open front verandah, though with mostly original (read "renovator's delight") everything else.

"I asked the vendors if they'd be open to a longer settlement than the usual 30 days and they said the longer the better. We struck a deal for a 90-day settlement," says Elin. "This gave me the time I needed to source finance to fund the deposit and begin the agonising process of begging for finance as a single mother. I knew it was going to be tough. A bank and two mortgage brokers weren't interested. They wouldn't count child support payments or Centrelink family payments as income. My own bank eventually came to the party based on a revaluation of my home at Ashgrove and my solid history of reliable payments."

Elin's plan was to move into the Windsor house for six to nine months, leasing out Ashgrove, which had a higher rental potential, and renovate and sell Windsor, then return to her home base at Ashgrove. This would give cashflow to help cover the renovation cost, also allowing the sale of Windsor without attracting capital gains tax.

"It wasn't till I had packed two boxes ready for the move that I realised this was not the right way to go. I'd received a promotion at work, making me my employer's first part-time executive manager (also job sharing, which was very brave of them). Suddenly I was struck by a flash of sensibility that perhaps starting a new management job, moving house and renovating might be a bit too much of a squeeze for a six-month window."

A couple of quick calls later the removalist was cancelled and the agent directed to rent out Windsor rather than Ashgrove. This also produced a long-term commitment to stay put, at least until the kids had finished primary school.

"I had plans drafted for a renovation but decided against it for the time being. Renting out Windsor, though, took a stressful month and finally a 12-month lease was struck at $240 per week. But I calculated that I could sustain the resulting negative cashflows for at least two years, if we continued to live frugally, buying 'home brand' everything, homemade clothes and entertainment."

Elin continued to look around at properties in Windsor, mainly to reassure herself that she'd done the right thing.

"I was worried that maybe I had paid too much. To my relief, property of a similar style in the area had escalated to more than $300,000 before we'd even reached settlement at the end of October 2001. We settled on my daughter's fourth birthday, a milestone in my personal development also, as I came to realise that I really could do stuff on my own."

It sold a year later for $356,000, a capital gain of $81,000 before costs. Not bad earnings for a single mum with a part-time job (it was more than her annual salary).

Investment property #2: Battling it out

But we're getting ahead of ourselves. Having done it once Elin had the urge to continue her property research, though she was not in the market. Hence her delight to be approached by her "time poor" best friend Mila early in 2002 to help her find a house in Brisbane's inner west.

"I was having withdrawal symptoms after weekends of chasing open houses. Now I had a goal to justify my combing the newspapers again, and searching the internet (which I'd now learned to use), and going to lots of open home inspections over the next couple of months. Bliss."

When Elin's friend happily settled for a newly renovated property in Ashgrove Elin decided to keep the appointments she'd arranged for a few other open house inspections.

"It was on this adventure that I found a beautifully restored and kept Queenslander on a mega 1012 sq m block of land in Enoggera," says Elin. "I began to wonder whether there might be more opportunities to add value to this property than my small lot in Windsor."

Elin was fishing for an asking price, but the agent was reluctant.

"This was the culture of property sales agents at the time," says Elin, "and it was quite nerve-wracking. He just kept asking me to make an offer, which back then I was very shaky about doing. These days putting an offer on the table feels like sending out party invitations."

With Elin being forced to shrug off her fear, her offer of $285,000, two weeks finance and 90 days to settle, though initially rejected, was successful after negotiating back to 30 days. The building inspection came up okay and the location of the house at the front of the block made this an ideal subdivision for a battleaxe block – a small lot at the front with a side easement to the newly created block at the back. So, apart from the small matter of finance, it was full-steam ahead.

"I was really excited by the prospect of this new deal but I had to jump through the finance hoops once again and I was not at all optimistic. It was pointed out, once again, that financial institutions just didn't trust single mums. A working man with a dependent wife and children was perceived as a much lower risk than a working single mother. The maths just didn't make sense, since I had better spread my income-earning risks."

But they obviously hadn't counted on Elin's determination (what her friends call her "stubborn streak") or maybe her share of good luck. Her current bank lender reluctantly approved her application for finance but only on the condition that she sell the Windsor property within six months. So at this stage, regardless of her capacity to meet the repayments, the bank wouldn't allow Elin to continue to hold all three properties.

"I was confident I could sell Windsor without a loss as the market was rising quickly."

Never the last word

While Elin agreed to the bank's deal, despite her frustration at being told how to manage her own investment portfolio, Elin refused to accept this as the last word. Once she had finance confirmed she let the contract go "unconditional" on finance and started to shop around for other options.

"This felt much better," Elin says. "I felt that I wasn't the 'beggar' any more, that I had some options. Feeling much more powerful I approached a number of lenders and brokers and invited them to bid for my business."

After coming up against a few more brick walls through one broker, Elin decided to approach another financial institution under her own steam. The lending manager was older and very experienced, and still had the paternalistic approach Elin had come to expect from financiers, but for once luck was on her side. Elin realised later that his miscalculation of income tax deductions inflated her net income stream to a level that qualified her for the loan on all three properties, based on refinancing her two existing mortgages and financing the new acquisition. Elin knew from experience she could afford the loan repayments so in March 2003, with a fond farewell to her old bank and a signed contract from her new one, she was back in business.

Elin's three properties were getting great capital growth. She continued to scrimp and save at home and took in a foreign "homestay" student, the first of several she took in intermittently over following years.

"A boarder is actually a great addition to our homelife, giving the kids an interesting socialisation and giving me an on-hand babysitter so I can get on with the domestics and my property research. Each one only stays a maximum of three months and they basically reimburse me for their cost of living. Since I cannot afford the cash to take my children overseas, it is my way of bringing diverse cultures and languages to our home. It has been an enormous benefit for the children."

At this point Elin felt she was ready to approach her bank about additional funds to finance the Enoggera subdivision and to do a bit of home renovation. It was brick wall time again.

"To my horror, the most they could offer me was $16,000, barely enough for my new kitchen. My reimbursements from homestay students, child support payments and family allowance weren't counted as income in the bank's calculation of my debt service ratio. Even though my equity was substantial, they wouldn't qualify me for further borrowing."

Elin's stubborn streak meant that she decided to press on with her plans to subdivide anyway, with the assistance of an increased limit on her credit card. She contacted her former brother-in-law for advice. He had some experience with subdivision and suggested she start with a land surveyor. After consulting a townplanner and a civil engineer and parting with $13,000, Elin had a development application (DA) in with the council. And now the waiting game began, but how to get the finance to fund the development construction?

Refinance, refinance, refinance

Elin is constantly on the lookout for opportunities not just to invest but to learn skills and strategies to improve her returns. She credits the ideas she picked up at one of the Reno Kings workshops as a major turning point.

"I left the workshop with an adrenalin rush," says Elin. "My personal beliefs about what was achievable were completely expanded, and I now had some relevant knowledge and expertise in my kit bag. Until you have a mental picture of what is possible you can't really think big when setting your goals. Nothing was going to stop me rushing out to buy more property that week. My eyes were now wide open. And one of the best outcomes of the workshop was meeting a mortgage broker who offered to do all the 'bank begging' I might require."

Elin's newfound broker introduced her to the concept of a "low doc" (low documentation) loan, in which the borrower provides details of financial status through a statutory declaration. They don't have too many criteria that limit the acceptable sources of income. Though these loans carry slightly higher interest, Elin was able to refinance to cover her kitchen renovation (which has not actually eventuated) and the subdivision at Enoggera, plus money to buy more property.

"The broker totally restructured my portfolio and found me borrowings of $500,000 to spend on investment property."

This clever (though expensive) refinancing had provided enough for up to two more houses.

Here are the numbers on Elin's portfolio.

	Description	Date settled	Purchase price	Reno, building, subdiv'n, sell costs	Purchase costs*	Total costs	Elin's share of total costs	Year sold	Sale price / current value	Elin's share of valuation	Capital gain
#1	Ashgrove (PPOR)	Sep-97	$235,000	$5,000	$5,875	$245,875	$245,875	held	$520,000	$520,000	$274,125
#2	Windsor (sold)	Oct-01	$275,000	$500	$11,000	$286,500	$286,500	Oct-02	$356,000	$356,000	$69,500
#3	Enoggera										
	original house and land	Mar-02	$285,000		$13,079	$298,079	$298,079	held	$370,000	$370,000	$71,921
	subdivision and new house	Feb-04		$251,000		$251,000	$251,000	held	$473,000	$473,000	$222,000
#4	Clayfield #1 (trans mortgage after Windsor sale)	Jan-03	$340,000	$2,000	$10,200	$352,200	$352,200	held	$430,000	$430,000	$77,800
#5	Ashgrove #2	Sep-02	$306,000	$18,000	$15,300	$339,300	$339,300	held	$430,000	$430,000	$90,700
#6	Kelvin Grove joint venture	Jan-03	$275,000	$60,000	$11,000	$346,000	$173,000	held	$400,000	$200,000	$27,000
#7	Shorncliffe joint venture										
	original house and land	Aug-03	$300,000	$70,000	$12,000	$382,000	$191,000	for sale	$485,000	$242,500	$51,500
	subdivision and demolition house	Oct-04	$33,000	$100,000		$133,000	$66,500	held	$400,000	$200,000	$133,500
#8	Clayfield #2 joint venture (pending council dev approval)	Jul-04	$575,000	$22,000	$23,000	$620,000	$310,000	under dev	$650,000	$325,000	$15,000
	Total		$2,624,000	$528,500	$101,454	3,253,954	$2,513,454		$4,514,000	$3,546,500	$1,033,046
	less #2 sale price									$356,000	
	equals gross worth									$3,190,500	

* Purchase costs are not generally given in totals. Elin's case is an exception.

Properties #3 and 4: Clayfield and Ashgrove again

So the next year was super busy for Elin. She was fired up and rearing to go to the next level. By the time she was ready to start on the subdivision of the Enoggera property she had sold the Windsor house and bought two more investment properties, one in the blue-chip suburb of Clayfield and another close to her home in Ashgrove.

Feel the fear and do it anyway | **117**

```
┌─ Reno Kings Tip ─────────────────────────────────────┐
│ Here we have Elin flat out getting enough money from a bank to do up │
│ her kitchen and another broker can get finance for the kitchen and two │
│ more houses. Never take no for an answer. Always use a broker to acess │
│ all the different banks and products available. │
└──────────────────────────────────────────────────────┘
```

Going blue chip

Elin studied more than 50 properties in an area that her research suggested was "hot", making offers on a few without success. Her agenda was to buy below market price with a view to getting capital gain at the front end, a very useful tip she picked up at the Reno Kings workshop.

"The vendors I was dealing with were not in any way desperate to sell. I got better at walking away from a deal without increasing my offer."

Then she started on neighbouring Clayfield. A small house on a large block of land zoned LMR (low to medium residential, suitable for unit development) caught her eye.

"I was interested to learn from the agent that the vendors had refused to allow a sign on the front of the house, refused open houses and refused to pay for any advertising. The agent expressed frustration at the lack of interest in the property through lack of exposure."

Elin's investigations with the council revealed that a substantial overland waterflow path existed in the back yard, and that further development was not likely to win approval. The agent confirmed that a number of developers had walked away from the property for the same reasons. Making her findings known to the vendor, Elin offered $30,000 below the asking price, with a view to future renovation and possible enlargement of the pleasant though small house.

"Even if not developable, it was still a big block of land in the heart of Clayfield – a blue-chip suburb close to rail, schools and shopping. My four-year-old daughter was with me on the second inspection and suitably charmed the house-proud Dutch couple, who insisted on being home for all inspections. Being of Dutch parentage, I was able to hold a friendly conversation with them in their own language."

A purchase price of $340,000 was agreed, with many conditions, including finance of three weeks.

"I have found that I really need this longer than usual 'cooling-off period' to allow me time to carefully consider all aspects of the deal, check my cashflows three times over, and change my mind if I want to. I also usually specify 14 business days for finance and building inspection rather than a straight 14 days."

Reno Kings Tip

Get to know how to use contract clauses to your advantage. The simple insertion of the word "business" means weekends aren't counted so she has at least four extra days up her sleeve.

But it's so cute

Even before the Clayfield contract went unconditional, Elin was out walking the dog and stumbled on a new listing around the corner from home.

"I wasn't even looking for another property, as I had the contract on Clayfield, but I was curious about local values, expecting this very cute Queenslander to be in the range of $350,000 to $400,000. It was open for inspection just as I rolled by, so I hitched the dog to the gate and wandered in for a sticky beak and a yarn with the agent."

The property looked great from the outside but on closer inspection turned out to be "a renovator". The vendor had not lived in Queensland for many years and needed the money fast to finance a property in Sydney. The agent was asking for offers above $300,000.

"A great tip I learned from the Reno Kings workshop was to 'secure the capital gain at the front end' by buying well. I put in a bid for $301,000 to see if the agent was serious about the $300,000+."

Elin's bid, renovator or not, still had to be up to $50,000 below market price for the area. The agent called back the next day to say there were three bids on the table and all were invited to better their offer. But then something unexpected happened.

"I found myself becoming emotionally attached to the place, and I know it's best to stay detached in these things. But it just looked so gorgeous and was opposite some beautiful parklands. I started envisaging how much better it would look with polished floors, a repainted interior, spruced up garden … as well as the convenience factor of it being just around the corner. I upped my offer to $316,000 based on a hint I thought the agent had dropped that a competing offer was at $310,000."

A call later that evening confirmed that Elin's offer had been accepted with two weeks for finance and building inspection and a 45-day settlement. The agent continued to open the house as the contract was not yet unconditional.

"I love attending the open houses of the properties I have already contracted to so I can eavesdrop on other interested buyers and just have the time to take everything in and think about my future options. So I dropped in."

Elin noticed a high-pitched hum coming from the bedroom window frames and when she tapped on the architrave it caved in completely.

"It was the first time I'd seen a termite in the flesh, and now I get why we call them white ants! This caused mild panic not only for me but for the agent and subsequently major panic for the vendor in Sydney."

The building inspection revealed damage to the architraves in the bedroom, and a narrow VJ wall between the bedroom and entrance hall had been completely eaten away. The roof in one bedroom had leaked at some stage and the stove needed a little work. The vendor came back with an offer of a $10,000 price reduction.

"I agonised over the choice between Clayfield and Ashgrove, then I looked at my options from a different angle, comparing Windsor with both of these houses. I came to the conclusion that both Clayfield and Ashgrove had greater opportunities for me to 'add value' than a house on a small lot in Windsor. So why not buy both of these and sell Windsor!"

Why not both?

Elin contacted the agent for Clayfield and requested an extra two weeks to arrange finance and a five-month settlement, half expecting that they would tell her to get lost. She was quite willing to walk away from the deal if they did, but they agreed within a day.

There were more issues with finance, however, despite the low-doc loan potential. Though the application did not request salary details, they wanted to sight six months of bank statements, which revealed of course that Elin received child support and family payments. "Oops a single mother!" The application was declined two days before the finance date. Yet another application was declined because Elin was a PAYE earner.

"My broker reassured me and quickly processed a new application but I hedged my bets by getting another broker on the case as well. There was no opportunity to extend the finance period and I knew there were other buyers in the wind. These two applications were looking much more positive but did not come through by the finance approval date. I'm not sure if it was my stressed state or pure insanity that I went out on a limb to go unconditional without finance approval. Thank goodness approval came from both a few days later. It's an experience I'd prefer not to repeat."

They settled on Ashgrove in September 2002 and Elin found a handyman to get the renovations under way immediately. The termite damage cost about $500 to repair, the roof $200 (because Elin had learned about short sheeting of roofs at the Reno Kings workshop) and termite treatment about $400 – making the $10,000 discount very much worthwhile.

> ## Reno Kings Tip
>
> *Termites. That strikes fear into most people buying property. Treat them as a plus. If you find termites all of a sudden vendors become very negotiable. Most old houses have been attacked at some stage or other. Even though the owners are shocked at the look of the damage and immediately think the whole house is riddled, often it's a case of replacing a few boards. So tens of thousands of dollars can be knocked off the price and repaired for a fraction of that. Sometimes the termites can pay for your whole reno. Just make sure there is no structural damage!*

"We painted the inside in light colours to 'de-brown' the place, polished the floors, landscaped a paved outdoor entertainment area in the back yard (cheaper than a deck), added new light fittings, curtains, fans, an air-conditioner, dishwasher and range hood, a lot of it secondhand to keep costs down."

The total renovation bill was $18,000 and my personal contribution was making the curtains, painting the window frames (nine panes of glass per window) and sourcing the various contractors and materials."

The house was rented by mid-November for $310 per week, and was revalued in July 2003 at $420,000. Ashgrove prices are still rising.

"I felt that this was a more than reasonable return on my outlay to attend the Reno Kings workshop."

Windsor for sale

Elin's next big learning curve was a selling experience. The Windsor house had been recently valued at $317,000 but Elin believed it had to be worth in the vicinity of $340,000, which would also help to cover the purchase costs of the Clayfield house, as well as some of the costs associated with the swap.

"I didn't shop around for agents (mistake #1), as I had a positive relationship with a Windsor agent. I accepted her advice on advertising strategy and an auction, and signed an 'exclusive' agency contract."

In the end Elin wasn't totally happy with the strategy and talked to the agency about getting out of the exclusive contract. That wasn't possible, for various reasons too complicated to share here, but the agency eventually bent over backwards to change her perceptions.

"In hindsight it was a good outcome. The open houses were overflowing each week, the agency managed to get an editorial printed in the local paper and we had a huge crowd at the auction. It sold at $356,000 on the day, which covered the buying and selling expenses, as well as giving me the opportunity to reduce a significant chunk of personal debt on my family home. The timing enabled me to transfer my Windsor mortgage to Clayfield through an 'exchange of security' that kept loan costs well down and I was not required to present financials."

Clayfield was settled in January 2003 and it rented within a month for $275 per week, after removing old carpet and polishing the floors.

Investment property #5: Kelvin Grove student housing

Elin had learned about the benefits of joint ventures at the Reno Kings workshop, so when her former brother-in-law suggested doing a renovation together in late 2002 she was open to sharing some of the stress and anxiety of decision making with someone else, not to mention some of the risks and hard work.

"He brought the equity to the deal and we agreed to borrow 80% of the purchase price jointly. My job would be to find suitable inner-city property, negotiate finance and legals, and be the gopher, while he would manage construction, 'subbies' and materials for the renovation. Our plan was to be in and out quickly and turn a small profit of $20k to $30k. If it worked we would look at doing it again."

Elin is on the mailing list of many agencies, and this is how she found the Kelvin Grove property, just 300 m from a university campus.

"It looked like a shocker in the picture, but it was the first inner-city property under $300,000 that I had come across for a good while. We checked it out, discovered there was potential and negotiated a contract at $280,000. We came up with a plan to turn the two-bedroom cottage into a four-bedroom, two-bathroom place for students.

"I'd read an article in the *Australian Property Investor* magazine about a similar set-up in New South Wales with good rental return prospects [see the Cash Cow Case Study in our free reports, page 235]. Our building and pest inspection revealed that the house was in an appalling state. The roof needed replacing and there was much rot in walls and floors. This led to a price reduction of a further $5000."

Beating the rush

Elin and her joint venture partner started work in mid-January and had students knocking the doors down to move in for the new semester in mid-February. They pulled all stops to get 90% of the interior renovation finished in time, removing masonite from walls and ceilings (the walls had another metre in height), removing carpets, plastering walls and ceilings, installing VJ villa board and rails (a Reno Kings trick to achieve great effect at a good price). They installed kitchen cabinets, carpet and fans in the bedrooms, polished floors and painted inside and out.

"I furnished all rooms, including whitegoods, with good-quality secondhand furnishings picked out of the *Trading Post* and the *Weekend Shopper* for just over $3500. My nickname soon became 'Queen of the *Trading Post*'."

The property was listed for rental on a per room basis on the internet, and was fully rented out in four weeks, cutting a separate lease for each student with guarantees from their parents.

"Our new tenants were delighted with the end result inside and we spent a further month outside creating a covered outdoor entertainment area and a new driveway and carport. The exterior is now bright yellow trimmed with blue and it makes a dynamic statement in the street."

The original tenant of the house was paying $180 per week. On completion the rent increased to $420 per week (inclusive of gas and electricity) on annual leases due each February. The renovation came to around $50,000 and the house is now valued at around $420,000. Good going for a couple of months' work, even though their intentions for a speedy sale did not eventuate.

Reno Kings Tip

If your property doesn't sell cut your losses and rent it out. Go for the best rent you can get. If you are in a rising market you will get the capital gain down the track. So get some cashflow while you wait.

What a result for Elin.

Cost: $275,000. Original rent: $180 pw or $9360 pa. Yield: 3.4%.

Cost + reno: $325,000. New rent: $420 pw or $21,840 pa. Yield: 6.7%.

New value: $420,000 = $95,000 equity gain and a 130% rent increase in just four hectic weeks.

"We learned that it was difficult to sell a tenanted property, particularly tenanted by students, who are largely messy and not inclined to tidy up for an inspection," says Elin. "Our highest offer was $390,000 and many buyers were suspicious of our high rental returns and lack of rental history at these levels. We chose to hold on a little longer, particularly with the profile of Kelvin Grove developing as an urban village precinct."

The property went into its second year of new leases, with all vacant rooms filling over three weeks, even managing a small increase of $5 per room plus the costs of gas and electricity. The leases were also tighter, with a cleaning levy of $20 per student per month (reimbursed if they cleaned their part of the house by the time of the monthly inspection).

"We haven't given up on the idea of selling but the negative cashflow is minor. Holding for a little longer may pay off in terms of growth, particularly if the reverse ripple forecast by research group Matusik's Property Insights occurs over the next year."

Reno Kings Comment

Capital growth normally flows from the inner rings to the outer rings much like ripples from a pebble in a pond. As a boom slows the ripples reverse back to the inner desirable areas: a reverse ripple.

The Enoggera subdivision

Elin's development application for Enoggera had been approved in late 2002 and in July 2003 the construction work began. This was new territory for Elin and a big learning curve. There was a lot to consider, including shed and tree removal, sewerage and stormwater infrastructure, retaining walls, earthmoving and landfilling, driveway, telecommunication, water, gas and electrical service provision and fencing. After a quote for a project manager came in at a massive $44,000 Elin decided to do it herself.

"My engineers told me which trades and services I needed and suggested I'd save a lot by doing the coordination and project management myself," Elin explains. "They gave me a rough idea of what should happen when, and suggested I find contractors via the Yellow Pages or contacts from people I knew. The tree lopper was an early starter and he recommended a concreter, who recommended a plumber/drainer, and off I went."

Looks like plain sailing from here? Think again. The first problem was the plumber, who turned out to be unreliable, delaying his start date three times. With no other plumbers available Elin was stuck with this guy to do the job.

Ask the right questions

Elin also learned the importance of asking the right questions.

"Nobody volunteers useful information. If you don't ask the right questions, you don't get useful information. So the engineers didn't mention that I needed a council permit (about two weeks to generate) before I got the plumber to start laying pipe work. Once the plumber finally dug his trenches, he asked me for the magic number from the council – and this started the first two-week delay. When I finally got the approval number from the council, the plumber was tied up on another project for a couple of weeks. He came back and laid most of the pipes but needed to wait for council inspections before he could go any further."

Frustrated by the delays, Elin tried her best to keep everything moving forward. She still had a tenant in the existing house, so when the earthmovers (drilling holes for the retaining wall stumps) drilled through the existing house's sewerage pipe her tenant had no sewerage facility. Luckily the tenant had moved in knowing that the work was to be done so was pretty forgiving. When the concreter came to start laying the access driveway, he told Elin that the tree lopper hadn't cut enough of the root from the big fig tree that bordered the driveway. So, another 10 days went by waiting for the tree lopper.

There was more drama a couple of weeks later when Elin discovered that the bobcat driver had also drilled into the newly laid sewerage pipe to which the existing house was about to be connected. Yet another delay while all this was fixed and more delays with the concreter, as he didn't want a heavy machine driving over his new driveway. Each delay took several more weeks as the tradesmen were cranking up for their pre-Christmas rush. Elin realised she needed some backup so she called in her trusty joint venture partner to help.

"I was just about to have a well-earned nervous breakdown," she laughs. "He fired the earthmovers and got in a new bobcat driver with manners, coordinated the laying of conduit and pipe for services, read the riot act to my loser plumber, told the fencing contractor to pull his head in and built my retaining wall with one of his mates (my usual landscaper had broken his leg and I couldn't find another to take on the retaining wall for three or four months). He also got a couple of casual guys in to tidy up the site (he's a Virgo) and finish off bits and pieces."

More hurdles

Elin's next battle was with the council. Under her DA she was liable for $3100 in contributions to Parks and Sewerage and Water infrastructure.

"I went to the council to pay when my DA was approved in late 2002, and the helpful officer said there was no need to pay until the end of the construction, when I would have the plans sealed. As this took the better part of a year, it was November 2003 before I again fronted up to pay."

Unfortunately there had been a rather drastic increase to the charges in the meantime, to $8,500, which Elin was not in the least prepared for.

"The council officer almost had to pick me up off the floor, and then he floored me again, saying that if I had paid them before 30 June I wouldn't have incurred the increase. It wasn't the amount so much as the principle that caused me a huge amount of stress. Much correspondence later led to the decision that I had to pay last year's rates plus CPI. Thank goodness for some commonsense."

There were more paper tigers to fight with Telstra. To get a compliance certificate for telecommunication services Elin needed to first deal with Telstra, then their contractor for laying cable (whose contract ended midway through the process) and a separate contractor who issues compliance documentation.

"Getting the lines in the ground was easy, but getting a piece of paper to verify that they were there took over a month," Elin says.

When it came to sealing the plan Elin was frustrated when inspectors came back with more requirements (such as mulching of the new site, replacing lids on manholes), causing another six-week delay. Finally registration with the Department of Natural Resources (DNR) brought another set of delays when the department sought amendment to the easement documentation.

Elin's solicitors had stated that the purpose of the driveway easement was for "access and utilities". She was told to change the word "utilities" to the word "services", at a cost of $30 and a further two-week delay.

"Finalising the construction work, approval of the submissions to have the subdivision plans sealed and registration with the DNR seemed an eternal process. In fact it took around eight months of heavy-duty learning experiences," Elin says. "Emotionally I felt like I had given birth when my confirmation of registration for the two blocks of land finally arrived in the mail in February 2004."

Was it worth it?

As for Elin's philosophy of being the author of your own destiny, Elin says, "While my frustration at the delays was endless, I was rewarded for my efforts by the market. The bank valued the new block of land at $270,000 and the original house that is now on a small lot of 412 sq m with an easement driveway at $370,000. The total costs of subdivision were around $48,000 and $285,000 for the parcel I purchased two years prior. I felt reasonably well compensated for the delays and frustration, even before signing the contract to build on the newly created rear lot."

Elin made $300,000 profit before she even started to build the house. That's 100% capital gain on her original costs.

Investment property #6: Bayside living

The Kelvin Grove joint venture had worked well for Elin and her development partner, and a revaluation gave them enough cash to do it again.

"One of the tradesmen we engaged at Kelvin Grove, Nev, invited us to look at the renovations he'd made to his own house at Redcliffe, a northern bayside suburb."

While there Nev showed off photos of a small renovator he had just contracted to buy at nearby Shorncliffe (he'd caught their renovating

Here are the numbers for the Enoggera subdivision before the new house was built.

Purchase price	$285,000
Subdivision costs	$48,000
Total costs	$333,000
Bank value, new block of land	$270,000
Bank value, original house on smaller block	$370,000
Total value	$640,000
Profit before house built	$307,000
Percentage profit	100%

bug). He was proud of his find and insisted that Elin drive past his new purchase on her way back to Brisbane.

"Nev's place sure was a renovator, but I was surprised by the extent of gentrification of the neighbourhood and the volume of renovation taking place. These were big renovations of high quality, and the place was starting to resemble some of Brisbane's inner suburbs in character."

Elin made a mental note to consider Shorncliffe in the future.

"Just as I turned the corner to head back I drove past a rickety old Queenslander on a big block right beside the railway line. A dirty handmade sign on the front stated that it was a deceased estate up for private sale. The writing was so small I had to get out of the car to read the phone number. I rang and left a message on somebody's messagebank."

A few days later Jim, the son of the former owner, called to say that he and his sister were looking for offers of more than $300,000. Jim shared that he had been badgered by developers who wanted to demolish the house for development and had made unacceptable offers. Jim (in his 50s) and his sister had grown up in the house and did not want to see the house go that way.

We started negotiations at $280,000 and over a month increased our offers bit by bit. He really hung in there, and we eventually signed a contract with his solicitors for $300,000 with a two-month settlement. The house was in a shocking condition, heavily eaten by termites (some of the mud balls in the bathroom were the size of soccer balls), rotting floor and wall boards, ancient plumbing, deteriorating wooden stumps. One side of the house sloped down significantly, but the roof was quite new and the house had a delightful character and charm."

Easements and flood levels

The railway line ran down one side of the block, with a long easement on the other to service three rear-lot houses. Title searches confirmed that the property had full right of access and use of the easement driveway.

"We planned a subdivision as a 600 sq m rear lot serviced by the easement and a 420 sq m front lot facing the street. Regrettably our back neighbour, and owner of the easement, was hostile to the proposal and took steps to object wherever he could."

The street is part of a demolition-controlled character precinct, so they planned to move the existing house to the rear lot and purchase a "demolition" character Queenslander to drop onto the front lot. The townplanners suggested processing both applications as part of one submission to the council to improve the prospects of winning approval, as well as saving time and cost.

"I went back to the *Weekend Shopper* and found a demolition house in beautiful condition and offering fantastic street appeal. The seller needed the house removed within six weeks so we went to work to find a house removalist with a holding yard. At the time the house seemed very cheap at $30,000, but adding on the costs of a double shift at $33,000 and holding fees of $125 per week I'm not so sure this was the way to go."

The subdivision application with the council was held up over the Christmas–New Period and completely stalled for a month. The council then required written permission from the back neighbour to use the easement driveway (even though the title gave right of access).

"We modified our plans to bring the driveway access for the rear lot onto our own land to create a battleaxe configuration as I did at Enoggera. The next hold-up was that the land at the rear was 30 cm below known flood levels, and the council requested a $20,000 private flood study of the entire catchment to assess the impact of bringing in 30 cm of land fill. This involved debate between ours and the council's engineers for about six weeks before reaching a solution acceptable to all relevant parties."

The subdivision was finally approved (without flood study) in February 2004, sliding the existing house from the front to the back. (Check out the Bonds story for more detail on sliding.) This meant completing the house renovation, installing all services and finalising plan sealing and registration of the new title before bringing the demolition house onto the front lot. The demolition house would enjoy its vacation in the holding yard for several more months.

"We have learned a lot from this project, and it's still going, and we eventually hope to realise a six-figure profit."

Investment property #7: Blue chip again

The Clayfield house was now also let to students on a room-by-room basis. Mowing the lawns there one day (she claims to enjoy mowing lawns for the aerobic exercise), Elin noticed that the house across the street had come onto the market. Her nosey streak came to the fore again.

"The agent advised it was a spectacular old Queenslander on 1012 sq m of land zoned low to medium residential (ie, we could build units) and that offers over $700,000 were welcome. I declined the offer for an inspection as this was quite outside my reach. I suspected that it would also be in a 'demolition-control precinct' so would not be removable and subsequently confirmed this with the local council."

Several months later the property went under contract and a town-planning notification went up out the front of the property advising that an application had been lodged for demolition. Elin was astounded and visited the local council office to inspect the "scrutiny file" (this provides information about applications lodged and is available to the general public, for scrutiny).

"I followed the application with keen interest. Some two months later the council turned it down on the basis that the house was not to be removed from the street. I figured that the new buyer probably no longer wanted the site and tracked him down."

But the property hadn't been sold to the new buyer. It was merely "under contract subject to the successful council application to demolish". Elin then tracked down the owner through the White Pages. The house was a deceased estate. The former owner's elderly daughter was very keen to sell at a reduced price. There had been two unsuccessful contracts over seven months and she now simply wanted to get rid of it, and preferably not to a developer.

"I explored options for relocating the home across the street to my other site, (since my place was not in a demolition precinct), but enquiries to the council were not promising. However, they suggested that if we left the old Queenslander at the front we could build two or three townhouses in the back yard with access via a driveway along the side of the house. I also discovered that new state legislation was soon to be passed allowing townhouses to be built on freehold title, meaning no body corporate!"

Enter joint venture partner. They reached agreement to buy the property for $575,000 with a six-week settlement and 15 business days for finance and building inspections. They also included a clause requiring the vendor to sign their townhouse development application to the council. This is a critical condition of lodging development applications during the purchasing period. The vendor's priority was for an unconditional contract and they were not overly concerned by the length of time to settle, as they had no debt over the property, providing that the lawns were maintained. Okay Elin, get out the lawnmower again.

"Our first viewing inside the house was not until the time of the building inspection and we were delighted with the superior condition and spectacular pressed-metal dome ceilings," says Elin. "We now felt more confident in getting a development application under way and managed to lodge it two days after the new legislation came into effect. Our design features two very up-market villas and a moderate renovation to the big old Queenslander."

With full confidence that the application would be approved with minor modifications in the next month, Elin and her project partner are back to their research, getting the goods on construction estimates, resale potential and development finance.

On solid ground: Building in the back yard at Enoggera

At the same time as the Clayfield purchase, Elin was agonising over her options for the newly created block of land at Enoggera. Her original plan was to sell it and use the cash to reduce the debt on the front house to make it cashflow positive.

The land had a couple of twists to it in that the council had designated the back quarter of the property to be an overland waterflow, separated from the front part with a low retaining wall. This meant that the building pad was quite small and needed a more creative approach in the design of a house. Elin had the land valued and was pleasantly surprised at a valuation of $270,000, which meant she could easily borrow another $200,000 or so to build a house.

"I was nervous about building from scratch as I had no experience in this domain and I'd heard from many people of their horrid experiences with builders unable to deliver to the budget they'd promised. I'd also heard that you rarely end up with what you really wanted the first time but by the second time most folk are much wiser about the process."

Up a pole without a ladder

Elin enjoyed visiting lots of display homes while the kids were at school and came to the conclusion that what she needed was a pole house. Council had no objection to building over the top of the overland waterflow path, providing that the floor levels were well and truly off the ground.

"My research around the rental market suggested there was insufficient supply of four-bedroom, two-bathroom contemporary homes in the inner city. Lacking contacts in the building field, I relied on the good old Yellow Pages to find a pole house builder. All the literature suggested obtaining three quotes from builders, but during a building boom I simply couldn't find three builders who were willing to give me a quote. The quote I got seemed reasonable compared to the spec homes I saw in the display villages so I went to contract with the first builder I met."

Elin's mortgage broker suggested to estimate high on "primary cost" items such as plumbing fittings, appliances and kitchen design, and for the builder to incorporate these higher figures into the quote. This enabled her to maximise her borrowing capacity on the construction of the house.

"Luck must have been on my side," says Elin. "Construction was completed in six months and I had quality tenants signed up on a lease to move in at the earliest possibility. I had developed an excellent relationship with the builder and any small variations, errors and 'changing my mind' were easily negotiated and resolved."

The completion date was six weeks later than planned, but the shortage of sub-contractors was a widespread issue impacting on all development work at the time.

"The absolute highlight for me was the vast amount of 'retail therapy' I derived from selecting kitchen appliances, bathroom fittings, tiles, carpets and more. By shopping around carefully I was able to bring the project in under budget. My fixed-price quote allowed me flexibility to choose less-expensive items than were provided for in the original quote and retain the savings. The savings allowed me to install curtains, sprinkling systems and landscaping, all within the original quoted price."

Elin plans to hold the property for five years to avoid a GST liability that would be incurred if she were to sell before then. The valuation on completion was $473,000. Just think what it will be in five years. In the meantime the rental returns are good, especially considering that the total development was well below market price due to the free block of land.

Managing the risk

"There have been days when I was so anxious about whether I could really pull it all off. I needed to remind myself to breathe," Elin admits. "At first it was quite outside my global view of what was possible. But I was so excited at the same time. It really gave me goosebumps."

Elin also acknowledges the support of professionals around her in order to build her portfolio, such as her mortgage broker, solicitor, architect and her accountant.

"A lot of it is about risk management," she says. "If you understand your current financial situation, especially your cashflow, and can adequately project where that's going to take you, you can analyse the reality of the risks. Often they're not as drastic or dangerous as you might have thought. It's important to run the figures through some property accounting software, or get your accountant to do this for you. The benefit of doing it yourself is a deeper understanding of the costs and benefits.

"We still have a couple of big renovations to finish and may revisit whether Clayfield has any real development potential as an 'affordable housing' project next."

Elin's preference is to keep to one or two developments per year as a means of generating cashflow to reduce debt on other properties she wants to hold for the longer term. But Elin hasn't been house shopping for a year or so now and is seriously getting itchy feet again.

The upshot

Elin's story shows the power of a positive attitude. Her determination, energy and enthusiasm are an inspiration. Elin's experience shows the importance of getting a clear picture of where you want to be in two or three years time and then going for it, in spite of the obstacles.

With two subdivisions under her belt, some tough decisions and a heap of experience along the way, Elin is reaping some hefty capital gains. She has built a property portfolio of around $3 million and is well on the road to financial independence.

Reno Kings insights

What's your background?
I grew up in Brisbane as a first-generation Australian of Dutch parentage. I went to university with aspirations to work in five-star international hotels. Graduating with a business degree, I left Australia for Europe (Queensland did not have international hotels in the early 1980s). Three years later I returned and spent five years working with the Sheraton Hotel Corporation in different locations, ending up as a human resources director. I left the hospitality industry when I began my family and spent a few years consulting on a freelance basis. I then joined local government, where I've worked as a human resources manager for just over 10 years.

Why did you get started?
After my divorce I felt I had lost control of my life. I was dependent on my employer for hours and pay, my ex-husband for child support and the government for parenting allowances. This wasn't going to be sustainable for a "control freak" like me. My ambitions are to fund quality education for my children and to retire with an independent income and, most importantly, to be around for my children while they are growing up. I saw property investment as a way to reach my goals. I had no cash to invest from the day I became single again, so my starting point was to refinance and invest the equity that had accumulated in my family home.

What was your greatest fear?
The risk of losing the family home. My home had become my castle and my emotional safe haven.

Did your parents show you how to get ahead?
My parents were small business operators. They taught us how to save and how to budget, so I can live quite well on a shoestring for substantial periods if I have to. I guess I picked up some business acumen from my

parents too. They were guarantors for my first car loan when I was still at uni and my first home loan in my early 20s, so they gave me an early education on how to borrow and negotiate with bank managers. They also instilled in me a value that "you can do anything you put your mind to".

What was your greatest mistake?
To think I could trade shares profitably. Another mistake was to cross-collateralise with the one financial institution. It limits your scope for further borrowings.

What would you identify as some pitfalls?
It's not really a pitfall I suppose, but having no cash can take a bit of getting used to. We eat home brand everything, and an overseas holiday means a holiday on Bribie Island (a budget holiday destination for the family market about an hour from Brisbane). My children haven't suffered any psychological damage from not having a Playstation at home or a television set in each bedroom.

What do you want to achieve?
I want my home to be debt-free and I want to spend lots of time with my kids during their growing-up years, especially after school. I'd like to be the one who tutors them with their homework and takes them to hockey and football training. As I get older I'd like to have the freedom to decide how much to work. At the moment I like the work I do and benefit from a progressive workplace that is supportive of families.

How would you describe your strategy?
I've only been doing this for a few years, so I'm still sort of making it up on the way. I try stuff and, if it works, I'll try it again. To date I've largely stuck to blue-chip inner-city and middle-ring houses. I've tried a student house and my next venture is affordable housing for the elderly, because I can see a need for this in middle-ring areas.

Any memorable experiences along the way?
On a big construction site near where I work, they were excavating and getting rid of huge truckloads of soil. I needed soil for one of my investment houses at the time, so I just went down to the site (in my suit and high heels) and asked the fellow driving the truck if I could have half a truckload of soil. A couple of days and a six-pack later the soil was delivered to my door.

Where do you find your deals?

Actually four of them found me! But mostly I talk to agents and do heaps of research. This could be reading magazines and journals like *Australian Property Investor* and the local paper of course. I make lists and search the internet and receive email listings from real estate agents. I must be on the email lists of 50 or so agents in the areas that interest me.

What's your best renovating tip?

Its amazing what a difference polished floors, window dressings and a coat of paint can make. Adding an outdoor entertainment area doesn't cost much and adds a lot to the value of the property. I'm also a big fan of the *Weekend Shopper* and the *Trading Post*. My other tip is to always be nice to tradesmen (ask for their advice), even the losers, because you might need them to come back and fix their own blunders. And I've discovered, on occasions, it helps to swear a bit and act like one of the boys if you want something done in the construction game.

Any other tips for investors?

Act on opportunities quickly. I always look for property on a large-ish block of land; subdivision is a great way to get a block for free. I always go for long settlements for time to refinance. It also pays to be decisive. Time is the biggest guarantor of capital growth. If you spend two years looking or thinking about investing in property, you've already missed out on at least 10% growth. There is no time like the present to buy property.

What would you do differently?

If I could rewind the clock I would start 15 years earlier. When I was married without children we had a very high disposable income, and we adopted the conservative view of "paying off the family home first". I wouldn't do that again. My aim would be to pay off enough of the family home to a point where I could refinance and buy investment property. We could easily have made significant gains in the boom of the late 1980s and now be riding our second boomtime. My biggest learning to date is the enormous value of leverage through using borrowed funds. I hope that I can get this through to my children early in their working lives.

How has your life changed since you began investing in property ?

Life's busy, and I have to be very organised with my time. I try hard to keep some sort of balance – work, managing the property stuff, and family life – it takes some juggling. I read every book, magazine and website that I can find about property investment and I talk to lots of different people about the strategies that have worked for them. My experience is that people who invest in property are very open and generous in sharing their learning and experiences. Reading novels is now limited to Harry Potter and other children's literature!

How do you picture yourself five years down the track?
Less intense; with more cashflow. A real overseas holiday would be great.

Elin's tips on dealing with bureaucracy

1. Get things in writing. When you think you understand the answers, put it in an email back to the person responsible for the decision.

2. Ask for the name of the person you are dealing with (and write it down).

3. Buy a large diary and keep notes (sit down each night and think it through – there may be things you forgot to write down).

4. Never take no for an answer (well maybe if everyone says no).

5. Ask different people (eg, a townplanner, an engineer, an ecologist, a plumber) the same questions.

6. Use data to make decisions on risk. It is readily available at reasonable cost from many sources, eg, websites, magazines, real estate institutes.

Reno Kings Reports

There are two Reno Kings Reports we'd definitely recommend for anyone having trouble with finance: Seventeen Ways to Get Finance when the Bank Says No; and Contract Clauses You Simply Must Know. See page 235 for details and how to order, or visit our website: www.renos.com.au

Going green ...
and getting cashflow

Scott and Sandie Elsom are part of a new wave of property investors, keeping a keen eye on the planet, as well as on the bottom line.

Scott Elsom laughs when we ask just when he became a greenie. "No," he protests, "I'm not a greenie." But, gee, he really is. He's doing a hell of a lot for the environment, advancing the interests of sustainable housing and energy efficiency. By the end of our conversation he comes to this conclusion himself.

"Inherently I suppose we all are," he says. "Most people will do the right thing by the environment as long as it doesn't cost them more. Being able to live from a productive garden instead of simply planting ornamentals, for instance, just makes good sense. I've even become a bit of a 'lightbulb Nazi'. It's amazing how many lights the kids leave on."

Scott and his younger brother Mark were brought up on a farm near Dimboola in Victoria, where growing your own vegies, using water from tanks and working in a way that meshes with your surroundings is just the way things are done. These days he's setting up The Green, which he describes as "possibly the world's first environmentally sustainable, relocatable home community for seniors".

The Green was once a traditional caravan park, which Scott's family purchased in 1998 as a multiple rental property, with leases on 40 caravans providing them with passive income. Now they are gradually replacing the caravan lots with environmentally sustainable houses. Each home will have its own solar panels for electricity, collect its own rainwater and recycle its own waste water. All will be equipped with energy- and water-efficient appliances and be built from environmentally sustainable materials.

Six homes are completed and another four are due to start construction, with a further 70 to be built over the next two to three years. But Scott says they have a long-term commitment to the development of a community, not just a property, with the focus on savings for the residents, the local community and the environment.

Over the six years it's taken to get this far, affordable and sustainable housing has become a bit of a passion for Scott. But the idea has evolved from another passion, finding creative ways to maximise the cashflow of an investment property.

Meet Scott and Sandie Elsom

Scott and his wife Sandie started pretty young. They were both just 24 when they built their first home in 1992 for $127,000. It was a four-bedroom, brick veneer house-and-land package in a new subdivision at Burpengary, about 30 km to Brisbane's north, an area that was tipped at the time to soon increase its value.

For six years they put up with the distance from city facilities, and the commuting, before deciding to try letting the house out and renting an older, smaller place for themselves back in the Big Smoke. They found a three-bedroom Queenslander in Nundah, a well-established northern suburb of Brisbane, where they stayed for three years, but the itch to buy had struck again.

"I'd always had the desire to own investment property. It was a way of earning income, as long as the outgoings weren't too high," says Scott.

In 1998, eager to learn about the property market, Scott and Sandie joined up with a two-tiered property marketing company and bought a new townhouse for $142,000 in Nundah, a suburb they were enjoying living in. It sounded so reasonable at the time. The set-up turned out to be something of a rip-off, with the developer acting as agent and double-dipping on commission.

"My method of learning about something has always been to jump in and do it," says Scott. "Well, we certainly learned a lesson from that experience. Rental income was $9360 per annum (giving 6.6% yield) and the place was costing me money, not earning it."

Interestingly Scott turned that situation around somewhat by offering the tenant a lease on whitegoods. Having priced the going rate for rentals on washing machines, dryers, fridges and dishwashers, Scott offered a nicely competitive rate and purchased near-new goods to fill their order, thereby increasing his rental income. The yield on the townhouse still ended up being 8.1%, but at least he was able to cover the outgoings. Look at the power of this strategy.

The rent increase from the appliances turned his rental cashflow from negative to neutral. The one-off capital cost qualified for annual depreciation tax write-off (more cashflow from the tax return) and the tenant was happy. Win, win, win!

"I soon realised this property was not a good long-term proposition and I searched around for better information and advice than I was getting. In 2000 I joined the Property Owners Association. I started to find out what other investors were returning and attended a Reno Kings workshop. It really got me thinking. There were quite a few discussions, some of them even a little heated, about capital gain over yield."

Reno Kings Tip

Each state has a Property Owners Association to represent investors. Visit www.renos.com.au and go to links for the POA national website.

A passion for cash

Scott was convinced that the earning potential in rental properties was there, rather than going for capital appreciation through buying in high-growth areas that also had, as a consequence, climbing property prices.

"Yield puts food on the table," he says. "That's why our family bought the caravan park in 1998, to increase cashflow through the multiple rentals it offered. Even with the cost of the on-site manager, it was working."

Picking the right area, and 14–21% yields!

The caravan park is in Greenbank, then one of Brisbane's lower socio-economic areas on the southside, west of the Brisbane–Gold Coast corridor. With that corridor saturated with development, the growth started filling out to the west, from there to Jimboomba, and the area now encompasses many of Brisbane's growing southern suburbs. Scott soon started looking for other properties in the area.

"In 2000 we bought in the nearby Logan Central/Woodridge area and decided finally to sell off the Burpengary property and the Nundah townhouse," says Scott.

Burpengary's value had earned them a pittance in the nine years they'd owned the property there, selling for just $10,000 more than they'd put into it. Scott reckons they just paid too much for it in the first place. The Nundah townhouse did a little better, but not much, and they were glad to be out of there.

Scott and Sandie found a former Housing Commission home in Logan, well worn but really only in need of a clean-up and a lick of paint, and at the cheap end of the area's market, at $56,000.

"The return was doing well at almost 14.4% yield. We also offered the same deal on whitegoods that we had introduced to Nundah, which increased it a little. The area began to pick up and the rental market was able to bear a gradual increase to a point where it was yielding almost 21% on the original outlay. But generally prices were rising faster than rents so it was going to be increasingly difficult to get the yield we were looking for.

"It was about this time we started getting serious about developing The Green in order to increase our returns. By building and selling affordable housing on common land, which is leased out under a perpetual lease agreement, you're getting the best of both worlds. You achieve capital gain through the development of the entire property, as well as rental yield that is higher per lot than standard housing, where you are paying for individual plots of land and the housing itself is more expensive.

"The homeowner can gain here also, by adding value to the house they buy, on top of the massive savings on their outgoings," says Scott. "Of course it would be another four years before we'd get to the stage we're at now, with everything in place, and there's still a lot to do."

Closer to home

In the meantime, between 2001 and 2002, Scott and Sandie were involved in renovating another two houses, within six months of each other, in Wavell Heights, close to Nundah, where they had rented for three years. One was to become their own home; the other was purchased for capital gain, with substantial improvements made to both properties.

"The experiment of renting in order to free up cash for investing was presenting too many limitations, so we started looking for a house to buy for ourselves, while keeping a keen eye out for rental propositions," says Scott. "By this time we had a good feel for the rental and home markets in the area. Yields were high and it was possible to purchase houses around the 10% rental yield mark. We looked at a number of places and made offers on a number as well. No one would come at my low offers."

Reno Kings Tip

When your offers get knocked back, that's okay. Keep making them and agents will know you are in the market, and you will get a deal as long as you keep looking and making offers.

Scott and Sandie's purchasing history.

Description	Year purch	Purchase price	Reno costs	Total costs	Current value	Year sold	Sale price	Comment
*Burpengary 4 brm	1992	$127,000	$20,000	$147,000		2001	$160,000	PPOR 6 years, then rented out, P&I
*Nundah 2 brm townhouse (in block of 4)	1998	$142,000		$142,000		2001	$186,000	Two-tiered marketing, I/O secured against Burpengary
Greenbank Caravan Park; in partnership with family	1998	$750,000		$750,000	$1,800,000	held		The Green; value on completion est $5m
*Logan 3 brm	2000	$56,000	$2,000	$58,000		2003	$181,000	I/O secured against this property – Mortgage Ins Paid
Wavell Heights 3 brm	2001	$120,000	$19,000	$139,000	$350,000	held		On two 500 sq m lots. Converted to 6 brm. PPOR P&I
*Newstead 6 flatettes; subdivision; joint venture	2001	$10,000	$5,000	$15,000		2003	$45,000	Costs and values of individual share
*Wavell Heights 3 brm	2001	$111,000	$18,260	$129,260		2002	$189,000	P&I secured against this property
Total		$1,316,000	$64,260	$1,380,260	$2,150,000		$761,000	
LVR=original loan/current value					65%			

* Homes sold to finance redevlopment of The Green

Reno case study #1

"The house we now live in was a property on a very busy intersection and it was so ugly I didn't even want to look at it," says Sandie.

But neither did anyone else. It had been on the market for six months without an offer and the price had just been reduced from $180,000 to

$150,000. Scott did some research and discovered that the house was on two 500 sq m lots, which the agent had failed to mention.

"We steeled ourselves to have a look and during that inspection I climbed a mango tree in the back yard," says Scott. "It had uninterrupted city views, which the agent had also failed to mention. I quickly got down out of the tree, without saying a word. We made an offer of $110,000, increased to $120,000 and we were in."

> ### Reno Kings Tip
>
> *A city view adds serious value. Tell the agent you want to examine the roof. While up there check out the view. Sometimes there is a city or, better still, water view just waiting to be captured by a roof window or by raising or adding an extension.*

"The house had a 1940s kitchen, bright orange curtains and brown carpet throughout. It sure was ugly," agrees Scott. "It had two large bedrooms and another smaller one and a number of other little areas. It also had two bathrooms. I knew there had to be a way to increase the number of rooms in the house, but couldn't think of how to do it effectively. I knew the house would rent, as it was, for around $210 per week. We made our first offer based on this rental return (a 10% yield), not imagining us living there ourselves. After a little bit of to-ing and fro-ing we settled on $120,000, a 9.1% yield. I felt that I could have done better; perhaps I had given in too easily."

"We weren't sure of the best thing to do with the house so we decided to move in to get a feel for the place," says Sandie. "After about six weeks of 'thinking' and asking other people for their ideas we were ready. We didn't want to overspend on it. Our aim was to add value and get out."

"We decided on a plan of action to get the best 'bang for our buck'," adds Scott. "It needed an entirely new kitchen – the old one was non-existent. We divided each of the two large bedrooms and the formal loungeroom into two, making a total of six bedrooms, which has added enormous value. We got a carpenter in for this, then added timber venetian blinds. We also got a professional painter in to repaint inside and out and hired someone to sand the floors.

"Then there was some heavy pruning to do in order to get the city view. We brought in a tree lopper. We laid a recycled concrete driveway ourselves and bought plants, soil and turf. I decided to build the deck myself to get some building experience and cut labour cost. We had been quoted between $18,000 and $22,000 to build the deck. Doing it myself cost $6000. By the way, a good tip for decks is to use galvanised fencing wire as an alternative to stainless steel cable – it looks good and is about 5% of the cost of cable."

Reno costs of case study #1.

Kitchen	$5,200
Adding 3 bedrooms	$1,300
Blinds	$400
Painting	$1,800
Sanding floors	$1,700
Tree lopping	$900
DIY driveway	$600
Plants, soil, turf	$1,100
DIY deck	$6,000
Total	$19,000

The house, familiarly known as the "House on the Hill", now had a huge deck with city views, six bedrooms and a study, a very large lounge, a new kitchen, a dining room, two bathrooms, a carport and a huge yard for their two kids.

"It even has its own traffic light – press the button and the traffic lights all turn red to let us out our front gate. The kids drove motorists crazy with that!" says Scott.

Scott and Sandie had set a budget of 10–15% of the purchase price and went over just slightly. The house is now worth $350,000 to $400,000.

"Our short-term renovation has turned long-term. We can't bear to leave now," adds Sandie. "We've been here for nearly four years and expect to stay for a while longer, though redevelopment of the site is a possibility in the future."

"While still looking for an investment property in the Wavell–Nundah area we also outlaid a small investment in a joint venture renovating an old Queenslander in Newstead that had been divided into flats," says Scott. We didn't restore it to its original one-dwelling form, as you might expect. We built a replica Queenslander behind it, as a second multiple-dwelling unit, which has worked really well." (See the JV story later.)

Reno case study #2

Drawing on the success of their first reno, Scott, with his brother Mark, attempted to duplicate it. They found a similarly ugly house on another busy corner a few streets away from their home and attended the open house. Once again this was a house that no one wanted. It had previously been on the market for about four months and hadn't sold. It was now back on the market.

"There were about six people at the open house," says Scott, "and no one seemed interested. I held back until everyone left to find out the asking price. The owner hadn't decided so I offered $110k and asked the agent to get back to me by the end of the day.

"I was determined to stick to my guns, after feeling that I had given in too soon on our previous property. The agent told me that I needed to give the vendor something to get it across the line. She wanted an extra $5k. I gave $1k and in the end we got it for $111k. The agent later told me that a thousand dollars was enough to make the vendor feel that they weren't being screwed. This was a good lesson in psychology. Everyone expects to get something in the negotiation process, even if it's just a thousand dollars," says Scott.

The house had an existing tenant and at the purchase price it was giving a yield of 7.8%, so it was paying its own way. The kitchen was 1970s style, with lime green benchtops, and the plaster walls had been covered up with brown ply veneer panelling. The back door opened onto a pile of broken concrete and the garden was overgrown. Scott and Mark decided to keep on the existing tenants for nine months and then do the renovation, which took three weeks all up. They sold it immediately when it was finished for $189k, a capital gain of almost $60k.

"With this one the biggest expense was the landscaping. Paving, plants and turf cost $11,000 with a landscaper, and we built up the broken

Reno costs of case study #2.

Landscaping	$11,000
Replacing fence	$3,500
Repainting	$2,200
Light fittings and power points	$870
Plastering	$690
Total	$18,260

concrete to make a paved patio and outdoor entertaining area. The old metre-high mesh fence was falling down, so we replaced it with a high Colorbond fence to block out the road noise. Again we got a professional in to repaint; same for the electrical work, light fittings and new power points, and plastering. We had once again set a budget of 10–15% of the purchase price and went over slightly."

Reno costs of case study #2

"One of the best lessons we learned from these experiences is to make lots of offers on houses that suit your needs until someone bites," advises Scott. "And don't make any decisions on a renovation until you're able to sit in the house and think about it. Talk to other people and get them to make suggestions on the best way to maximise the return on the money you spend. Appearance is everything when selling a home. Spend money on landscaping, painting, kitchens and bathrooms – but not too much."

Here's a comparison between Scott and Sandie's early purchases and the renovations.

	Nundah townhouse	Logan house	Wavell Heights PPOR	Wavell Heights investment
Year purchased	1998	2000	2001	2001
Purchase price	$142,000	$56,000	$120,000	$111,000
Reno costs	$-	$2,000	$19,000	$18,260
Total costs	$142,000	$58,000	$139,000	$129,260
Original loan	$136,000	$50,800	$110,000	$95,000
Rent pw at purchase	$9,360	$8,580	N/A	$10,140
Yield at purchase	6.6%	15.3%	N/A	9.1%
Rent pw at sale* / current	$11,440	$12,480	N/A	N/A
Yield at sale / current	8.1%	21.5%	N/A	N/A
Year sold	2001	2003	N/A	2002
Sale price / current value	$186,000	$181,000	$350,000	$189,000
Capital gain	$44,000	$123,000	$211,000	$59,740
	*Includes $20 pw for whitegoods	*Includes $25 pw for whitegoods		

Yield at purchase=rent/purchase price
Yield at sale or current=rent/total cost
Capital gain=current value-total cost

Moving on and up

In 2003 Scott and Sandie sold both the Logan and Wavell houses, keeping the House on the Hill, and sold their share in the Newstead flats, which allowed them to raise the funds needed to develop The Green.

The last four years have involved much painstaking work in getting council approvals for all sorts of aspects of the property, as well as designing the houses themselves. The caravan park was equipped with its own sewerage system, but Mark and Scott then had to ensure a high level of treatment of the waste and work out ways to use the treated effluent on the property, such as in gardens, for toilet flushing and washing clothes.

"Beyond that we've developed entire systems of supplying the services you normally take for granted: solar panels for electricity, large-capacity rainwater tanks for drinking water, even buying in building products that are non-toxic and long-lasting, with limited use of plastics and glues."

The ceilings and some walls are made from compressed wheat or rice straw that use no chemicals to manufacture, and the material is totally renewable, with new crops grown each year. As a result, the houses should never require air-conditioning and will require very little heating.

Mark developed a simple and cost-effective method of replenishing the ground-water, using a series of absorption pits. This has helped them realise one of their development goals of retaining all stormwater on-site. We have a natural aquifer on the property that is now replenished by the stormwater that falls on the site. Previously all of the stormwater ran into the council drains, into the Logan River and into Moreton Bay. Now the plants can tap into this water supply and this reduces the amount of watering required by our homeowners.

"We owe an enormous amount to Sydney-based designer Michael Mobbs. We saw on his website the 120-year-old terrace house he'd renovated. It was totally self-sustaining and energy-efficient and we were just amazed. He joined forces with us for a while, helping us to set up the basic designs. We ended up establishing SALA Homes to build the houses."

"We've kept the old Queenslander feel to the houses by using wide eaves, high ceilings, timber walls and lots of cross-ventilation. Not only are the old Queenslanders pleasant on the eye, they work well with their environment – not like the brick boxes that tend to be built today. We're finding many in the seniors community relate to the Queenslander feel of the houses because it is what many of them grew up with," says Scott.

They're also quite at home with the concept of vegie gardens and rainwater tanks. Many were brought up in the Depression years so saving money on electricity and water bills is definitely appealing.

"Many seniors are concerned about their health, so the fact that our homes are healthy to live in appeals also. We use non-toxic paints and minimal glues and plastics, and the home design allows maximum ventilation. We also provide various air-cleaning plants, which act as an air filter for the homes, extracting commonly occurring substances such as formaldehyde, benzene, trichloroethylene (TCE) and carbon monoxide."

For young and old

"We've started thinking about extending the idea of community developments for young families," says Sandie. "We're considering building small houses around a communal park/playground area in order to fit more families into the space available while keeping the amenity of the place. It would mean cheaper living expenses, while fostering a community feel.

"Young families, particularly in low socio-economic areas, tend to find it difficult to buy a house. Using our model, buying a home becomes a partnership between the landowner and the homeowner. The cost of buying a home is reduced dramatically because the homeowner is not purchasing the land component. Any improvements they make to the home remain theirs. It is a great way to 'get a foot in the door'."

According to Sandie, in the seniors market people tend to like this type of community because it frees up their cash, so they can enjoy retirement with the money they save.

"I see no reason why the model can't be applied to the opposite end of the life cycle for those who don't have the cash."

"It's funny, once you become conscious of saving energy and water, doing things that are better for the environment, you look at the way your own family lives, the habits you get into," Scott adds. "Hang on a minute – just got to turn off a few lights." And the lightbulb Nazi's away.

The upshot

We see many investors who are thinking GRQ (get rich quick). We understand that, and we used to be that way ourselves. Scott and Sandie now have an eye for a deal, for cashflow, but also consideration of the big picture, the next generation, and an attitude to lessen their impact on the planet. They are a new breed of developer, one eye on cashflow and the other on its balance with sustainability. They save you money on water and heating and electricity and you reward them by buying their houses. It's an eternal cycle of win, win.

Reno Kings insights

What's your background?

Scott: I worked in the IT industry until July 2002, but always had the desire to become financially self-sufficient. Sandie and I tried investing in shares (unsuccessfully) and we have tried multi-level marketing. I had always been interested in property investing and purchased an investment property through a two-tiered property marketing group in 1998. I got more involved with this group with the aim of learning more about property investing. I learned what *not* to do.

Since then we have been on a journey to find higher yields and greater security in property. We've owned houses in new subdivisions, we've bought and renovated, we've purchased high-yield homes and we've bought lower-yield homes in high-growth areas. For the past four years my brother Mark and I and our wives, have been redeveloping our caravan park into an environmentally and socially responsible community for seniors.

Sandie: I have worked in travel forever. Our first home was in the very outer suburbs, standard four-bedroom, two-bathroom, but it always felt a bit sterile. When we moved and renovated an old house it seemed much warmer and more homely.

Why did you get started?

Scott: I didn't want to be dependent on my employer for the rest of my life. I wanted more control over my life.

Sandie: Out of necessity. We wanted to move closer to the city and an old house was all we could afford.

What was your greatest fear?

Scott: Napoleon Hill, through his book *Think and Grow Rich*, taught me that fears are nothing more than a negative state of mind that get in the way of you achieving your goals. I would rather focus on my life goals than my fears.

Sandie: That we would be living for years with unfinished jobs. This has happened, but not to the extent that I feared.

Did your parents show you how to get started?

Scott: Yes. My parents were farmers. They wanted to get off the land and saw property investing as a way of achieving that. They invested in property and involved us in the day-to-day management of those investments and the household. They would often ask us for our opinion on both major and minor financial decisions. Sharing these experiences with my parents from an early age was invaluable. We are still learning from Mum and Dad today.

Sandie: No, my parents have never renovated or involved me in any of their investments.

What was your greatest mistake?

Scott: Trying to make money the easy way. I believed the hype of the marketers and convinced Sandie to agree to purchase a sub-standard investment early on in our investing career. They promised to do all of the research, source the properties, help us with finance and help us manage the property. In reality the only person who can find *you* a great deal is *you*. The best manager of your investments is *you*. Believing salespeople cost us a lot of time and money.

Sandie: Trying to do our own tiling. I recommend you leave this to the professionals unless it is a very small area. Of course, I would never use tiles again anyway because of the immense energy required to manufacture and lay them. There are more environmentally sensitive products available.

What do you want to achieve?

Scott: I want to be able to provide an ongoing income stream that will support my family indefinitely, without taking advantage of anyone. I want to show that it is possible to make good returns from investing, without screwing the community, the environment or the people living in our houses.

Sandie: I want to create a house that is 100% gentle on the environment, and costs no more than conventional housing. I want environmentally sustainable building methods to be standard. I want world peace too!

How would you describe your strategy?

Scott: We have tried picking the market, we have tried picking growth areas, we have tried renovating and we have tried investing for yield. I think the strategy that we have settled on is a combination of all of them. We will continue to buy properties in growth areas based on yield and add value to those properties where possible. The Green illustrates this combination. We are situated in a growth corridor, with a growing market (seniors). We have added value to the property by offering environmentally and socially responsible housing at an affordable price. We are getting both short-term capital gain when the homes are sold and we are also getting a secure, long-term income stream by leasing the land to our tenants. When complete the yield will be well over 30% per annum on purchase price and we will be debt-free.

Sandie: I listen to Scott's ideas, weed out the more outlandish ones and go with the rest. He has a great passion for what he does, and his judgement is generally very good.

Any memorable experiences along the way?

Scott: In 1991 when I met Sandie I told her that I wanted to stop work by the time I was 40 and spend my time with my family and looking after a portfolio of investment properties. I think she thought I was joking. I love proving people wrong!

Sandie: We thought we had a big rat that was tearing the kitchen apart at night. We couldn't seem to get rid of it. After a while we discovered it was a cat that was sneaking in the cat door, a legacy of the previous owners.

What's your best renovating tip?

Scott: Don't try to do all the work yourself – life is too short. Do one renovation yourself and, once you know what is involved, pay someone to do the work. This will free you up to spend more time with family, or find the next deal, or new products, or anything else. Qualified tradesmen will probably do it quicker than you and it will probably be a better job.

Sandie: Do you really need a formal lounge and dining room? Consider what rooms people would really use and work them in, even if it seems a bit strange. For example, our house has three large bedrooms and three smaller bedrooms used as studies. It works wonderfully.

Any other tips for investors?

Scott: Try to buy a property with a special feature, a view, a great location, a desirable zoning, large block, etc, but try not to have to pay for it. When we bought the house we live in, no one, including the agent, knew that it was on a double lot with a view (once the mango tree was pruned). If your property does not have a special feature, try thinking outside the box to see if there is something that you can do to give it a special feature. The Green was a small caravan park with no special features. Turning it "green" gave it that special feature. There is no reason why someone couldn't carry out a green renovation on their investment house and market it as an eco-rental with low running costs and a healthy indoor environment.

Sandie: Normally when people renovate a property they start inside and do the landscaping and outside painting last. I say do the opposite. Start in the front yard with the landscaping and painting. Once the front is complete, put up a "For Rent" or "For Sale" sign and wait for people to come knocking on your door. When people see a drastic change in a house it sparks their interest. You would be amazed at the number of people who notice the change and stop to ask what you are doing. By carrying out the most visible part of the renovation first you arouse that interest early on. You never know, that interest may result in you selling or renting the property without the need to engage an agent (that can save you some serious dollars).

What would you do differently?

Scott: In future I will try to ascertain people's credentials before taking advice from them. Only listen to those who have done what you intend to do. I listened to salespeople and others who gave the impression that they knew about renovating and investing. Believing people without checking them out cost us a lot of time and money

Sandie: Close up the cat flap sooner.

How has your life changed since you began your property investment?

Scott: Investing equates to taking on a second job. While I was still working in my job I worked very long hours after work and on weekends. Looking back on this period shows me that you really do get what you put in. That hard work has now left us with no personal debt. This could not have happened without our property investments.

Sandie: It's made me look at working in a different light. I had always envisaged myself as a loyal employee until I retired, and then living off my superannuation. Now I look forward to the day, in the not-too-distant future, where I will not be working for an employer at all. It's also made me think twice about large expenses like cars. Previously I was quite happy to borrow for a car. I cringe now at the thought of owing as much as $30,000 on a car, when you know you will never make a return on it.

How do you picture yourselves five years down the track?

Scott: I see us doing exactly what we are doing now, except that Sandie will be able to also work in the business. I expect that we will have less of a hands-on role than we currently do. We will have a number of green investment properties and communities that will provide us with ongoing passive income and the time to experiment and improve the quality of our work.

Sandie: SALA Homes and The Green will be leading Australia in environmentally sustainable development. I will consider going back to uni and studying environmental law so I can help make our product range better and broader. I'd like to be more involved in sourcing products and upholding our standards in environmentally sensitive products developed through non-exploitative work practices. I want to have more time to spend with our children, and to encourage people to embrace a lifestyle that minimises their ecological footprint.

Visit Scott and Sandie on the web

www.salahomes.com.au and *www.thegreen.com.au*

Every deal has a story

Paul Eslick might be best known as one half of the Reno Kings, but he built much of his portfolio way before he met Geoff Doidge, the Reno Kings' other half. And their strategies do differ, which just goes to show that there is no single way to make money through property investment.

Paul reckons he was destined to work with his hands: his mother thought he should be a surgeon because of his delicate digits. Mind you, his father thought he should be Prime Minister, but Paul says he's made more money than he would have in either of those options simply through wise property buying and value adding.

"If I have a gift it's the ability to know a good buy when I see one and know instinctively how it can be quickly improved. Why wait for four years to get a hefty capital gain on your investment property when you can get it in four weeks?"

That philosophy has helped Paul build a property portfolio in excess of $8 million.

"When I buy a property and renovate it, I like to have the renovations finished within four weeks," Paul says. "The best I've done is 10 days. But, whatever way you look at it, time is money."

Meet Paul and Helen Eslick

My wife Helen and I have been involved in buying and renovating property for close to 26 years, but it was only in 1995 that I decided to "get serious" and give up my job as manager for a large hardware company. I'd been doing up houses in my spare time all these years. It was when I realised that I was making more money and having more fun with the renovations that I decided to give up the corporate world and focus on property.

My main secret has been to buy good value properties with a twist. I've never been interested in negative gearing. As far as I'm concerned, a loss is a loss whatever way you look at it, even if you're sharing the loss with the tax man. Unless, of course, there is an ulterior motive, like finding the worst house in the best street and "land banking" on it until you get round to D9ing (demolishing) it and rebuilding. (I'll be doing this to an old dongar I've got sitting on what will soon be a million dollars worth of dirt on a deepwater canal.)

Every property deal has a story, and a reason behind it. The one criteria I have for property is that it has the potential to add value. If it doesn't you shouldn't go to first base. Don't buy it.

My first-ever property, though, was bought in 1979, when I was 28 years old. I'd returned from "OS" back home to Beaumaris, an outer suburb of Melbourne on Port Phillip Bay. I was broke, with no car, living at home with Mum and Dad. So I made my way to the dole queue.

I never did pick up that cheque. There was a massive storm over most of Victoria on the first Tuesday in November 1976, Melbourne Cup day. I'd stopped at the Portsea pub to watch the big race. The reports on the news said it had caused a million dollars worth of damage.

A local building firm that specialises in insurance damage repairs was snowed under with work as a direct result of the Melbourne Cup Storm and the ad in the local paper caught my eye, especially the bit that said company car included! Their staff were mainly older builders. They had all the knowledge but couldn't put two words together on paper. They believed it would be easy to train a person with little building knowledge to do all the investigation and written reports.

In my previous job as a trainee accountant and office manager for Repco I'd done some cost accounting work, studying accounting at night, and been involved with some minor insurance claims on behalf of the company. I signed up.

New tricks

I was the new kid learning new tricks. I crawled over every leaking roof there was, and under them, looking for major structural problems. The old chippies were my eyes and I was their mouthpiece. Imagine the benefit of this type of apprenticeship. That's where I learned the building side of things. I stayed with the job for four years, writing up reports and organising the tradies around it, learning every trick of every building trade to do with fixing faults and solving problems.

So many apparently major problems, like plaster ceilings falling down, were easy to fix if you knew how. But you also had to know when the work *was* major and beyond you and call for help. This was my groundwork and it's kept me in good stead ever since, given me that "gift" to know a good buy and how it can be quickly improved.

In the meantime my girlfriend at the time worked for a stockbroker and she was given some vital insider goss that the barrel price for oil was going to move upward at a great rate. There had been a push for Victorians to move out to bigger blocks and the small inner-city properties had lost their appeal. The girlfriend's guess was that people would start moving closer to the city as the price of fuel began to rise. It's a phenomenon that's occurring now also.

I have always been a sad observer of the "back to the womb" theory of most Australians when it comes to buying their first property. Many think they must live where they've been brought up, right near Mum and Dad, because they respect their parents and the decisions they've made. But their decisions were not made with hindsight; they were made out of necessity, often with funds generated from war service loans. I meet a lot of people today who are still resigned to buying their principal place of residence and investment properties all within 10 minutes of where they were brought up.

I hurdled that great barrier and discovered that there were suburbs other than Beaumaris that had just as much to offer. I could also go home on a Thursday night for tea with the oldies. The great metropolis of Melbourne opened up.

I can tell you there are lots of fab places and people out there. Just go and do your research. With good research there is no reason why you can't buy in any suburb in any state, or in any country for that matter.

There's got to be a first

Inner suburbs started opening up and I bought 4 km from the GPO and nine seconds from the beach, in Albert Park. I had considered the next suburb, Port Melbourne, but Dad reckoned I was "too soft" for that tough area. "Any bloke from Port with two ears is a sissy," I recall him frequently saying. For once I took my father's advice. I quite like my ears, both of them.

There were plenty of houses to choose from that needed renovating, though they were structurally sound. This was an old suburb with old inhabitants. Gentrification was just beginning. I bought my first property direct from an elderly lady who was moving back to be with her family. It was my first encounter of buying a house that was not for sale. I had let it be known that I was in the market in that area and one of the chippies at work had an aunt who was unsure of selling. We were introduced. She liked me and I liked the house. She wanted $30k and I offered $29k. (I wasn't too skilled in negotiating at this stage.) All was agreed and the rest is history, as they say.

This is when I began to develop my current belief in "cosmetic" renovation, what Helen has dubbed the "hair cut" look, as well as in "cannibalising" the existing house for materials, using the materials you take from one part to renovate another. We also always try to take a house back to what it was originally, stripping off imitation-brick cladding to reveal original timber, for instance.

I had discovered another world doing up my first property, working hard during the day and racing home to start work. I just loved it, especially on Saturdays, because if I kept up with my strict building schedule (some refer to this as a Gant Chart) I would reward myself with a two o'clock knock-off and down to the Golden Gate, a local pub with a great band and great people. I made new friends, adopted a new suburb. There would be no turning back.

When I had finished my cosmetic makeover the transformation was unbelievable. One of the locals remarked that my home was the smartest house in the street. I had accidentally discovered street appeal! I had achieved what I had set out to do and sat back in my glory, when in hindsight I should have been on the prowl for more property. I had yet to learn about good and bad debt.

I loved my job, loved my house, but I didn't love the weather and with that in mind rented out my joint and headed north to become a Queenslander. Twenty-three years later my local mates reckon maybe next year I will become one; they're tough on us Mexicans. Two years into my Queenslander apprenticeship I severed the Melbourne umbilical cord and sold up for $57,500. Not so long ago I visited my old street to find that a house a few doors up had sold at auction for $503,000. There is no profit in looking back.

To warmer climes: 1980–83, #1–2

My stockbroker girlfriend (yes, it was Helen; we married a few years later) decided to flee the Victorian cold and landed on Queensland's Sunshine Coast in 1980. I started work with Monier Roof Tiles as a supervisor, then sales rep.

We bought our first Queensland house for $55k soon after arriving there. It was in Buderim, up the mountain behind the main beaches of Mooloolaba and Maroochydore. It was on the main drag, my first purchase in what I call "the 'ways", main roads and similar busy and noisy spots. I don't mind buying on these sites, providing I get them at the right price. They might not have as much capital growth as the next street back but they're cheaper to get into and they rent out quickly because they are slightly lower in rent. All my properties on the 'ways have still gone up three times in value since purchase and they're always rented out first.

The house was a cute skillion-roofed cottage on two and a half acres [1 ha] on two lots. The house, much to my surprise, straddled both of them. When I ran a tape along the roadway boundary I discovered the lounge was situated on lot two.

> ### — Reno Kings Tip —
> *Be super careful in surveying your purchase to confirm without doubt that what you are purchasing is actually reflected on the title, and not by fence boundaries.*

We did a deal with the vendor and split the cost of reconfiguring the boundaries: our first subdivision, and another twist! The existing house was on a wider block with less depth, giving great access to the back, where we built two years later.

As construction work on the house began, there was a slump in the building industry and I got laid off through a restructure based on "last in, first out". It was a social shock to lose my job and some people would see it as a negative, but all of a sudden I had time on my hands and no income to pay for building, so I did it myself.

We sold the little cottage for $55k to pay for the new construction and discovered another bizarre consequence. We bought the cottage on two and half acres and sold it on half an acre, giving us two free acres! What a positive!

> **Reno Kings Tip**
>
> *This happens again and again. Subdivide the yard, get a free block and the original house maintains its value. It's the most underrated and little-known money-making strategy in Australia.*

I can remember very clearly digging the footings for the new house. The next day 250 mm of rain bucketed down in just over three hours, on what was to be then known as "Wet Wednesday". The deluge caused millions of dollars damage across the Sunshine Coast, and cost me about $1000 for extra concrete to fill in the trenches gouged out by the rain.

I had a go at all the trades and found out I was no good at bricklaying but not bad as a brickie's labourer. The solid brick construction and timber VJ-lined internal walls took six months to build, at a cost of $74k. A few years later we sold it for $182k. I always knew there was a truckload of capital gain here because I got the land for free, a clear example of making your money when you buy not when you sell.

Off to the beach: 1984–89, #3–5

I'd been working for McEwans as a hardware rep since 1983. Then I discovered they were moving out of supplying the hospitality industry. I couldn't understand this as that particular field was under-catered for at the time. Another opportunity! I started my own business, importing and selling hospitality equipment to restaurants from my garage. I don't know how many of the same restaurants we refurbished, all with new owners, but what a great little business.

In 1988 we were looking at property again, this time closer to the beach. We bought a "four-pack" block of units from an interstate vendor for $106,000. They were well under-rented. The rear two-bedroom unit had its own in-ground pool and was rented for only $75 per week; a small, noisy front flat went for $65 pw. An exterior paint job and a bit of a tidy-up cost $3000 in the first two weeks. The tenants agreed to a higher rent due to the improved living conditions and, with the rent up, the yield was much higher, just ripe for another investor.

It sold immediately for $134,000 to a chap who was on the lookout for an investment property for his interstate friend. His mate never did get that property. "No bargains up here," I bet he told him. The bloke snaffled it for himself! Under-rented properties equal undervalued properties.

> **Reno Kings Tip**
>
> *Always be on the lookout for under-performing properties that can be easily and quickly made to look much smarter by the use of paint to increase the rent. That way you "revalue the devalued".*

The next year we found a vacant duplex block up near the Maroochy airstrip at Marcoola, once again purchasing directly from the vendor. I can't emphasise enough the importance of letting everyone know you're in the market. This one came via our carpet layer. It was only 551 sq m and I bought it for $19,000. I teamed up with a builder mate, who built at cost, for $98k for both the units, and we divvied up the profit at the end of the project: my first joint venture with someone other than my wife.

We ended up selling them for $79k each, one to a bloke who was a plane-spotter and the other to an investor who didn't care about the position because he wasn't living in it. The owner-occupier didn't care about the noise of the aircraft. It suited him down to the ground. This confirmed my belief in buying on the 'ways, locations that a lot of people think of as detrimental but are a real joy to others, like the plane-spotters, the bus-spotters, the train-spotters.

Home, sweet deal

Around this time I was working for a builder at Mooloolaba who knew I was keen to leave the Buderim bush and take up an aquatic lifestyle to continue my love affair with sailing. He casually remarked that a place two doors up had been sold.

I couldn't believe it. Here's the worst house on the best street and out the back there were 2 ha of deep tidal broadwater. I rang the agent, to discover that it was only a verbal sale for $190,000, no contract. I offered $193,000 with no hesitation. Helen hadn't even looked at it.

When you find a bargain, get it off the market immediately, but make sure your solicitor builds in an escape clause. This property is now our home and I like to get it revalued regularly to increase my line of credit. It's now worth about $1.5 million. It's really the land value that goes up.

There's a great difference between "good debt" and "bad debt". Good debt is for investment properties, IPs, bad debt is for your home, as the interest is not deductible. Establishing a line of credit worth $220,000 a few years later on my principal place of residence has been the best thing. By the time we had acquired six properties it only cost me $100 per week to hold them before the quantity surveyor's figurework kicked in.

Reno Kings Tip

Most people slaving to pay off their home loan are stunned to find out that it can cost less than $100 per week to control the debt on six investment houses.

I know of numerous investors who are paying more than that to hold just one negatively geared property. Going back into debt to make money is the best thing I could have done. It's the power of leverage. The fewer negative-geared homes you buy, the more homes you can acquire and, using all of the depreciation allowed for under the tax rules, the more your personal tax will drop.

1990–94: The learning years

Between 1989 and 1995 I slaved hard at the hardware shop, working my way up from sales rep to branch manager. During this time I attended as many courses as I could in relation to building and timber products, estimating, quotes, and had vast exposure to the TRADAC [Timber Research and Development Advisory Council] manual, the Bible for using timber in the building industry in Queensland.

Also during this period I went back to night school to obtain my builder supervision accreditation. I was the oldest one in the class, with the majority being apprentices, who could have been my sons, in the final legs of getting their building licences. I was at first looked on as the outsider and mocked by the back-seaters. (I always sat at the front due to my eyesight.) But as the course continued, and nearer exam time, I do recall a few round at my place getting extra tuition in wind- and stress-loading calculations. Some of these guys have gone on to become major builders on the Sunshine Coast.

I was a bit bored being a branch manager. The company had gone through a few new owners and the market had started to wane. You're a god when you make your budget and a bastard when you don't!

The fast-track Ferrari: 1995–96, #6–11

So we decided to look at properties in Brisbane, entering what you might call "a busy period". We bought six properties in 11 months, all in the inner-Brisbane area and all cash positive. That's where I got the nickname the "Fast-track Ferrari".

The first one was back on the 'ways again. Helen calls it "the yellow brick road", because the major arterial roads are coloured yellow in the street directory. We were so excited we got our neighbour up early on a Sunday morning so we could use his fax machine to send the contract back. Talk about eager and green!

Emotions were running high. We both loved the cute, artistic, pleasing little Queenslander and couldn't get our money out of our pockets fast enough. Purchase price was $85k, with 80% supplied by the bank and 20% supplied by our line of credit, also funded by the same bank. This appeared to be a very good buy at the time, as most other properties we had researched and viewed were asking another $15k.

> **Reno Kings Tip**
>
> *"Fall in love with the deal not with the house"* (with thanks to Jodie, a past student).

Three weeks later we purchased the second one, by accident, when we dropped in to a deceased-estate auction round the corner from the first house to check local values. We were doing our research in reverse.

The contents were also being auctioned and we were very keen on a marble washstand. On the third and final call on the house I felt a dig in the ribs. Helen murmured, "Gee, this is a good buy," and I shouted "$76,000." Thirty seconds later we'd bought a house instead of a washstand, which ended up being bought by the auctioneer.

Still, it did confirm that either this was a bargain or I had paid too much for the one on the 'ways. Rents were the same at $150 per week, so the yield on the second purchase was far better, but the dwelling was in worse condition. A few years later we sold both properties, the first purchase for $112,750 and the second for $115,000, which ultimately confirmed the second purchase was the smarter one.

The third was another main road property in nearby Norman Park. It was being sold as part of a divorce settlement. We negotiated to $79,000 plus a thousand cash straight to the vendor so his wife wouldn't know. As it turned out the vendor was the selling agent's father-in-law and I wouldn't be surprised if the full details of the purchase circumstances have since been made known to both the divorcing parties. However, it's a clear and evident example of fulfilling the seller's special requirements. Sometimes it pays to deal direct. You get to know what they really want.

> **⌐ Reno Kings Tip ⌐**
> *Talk to the seller. Find out what they want. If you can give them what they want, you will get what you want.*

The Ferrari halfway round the track

Another auction in Moorooka found me bidding against an unseen person in an adjoining room. I had gone there because the agent's ad was adamant it would sell for $64k. So how come I ended up purchasing this property for $76k? And I would have kept on going if the brakes hadn't been firmly applied by Helen. Nothing would have stopped me from beating that other bidder. However, one thing did stop the other bidder: when I stopped.

To this day I still don't know for sure, but I was positive I was bidding against the vendor. Another valuable lesson: always identify the sellers and get yourself in a position where you can see all the bidders so you can be sure the auction is "legit". I've been to auctions where a fence paling and the dog have opened up the bids.

> **⌐ Reno Kings Tip ⌐**
> *Dummy bidding is everywhere. Get there early to see who is in cahoots with who. Stand so you can see the auctioneer and every bidder. Don't be afraid to ask the auctioneer if that was a vendor's bid or who made the bid. Bidder registration is encouraged but not mandatory in Queensland. When they have taken a bid off the rosebush they can get a bit "prickly".*

The only thing this post-war non-destructible home required was repainting of one of the bedrooms. Being in a working-class area it rented out immediately and the same tenant stayed for three years, giving a gross yield of 10.3%.

We sold this house in 2001 for $93k, and I would consider this to be one my lowest-performing properties, but we did need the cash to free up our overall position to start developments. Not long after the sale the Moorooka area had a surge of growth and the new owners will have made more than we did on it, and in quarter of the time. The longer you hold a property the better it performs, confirming the old saying, "The only way to lose on property is to sell it!"

Hidden treasure

The next purchase, in East Brisbane, was for $89k and it got me really excited. This offered a major cosmetic makeover to complete during my four weeks annual leave. No point wasting valuable time and money on holidays and consumables.

It came up a treat. We found original balustrades and verandah finials hidden under the sheeting and beautiful pine floorboards beneath rotting floor coverings. This turned into a thumping money-making project in which I thoroughly enjoyed myself. So did the family (we had two kids by then), as they were all roped in. Just as well; this forced apprenticeship has now given my son the tools to go it alone with his own house make-over. There's nothing like having fun *and* making money! A few years later we sold it for $154k, a nice little windfall conceived during my annual leave.

> **Reno Kings Tip**
>
> *In just four weeks Paul made equity equal to his annual salary and had fun doing it. Most people spend more than half a year's savings on their annual leave.*

The sixth purchase in this period was a house on a block in nearby Morningside that was advertised by the agent as being suitable for building units. I'd dealt with this agent a number of times before and trusted him to do the right thing. I was pretty shocked when I discovered it wasn't wide enough for unit development. But the asking price was only $99,000 and I negotiated this down to $80,000.

Don't believe the agents; do your own research. I ended up renovating to turn it into a cash-positive property, but it was a valuable lesson.

> **Reno Kings Tip**
>
> *There are no problems, only opportunities. This apparent setback was to become the first piece of the creative jigsaw puzzle that made Paul a motza. Read on.*

Then there was more: 1997–99, #12–16

The next buy, for $74k, was in Murrarrie, a little further out than I usually prefer. The house had been moved from up-market Hamilton onto the new site. The area had been home to a tannery. With the industry gone it was turned into new residential building sites. The new houses had lifted the value of the area and it was still a high-employment zone. Factory workers, they're the salt of the earth; always pay their rent on time and really look after the houses. And this one was a beauty.

A lot of people shy away from houses that have been relocated, but look at the value here. Moved houses have been completely rewired, replumbed and restumped. The stumps, bearers and joists are, of course, the basic bones of any dwelling. Don't let the stigma of buying a "relocated home" put you off buying a great deal. In fact, look for these homes and use the stigma to steal a deal! We sold this property in 2001 for $108k to get cashed-up for the big development, making money, but not big money. Still beats working in a hardware shop.

Going, going …

Another trek to the Public Trustee auctions netted me a great property in Woolloongabba. It was walking distance to Stones Corner, which was in the transition of gentrification from a sleazy suburb to a new glam one with trendy people taking up residence. I'll never forget the local pub, a ruff and tuff, all-tile main drinking bar, with crisps being the only food on offer. I used to order beer and duck, as in "duck the punch", but now it's Chards and whitebait, a fantastic renovation to the old pub attracting new clientele with no money problems and no attitude problems.

I really liked the start of this auction. It was made quite clear that this was a property that required major renovation, which would put a lot of punters off. And looking at it, at first, I certainly agreed: there was rubbish all over the place, torn and missing window furnishings, and decking rotting out in places.

But the position and the bones – the bones, never forget the bones – were in great shape! The place had been restumped with concrete stumps and the hardwood bearers and joists were in excellent health. The pine timber flooring showed no white-ant damage and were also in excellent condition. The wall and roofing framing and roofing iron were all solid.

I became a little concerned that I had missed something from the general description given by the auctioneer; however, my due diligence had paid off. This was a grouse house and after only two bids we purchased this dump for $129k, quickly turning it into a diamond. Eight months later we sold for $189k. Now, out of all the properties we have owned and sold, this is the one I most regret. I have often remarked that sometimes you keep the mould and sell the gold. This was a prime example.

Another auction and another property, this time at Coorparoo for $95k. This is a trendy inner-Brisbane suburb 4 km from the city and a favourite with the renters. The place was structurally disadvantaged through some previous termite attacks. The neighbours even remarked they had demolished their property and completely rebuilt: a concrete slab, brick and tile box, an eyesore. They believed the white ants had nothing left to eat at my joint and would have invited themselves to lunch at their place.

Notwithstanding, I could visually see the finished product and replaced all that I could that had been damaged. I put it back on the market 16 weeks later and sold it at auction for $147.5k. Not bad money. I noted in 2003 the UCV [unimproved capital value, ie, the land only] of the property was $180k, which goes to show that land appreciates, while buildings depreciate.

Completing the jigsaw

The Morningside area had always been a favourite of mine. I still hold four properties there. I may have been putting too many eggs into one basket, buying so many in one area, but it has always been a good hunting ground for me for the purpose of gaining rental properties that usually give a yield in the vicinity of 10%.

Several neighbouring suburbs had generated excellent capital growth rates over the previous couple of years and a little bit of capital gain usually rubs off on property close to these hubs. Morningside is only 6 km from the CBD and is close to all major transport and tertiary institutions.

Just back-tracking a little, in 1997 the property next door to the Morningside "future unit block" house that I'd bought a year earlier had luckily come onto the market. We quickly swooped on it and paid the market value of $111.5k. No use haggling over a few thousand dollars.

It was far better to achieve the greater goal of our first development. I am often asked what the best location is for buying property and my stock answer is, "Beside and behind wherever you own," because, you never know, maybe one day it could be a development site. The two adjoining allotments were long and rectangular and abutted a major rail line. Another purchase in the 'ways.

And this time I had struck gold. Now, with the acquisition of the second piece of the jigsaw, I could demolish the two houses and start my long-awaited trek into the mysterious world of development. These two adjoining properties were one down from a side street where a vacant block of land had been on the market for some time. The owner approached me to see if I would sell, as he wanted to take off the back two sections of our properties and combine the lot into one large development site.

How smart he was, but with greed on both sides of the ledger we could not agree on a price and I went back to stage one of demolishing the houses to make way for the development. I did say he was smart; well, the house he intended to move onto his empty block of land was too big to get down the street and the block was back on the market.

No dealing with the vendor direct this time, and the full asking price of $56.5k was quickly settled. This unexpected acquisition was piece number three of the jigsaw.

Keeping the lot, three of them

It's not often that you piece together a property subdivision jigsaw where you end up still holding the original rental properties you were going to remove and also still have the opportunity to build five new townhouses. It was just a matter of reconfiguring the puzzle.

The combined rent on the two properties gave positive gearing. The beginning of the GST building boom emerged. Prices for both materials and labour were skyrocketing and we were happy to sit back and go against the "herd" mentality. The increase in materials would eventually be compensated with competitive labour costs. Material costs could even drop as manufacturers and distributors competed for market share in sales (though this didn't eventuate).

With the acquisition of the third block we now had the beginnings of our subdivision, which as it turned out was going to be easier to undertake because we were not combining two sites into one, just reconfiguring the boundaries. We had three separately titled properties before the subdivision and we still had three separate titles after the subdivision. They were just different sizes and the two original properties no longer abutted the railway line to the rear. That's where the new development was to take place.

Having two properties that now did not abut a railway line would turn out to be an absolute windfall for their valuations, but read on.

Assemble your army

To get to this stage you need to assemble your army around you to ensure that a clear and safe path through the development minefield is achieved. The important professionals are: townplanners or development consultants, an architect or a smart designer (my preference is a smart designer), hydraulic, acoustic and structural engineers, surveyors, valuers and lenders.

A development site adjoining a major railway line can realise some major problems, like over-capitalising and noise problems. Hence the importance of an acoustic engineer, to enable you to build in lightweight, and therefore lower-cost, construction materials, and a switched-on designer, to keep the window and door openings away from the noisy, offending railway side.

I was astonished to discover my flat block of land, in fact, had a 2 m fall to the rear. Viewing a large piece of land over a distance can be deceiving. One of the first rules in developing is to bear in mind one of the council's main concerns: that you can demonstrate stormwater run-off to existing or approved new outlets.

One of the smartest people in my army was the hydraulics engineer, who suggested that we visit the property on the other side of our two houses and talk to the owner about us gaining access to install a stormwater pipe through her property to a discharge point on the roadway. We advised the owner that the only other way we could achieve council requirements was to fill the rear 2 m of my property to allow for natural run-off to my roadway. This, however, would result in our units overlooking her property, which she decided would be detrimental.

The final agreement was to hand dig the stormwater line, replace any damaged vegetation and restore the landscaping back to its original state, providing $200 worth of plants. What a great outcome. I must have saved myself $20,000, with the help of a very considerate neighbour.

The only correct and acceptable form of confirming your land's position with regard to water run-off is to have your surveyor draw up a detailed contour map. Do this during the due diligence time. You may not be as fortunate as we were.

Always allow for the unexpected. Most builders call that a contingency, which is a fancy word meaning "things I forgot", like us getting slugged by the council to install a fire hydrant for the street at a cost of $12k: no fire hydrant, no development approval. Get used to it, it's the cost of doing business. I used to joke that the only use that hydrant would get is by my dog! But, as you probably know, modern hydrants are flush with the ground. I was only having a lend. And when I did take the dog round there he was *not* happy.

We got to do our development and instead of demolishing the two homes we demolished an old garage along the fenceline and replaced it with a repositioned carport. The development proceeded quite quickly and the finished product was magnificent, so much so that a couple of the tradespeople decided to purchase two of the five units, and I sold another to a mate whose daughter relocated to Brissy.

Sell, or hold and refinance?

The construction loan was 60% of the valuation of the completed townhouses, on a per-unit basis, and this loan to value ratio is what would be considered the norm. Our loan had no presale conditions but it was on the understanding that the townhouses would be sold to repay the loan amount.

After numerous discussions with the bank's valuer and their thorough investigations into my building costs, it was obvious that the value of my proposed project at planning stage was a lot lower than what it would be at the completed stage. I believe that plans do not express the final product outcome when taking into consideration the quality of workmanship and inclusions, and this may have been a contributing factor in the original construction valuation.

Let's take a look at some of the numbers. The construction loan was for $429k and after selling three of the townhouses for $180k each I was about to repay the bank's loan, which left me $111k ($540k less $429k), when I remembered a basic principle of saving. Pay yourself first.

I had undertaken all the risk, done all the paperwork, done the hard yards to get it to the building stage, and here I was paying off all my hard work back to the bank. I called the bank and invited their valuer to view the finished product. The valuation of the two townhouses that were not already sold came in at $185k and $190k. The total of $375k, which was not much less than the previous value of the entire five-townhouse project! Funny about that, seeing the new valuations of the completed project are over 30% more than the valuations at the planning stage obtained some eight months earlier.

Back to the bank to convert the building construction loan to home loans, 80% of $375k = $300k. The existing loan was for $429k so I had to bring that back in line so as not to exceed the bank's new valuation of $375k ($429 less $300k = $129k), which was paid back to the bank. I kept the difference ($540k less $129k = $411k), which I ploughed into another property.

Reno Kings Tip

Now, I realise that you are thinking I still have to pay off the loan, and quite rightly. But I can choose to do that when and where I feel like it. Remember to PAY YOURSELF FIRST.

We still own the other two parts of the jigsaw, the two smaller front blocks with the existing houses, and looking at the bank valuation of one of them, obtained before the subdivision, is quite unbelievable. We have gone from an allotment of 688 sq m valued in October 2000 for $150k to the same allotment on 369 sq m with a bank valuation of $300k at the end of June 2004.

The adjoining property has performed just as well and, being on a slightly larger block, I could easily sell that tomorrow for $315k, and that's a conservative estimate.

Wow, what a development. We keep two of the townhouses and have fantastic appreciation and unbelievable rental yield. We keep our two original houses on smaller allotments, which have exceeded my high expectations for capital growth. This has just been a win, win, win project and I'm hungry for more.

A new century: 2000–03, #17–25

In 2000 it was off to Newmarket, on Brisbane's northside, for the "fugly", a solid brick house that only the original designer could love. With its new, green corrugated iron roof, the whole streetscape was nothing but disastrous. However, being less than 4 km from the GPO, this was our closest purchase to the CBD. At $134k it represented really good value, mainly due to the fact that nobody knew how to tackle the "fugly" aspect, but I had a simple idea to change that.

No mucking around; again I could feel the heat in the market and after a small amount of negotiating we took the property off the market. It was a good position near a park, Ballymore, and bike tracks to Kelvin Grove campus, and it was on a quiet street.

After a quick "haircut" to paint inside and polish the floors and an aggressive landscape plan of quick-growing, small but bushy trees, we managed after a short time to hide the not-too-appealing residence and achieve some form of street appeal. Appeal or no appeal, the conservative value of the property today would be in the low $300k ballpark and it has had the same tenants since day dot. Even the ugly can revalue quite handsomely! We still own this property today; it's just sitting there getting older and richer.

> ## Reno Kings Tip
> *When planning landscaping the tree should be planted at a distance equal to the mature height of the tree from the dwelling to ensure no footing structural problems in the future.*

Closer to home

It was then time to move back to the Sunshine Coast, where we bought a simple timber house constructed in that lovely period when you can claim 4% building write off (see Galvo's story earlier in the book). The house had been tenanted and was in good condition, except that it was rundown and had been on the market for some time.

I like this type of deal. The longer it's been on the market the more negotiable the seller becomes and the less negotiable you become. I said, "Here's the deal, take it or leave it." They took it for $85k and a 30-day settlement. I recall the agent saying she couldn't believe we were making an offer, as is.

It was the same deal with the "haircut". A quick paint job with all the family one weekend and she's back on the rent roll and leased to only two tenants all this time. The biggest problem to date has been a water-affected bathroom floor that required the section to be cut away, replaced and tiled. We got a quote for a few grand to fix it, so I did it myself for a few hundred.

Once again we still own this property and it's just been revalued by the bank to get access to the equity. A conservative value came in at $240k so I'm using the money for other projects while not selling the property and incurring zero capital gains tax.

The Public Trustee beckoned again and we bought a structurally fantastic, well looked after house for $80k on the main drag in Stafford (back to the 'ways), another northern suburb of Brisbane.

I haven't had to do a thing on this one. I can't even remember what it looks like. In fact, sometimes we unintentionally leave it off our assets and liabilities statement because it's just one of those unvisited, uninspirational average homes in an average area suitable for the average Aussie. However, it does have above-average capital gains and today would be valued at the high $200k mark and is still held by us.

Further afield

In 2003 we checked out Ipswich, to Brisbane's west, which the Reno Kings research had shown as a "hotspot" (see Brenda and Les Irwin's story). We found a traditional Queenslander for $94,000 that needed a bit of structural work. This was in a "black-soil" area, where you get a fair bit of subsidence. But, being a high-set house, it can be jacked up, and the house restumped and levelled. You can't do that with a concrete slab, so if you're thinking of purchasing in a volatile soil area keep away from concrete strip footings and brick bases unless they are engineer designed. When these break down you'll have huge underpinning and rectification costs and get little rent yield for your outlay.

We are yet to do the relevelling on this one, but the tenants are quite happy with the few sticky doors and prefer that inconvenience to that of major works being undertaken. Nonetheless, this property has been our best performer during the last year, with a whopping 62% capital gain, and I haven't even got round to adding some value yet!

The same year, after more research, we looked even further west, to Toowoomba. After talking to a lot of the local residents and businesses it was evident that everybody was positive about growth in this region due to the break in the drought, meaning more employment. Toowoomba has one of Queensland's largest regional universities, with many overseas students undertaking courses there.

The track record for this region has not been that good, but of course things can change. If you are an investor, be there when they do, for the better, and try not to be there when they change for the worse, such as drought.

We found a 19-year-old brick veneer triplex with a couple of twists. It was under-rented and therefore undervalued, and the units have the capability of being strata titled easily and cheaply.

The units were rented for $110 per week each, representing a gross yield of 7.4% at the purchase price of $233k. The rents have since been increased to $130 per week to keep in line with the current value, giving us a yield today of 8.7%. The current valuation would be around the low $300k mark.

We are yet to strata title the units and will probably get round to this when the heat during the current boom for townplanners and surveyors has abated and the property cycle clicks on to a new time. But there's no real rush; the units are cash positive by a country mile.

More sunshine

Returning again to the Sunshine Coast we found a real gem right on the waterfront at Mooloolaba, for $700k. This is a "knockover" that can rent out easily to help compensate the interest payments while waiting to build a new Taj Mahal when the time is right.

This is my land-banking gemstone; the longer I wait, the higher the land value will be. Good positioned property like that with deep water in its back yard will all always appreciate more quickly than less well positioned properties. And there is a premium people will have to pay to gain access to these areas. Although negatively geared, which really doesn't affect me due to my entire portfolio being positive, this house has had tremendous capital growth over the past 15 months and will continue to do so. Just another project to put on the stove and stew the capital growth for a while.

Back to our beginnings at Buderim, we made quite a rare find for the area, a Queenslander with traditional VJ walls and narrow strip floorboards. It was originally the Mooloolaba pilot's house, built in the late 1940s and moved to the site in the late 1980s. Again, this house had been restumped, rewired and replumbed.

We picked it up for $220k and it would probably achieve around the near $300k mark if put on the market today. It's a bit unusual to find an original home like this in this area. Most of the adjoining properties are brick and tile construction. This place just oozes charm and is in high demand from renters chasing that wow factor. And there are plenty of twists on this one: another bedroom under the huge front verandah roof or extend out the back. It's currently rented for $225 per week. Another one plodding along!

Joint ventures in between

On top of all this, and in amongst it, we've taken part in a number of joint ventures, including a house on Fraser Island with a group of mates. This was rare freehold land on an island that is mostly national park.

Gone fishin'

This was another property purchased directly from a vendor who didn't realise he wanted to sell. I have been fishing Fraser Island now for more than 20 years. Helen and I both fell in love with the place not long after arriving in Queensland. The idea of driving a four-wheel-drive along a beach sounded farcical to a Melbournite but one trip was all it took for us to buy a brand new Jackaroo (new car for beach work; was I mad? Yep.)

As you get older the camps get harder to set up and the more luxuries you crave. We then started renting. It was 10 years of just plain madness. The idea of a non-profitable holiday home is beyond my comprehension but, if we can break even and keep it for our kids to use, what a great investment. It's not every day you get to purchase a bit of freehold land on a designated national park.

Our fishing mates consisted of six people from varied backgrounds: a barrister, a retired chief flight engineer, builders, a pharmacist and an executive, all with varying degrees of expertise. This makes for a good JV. I'd hate to do one with a group of hairdressers; they'd be only good in the goss department!

We all preferred the top end of the island around Orchid Beach, as it was too far away for the daytrippers to access. We sent out a letter to all the vacant landowners inviting them to sell. It wasn't long before we anglers had a bite and what a deal.

The block was 3048 sq m with ocean views, all tied up on a small deposit with a six-month settlement. In that time designs were agreed upon, geothectical analysis (that's a soil test, and I can tell you at 150 feet down it's still sand!) completed and plans lodged with the council.

The day after settlement our first truck arrived with the building materials and we completed the first section in four weeks. The main pole home took another four months to complete by our subcontracted builder mate. Our best year's rent has been $55k and it is one of the most popular rental homes in the area. If you want to have a look at the eighth wonder of the world go to www.orchidhouse.com.au. Nothing is sweeter than a fantastically yielding holiday home that gives you so much enjoyment.

Townies

Then there was the Newstead JV (subject of the JV story later in the book), as well as a couple of projects I've undertaken with Geoff in Kangaroo Point in Brisbane's inner city.

I had driven past this massive, three-storey, tilt-up slab property many times without noticing it. Funny how an auction sign can grab your attention. What impressed me the most was not the three-year-old structure but the land at the rear.

The block was only 708 sq m, which under normal circumstances you can't do much with unless the zoning says something different. This is a clear example how your army can make correct money-making decisions. For an outlay of $550 I was given a 99% success rate for subdividing off the rear block. With odds like that you just gotta have a punt.

The existing building had off-street, secure parking for four cars, a first-floor, three-bedroom super apartment and top-floor open space with two offices and separate lunchroom, quite an unusual combination. The more I looked, the more I was amazed. There were two separate air-conditioning units, powered venetian window blinds and the list went on and on. The quantity surveyor had a picnic here, with the depreciation of the plant plus the three-year-old building write-down.

The auction

The auction was one week away. Geoff and I had agreed on a pre-auction offer of $440k. I don't know why so many people wait for the auction day before making offers. Wouldn't it be simpler if you were the only one negotiating? Our offer was rejected but we were close to the mark, as it was passed in for $450k. The vendor believed it was worth $550k and that was $100k away from what was on the table.

The owners were builders and a quantity surveyor and, from what had started out as a fine partnership, they now wanted out. I couldn't remember a time when we had purchased a property well above the passed-in price, but we did on this one, and with no hesitation went to contract for $510k. We had commissioned a thorough due diligence and we understood once again that we had made money when we bought not when we were to sell. A free block of land 1.5 km from the heart of the city on "Torrens title", a completely separate title, is what we had negotiated. We had once again become land creators.

There may be a time when there will be oversupply of inner-city units, but there will never be an oversupply of land!

With any development, from conception to getting all approvals through, to commencing construction, there may be a time lag of up to 12 months. We try to find development blocks that already have a holding income during this time, and we struck gold with our first and only tenant, who insists on paying one year's rent in advance (currently $29,767.50 per annum).

The development

The rear development moves forward, ever so slowly, due to the high demand for subcontractors, especially chippies. Our supervisor employed a number of final-year apprentices to keep the job progressing and this proved to be a blessing in disguise. Some of these young men under supervision are great workers and very cost-effective. You just pay their contract labour supplier an hourly rate, which covers everything.

On the last day of the job we had two agents from the same firm, but different departments, fighting for the right to either sell it or rent it. The selling agent believed in one week she'd have an offer of $700k; the renting agent was a bit more conservative with a mid-$600k call.

We decided to rent, which, after the bitter experience of "selling the gold and keeping the mould", was an easy decision.

An accurate, detailed cost for a development of this size is something most large construction firms and builders guard with their lives. So have a good look at the numbers opposite for a subdivision development.

For a total cost of $247,731 we have a brand new Queenslander 1.5 km from the GPO, standing on its own freehold-title block of land in a sought-after area with massive annual capital gains. And it rents out for $550 per week, a gross yield of 11.5%. How sweet is that?

The upshot

Paul is a living example of the power of property. Make no mistake, he has paid a price to get to where he is today. If he didn't "have a go", if he didn't make some mistakes, then find a way through them or round them or over them, he would still be in the JOB, "just over broke", as a wage slave. The great thing is how he is willing to openly share those mistakes so you don't have to make them. Best of all, I've personally tried and tested his strategies to make huge capital gains and cashflow. Thank you Paul. And following he explains even more of his system.

Geoff Doidge

ReBATES explained

Through all this I was using sound principles that I apply to all my property dealings. When I teamed up with Geoff, who had been presenting seminars and workshops for quite a few years by then, Geoff structured it so other investors could profit from the strategies.

Now it is well entrenched as the ReBATES system for buying and selling properties, a system embraced by the many property investors who have taken part in the Reno Kings workshops. Here's a basic explanation.

Re: Research

You need to know the area where you're buying. In fact, you need to become an expert in it. If you can't go to an auction and be within 5% of the price you haven't done your homework. By knowing a suburb, and what the properties are worth, you can then identify a good value buy when it comes along. And come along they do. I would say the "once-in-a-lifetime bargain" crosses my desk once a week.

Development costs on the JV.

Preliminary costs	
Subdivision viability study	$550
Surveyor	$4,235
Sewerage and stormwater	$17,435
Hydraulics engineer	$1,974
Insurance	$1,257
Council water supply fees	$1,749
Council subdivision plan fees	$600
Structural engineering	$220
Council sewerage plan	$330
Council water design	$200
Council lodgement fees	$1,000
Certification	$1,485
Designer	$2,091
Soil engineer	$280
Site survey	$220
Q Leave (superannuation)	$280
Subtotal	$33,906

Building works	
Earthworks	$3,838
Backhoe	$244
Bricks	$2,177
Blocks	$517
Brick/block layer	$3,826
Slab plumbing	$2,860
Reinforcing mesh (reo steel)	$1,619
Termimesh	$324
Concrete pump	$1,130
Conrete labourer	$8,763
Concrete	$7,190
Steel posts	$3,445
Windows	$10,132
Fix out plumbing	$3,300
Building supplies	$574
Timber, hardware	$22,644
Timber strip flooring	$3,127
Scaffolding	$1,496
Trusses	$3,806
Carpenter	$16,503
Apprentice carpenters	$9,024
Supervisor	$4,664
WC hire	$352
Engineering inspections	$726
Subtotal	$112,281

Lock-up	
Roofing	$7,971
Waterproofing	$754
Stairs	$2,706
Electrician	$5,068
Plasterers	$10,833
Colour consultant	$275
Painting	$11,594
Rollerdoors	$2,057
Tile labour	$2,689
Tile materials	$2,085
Shower screens	$944
Cabinetmaker	$8,195
Driveway excavation	$968
Concrete cutter	$183
Plumbing finals	$1,914
Hire equipment	$629
Subtotal	$58,865

Fitout	
Fitout materials	$9,740
Lights	$1,435
Taps	$670
Plumbing items	$2,882
Whitegoods	$3,036
Window tinting	$594
Insulation	$646
Subtotal	$19,003

Final	
Landscaping, fencing, plants	$10,723
Carpets	$2,130
Flyscreens	$1,205
Blinds	$1,226
Final clean	$880
Plans for stamping	$820
Council compliance fees	$1,150
Council sewer, water fees	$5,181
Titles office	$361
Subtotal	$23,676

Summary	
Preliminary costs	$33,906
Building works	$112,281
Lock-up	$58,865
Fitout	$19,003
Final	$23,676
Grand total	$247,731

B: Buying

You don't want to be competing with everyone else. Look for properties that other people are likely to pass up. I have a saying, "Where there's mess, there's money," because most people will look at a mess and decide that it's too hard to tackle. Actually, cleaning up a mess is usually easy.

A: Adding value

This is where cosmetic renovation comes into its own. It immediately enhances the appearance of the property and value of your investment. The banks love you because within a very short space of time you've increased the value of the asset. That was how I managed to get those six properties in 11 months. In each case the value was increased with renovation, and so I was able to finance the next purchase.

T: Time

You need to be able to get in there and start work the day after settlement; before settlement is even better if you can have it written into the contract. And to do this you need to have built up a reliable support team.

I have good solicitors, good accountants and good builders who I can call on when necessary. It's important that you recognise where your own skills fall short, and make use of other people's expertise where appropriate. It saves you both time and money in the long run.

E: Expenses

I work to very tight budgets and over the years I've developed what I call a "cookie cutter" system of tackling a reno. I only use two paint colours, for example. I also use the same kitchen style every time. The same goes for the fence out the front. By finding a standard and sticking to it, you get to know exactly what you're doing. That's how you save money and ensure your projects deliver the bottom-line profits you expect.

S: Sell, or hold and refinance

You need to know what you're going to do with the property before you start out. The changes to capital gains tax legislation, known as the Ralph Report, which made it more cost-effective to hold a property for 12 months before selling, need to be taken into account before purchase. It means that you should consider holding and renting out the property for 12 months to take advantage of the 50% capital gains tax exemption.

It may be possible for people in a low tax bracket to turn a net $48,000 capital gain from a reno into $40,000+ after tax if structured correctly. Check with your accountant.

A quick example of how a reno turns theory into profit is the Woolloongabba property I purchased in 1999. I was actually there for six months, as I used it as a base while I had three properties on the go at the one time. I bought it in March for $129,000, spent $15,000 and then sold it in November for $189,000. These days I hold my properties for a minimum of 12 months and, if possible, do not sell at all.

One of my strategies is to seek out houses that have been modified, usually to their detriment. You find a lot of older houses where areas such as verandahs were enclosed during the post-war period when money was scarce and people tended to have large families. What generally happened was that people would enclose their verandahs and put beds in there. I've come across places where verandahs were turned into five tiny bedrooms. It's very easy to open the place up and show it off in its original state, usually creating a substantial improvement in value.

Reno tips and tricks

Over the years I've been able to combine my experience in renovation with my knowledge of the hardware industry to come up with quite a few cost-cutting tips and tricks. Here are a few of them.

I'm not a purist. If I can achieve the same effect with a sheet of VJ board instead of individual tongue and groove [VJ] boards, I'll go for the VJ sheeting board and save time and money.

Similarly, I tend to use a standard picket fence for most of my renovations. They're like the frame around the Mona Lisa. I've settled on something that looks a bit different, something people like, and because I've standardised I can put up a nice little fence with a minimum of time and money. There are another 31 ways to add value. Read on.

Reno Kings Tip

Always look after your "street appeal". It invites prospective tenants to get out of the car and into the house. A fence will appeal to different groups. Pet owners love fences, so the place will rent fast. Real estate agents and prospective buyers like them. First impressions count, most importantly to the valuers, when you are extracting the equity to do it all again.

Knowing when to ask for help

Be careful. If you lack the knowledge, experience and confidence in determining if a house has inherent structural problems, obtain both a building and a termite inspection before committing to the purchase. The cost of these inspections is very reasonable when compared to the total cost of the house.

It's your safeguard to ensure you're not biting off more than you can chew. You cannot, for example, renovate a termite-infested wall. All your careful calculations, budgets and profits will go right out the window if you suddenly discover the house has a serious structural problem that you hadn't taken into consideration when doing the costings.

Buyers will often get a report that states that the building construction is not up to today's standards, usually regarding undersized bearers, joists or other outdated building practices. This is to be expected, given the change in building standards over the years. To me a good report should always state this fact, if the house was constructed say in the 1900s when the building codes were different. If it's structurally sound and has stood for 100 years and is in good structural condition, there's no reason why you should not proceed with the purchase.

Floors and doors

Floors are another area to examine carefully. If a floor is in poor condition, sanding will not be able to restore it to an acceptable finished product and you'll have to cover it with a floor covering such as vinyl, carpet or cork tiles. However, the general fashion of floors over the years has been that good timber floors have been covered with carpet. So if you lift the cover in one corner of all the rooms you'll usually discover a beautiful timber floor of either hardwood or pine that basically requires only a simple sanding and coating to achieve a beautiful product.

It's easy to hire sanders from most large builder's equipment suppliers. The cost is quite reasonable and the average person can obtain a very good DIY result, particularly if they always follow the practice of a rough sand followed by a fine sand. Hire companies can supply the correct sandpaper and provide instructions on how to use the machines. However, for those who are not comfortable with undertaking this work, professional floor sanders are readily available at a cost of around $25 per sq m.

One mistake many people make is to rip up the old carpet as soon as they go into the house. I'd suggest leaving it there until the very end, until you're ready to sand the floors. It's the best covering you're going to get while you're working.

When it comes to doors I prefer to make use of the original front door where possible. The front door is the first impression people get of your house, and the one that people will remember. If a modern door has been installed, I'd attempt to obtain an original from any secondhand window and door specialist. For internal doors I prefer a new replica type. I find these are easier to install as they're of a lightweight construction and paint up extremely well to give an excellent finished product.

Kitchens and landscaping

When it comes to kitchens I prefer a cafe-style look, which consists of a "Swiss Pear" top combined with teal-coloured drawers and doors. This particular design usually gives a well-presented appeal to most houses and blends in extremely well with polished floors.

After you've installed a kitchen, always ensure a tiled splashback is installed to prevent water penetration and ultimate damage to the bench, and always ensure the join between the tile and bench top is sealed with a silicone product. If it's a rental property ensure the edges of drawers and doors are fitted with a 2 mm PVC edge strip to reduce chipping and damage.

Landscaping is an important concept in any renovation and one that will have a significant impact on the final value of the property. By using established plants and suitable ground cover, such as tanbark, it's possible to create an instant, low-maintenance garden. If you're renting the property out, definitely consider the low-maintenance factor, as tenants aren't likely to put great effort into maintaining the gardens.

Painting

Painting is one of the most important components of a cosmetic renovation, as it can add instant value and enhance a house's aesthetics dramatically. It also has the advantage of being a very simple process with considerable DIY potential.

To ensure a satisfactory and beautiful finish, make sure all the preliminary work is done right. All the walls and ceilings need to be cleaned down with "sugar soap" to remove any buildup of grime, smoke or mildew that may have occurred. You also need to ensure that all VJs that have opened up are "gap filled", using a filler specifically recommended for this particular application. Not all gap fillers are made for filling vertical gaps in lining boards.

I've used two colours for internal use for a long time, and found that these two match most common original colours. These are Berger Shortbread as the main colour, and a contrasting Berger Cream, which I use on picture rails, door infills, archways, architraves and skirting. And for a final hint from my days in the hardware industry, I suggest always standing new paint brushes in very hot water before you use them. This will reduce hair loss and make the job proceed much more quickly.

There is dramatic profit potential in carefully planned cosmetic renovations of carefully selected properties. Suitable properties exist in every city and town around Australia. Prospective renovators just have to know what to look for, and what they're going to do when they find one.

My best-ever buy

Thank God for the ReBATES system. It helped with my very, very best-ever buy and that was the one I never bought!

Imagine a large parcel of inner-city land zoned for development coming onto the market, with a couple of interested parties going hammer and tong trying to whip it off the market within the hour. This is where I found myself, even down to an unconditional contract. Providing I get the development through and watch the pennies during the development phase, I'm okay. And once the development is sold it's payday and for a long time I'm back living on the hog.

My signature is about to be scrawled on the contract when the "Re" in the ReBATES bell sounds. I make one call to one of the army for a drainage map of the situation. Five minutes later I'm looking at a cross on the plan and I'm sure it marks my grave. Two of the biggest stormwater drains you can imagine transverse the block, making subdivision impossible! I walk away from the deal, the best deal I've ever had or thought I had, and save myself from financial ruin.

Being a property-savvy investor and learning from some of our tips, the average investor can transform themselves into the above-average investor. The average investor accepts average results, and you're not one of those people – you're reading this book aren't you? So get cracking and accept nothing less than what you deserve.

Do not strive to be average. I meet too many average investors. I want to start mingling with the better ones. Why can't that be you?

Reno Kings insights

What's your background?
I started in an office and worked my way out via sales, renovating and investing.

Why did you get started?
We just couldn't live on a hardware manager's salary. We had two kids in private education and I was sick of cask wine!

What was your greatest fear?
Not being able to afford the best education for my children.

Did your parents show you how to get started?
They taught me how to save.

What was your greatest mistake?
Selling too many properties instead of holding them.

What do you want to achieve?
I'd like to help all those who want to achieve in the property market.

How would you describe your strategy?
Very cautious, with little room for error. All properties have to have the ability to produce skyrocketing capital gain. I never spend a fortune doing up an investment property; the capital gain on the land will do that for me. Remember, the worst house in the best street will outperform the best house in the worst street.

Where do you find your deals?
Most by word of mouth. I talk to everyone, even my lawnmower man, who's always got the goss on who's thinking of selling.

Any memorable experiences along the way?
Telling my son to start at the bottom and work his way up, which he took literally when painting a roof and he got stuck at the top. "Help Dad, help," I can still hear it!

What's your best renovating or money-making tip?
Buy well and don't underestimate the power of paint.

What would you do differently?
Not sell.

Has your life changed since you began your property investment?
You bet … more time, more choices. The surf's always better mid-week around 10 am!

How do you picture yourself five years down the track?
Not much different to today, except probably as a grandparent with a few more properties. They say happiness leads to success. I intend to invest in being happy!

Reno Kings Reports

If I were to recommend four Reno Kings Reports for people starting out they'd be: Thirty-three Ways to Add Value; the Gutter Money Report (your equity – money that's just lying in the gutter ready to pick up); the Gant Chart; and How to Buy a House that's Not for Sale. Oh, and Buying in the 'Ways, that's five! And How to Fast-track Your Approvals, six. If I were to recommend six …

See page 235 for more information and details on how to order, or go to our website: www.renos.com.au

Paul's 10 top tips for buying bargains

This is just a brief version.

1. Do your research otherwise you won't know it's a bargain.
2. Buy in a suburb next to one that's already gone ahead.
3. Buy in the 'ways.
4. Buy a house that's not for sale.
5. Buy an aesthetically challenged home with good bones.
6. Buy properties with high land value and low house value.
7. Get yourself on the first-hit lists of your real estate agents.
8. Only buy properties with a twist.
9. Cash + uncomplicated short-term contracts = bargains.
10. Look long term; a reasonable buy today could be a bargain in a year or so.

I must have failed my way to success

Compared with the "Fast-track Ferrari", Reno Kings partner Geoff Doidge has taken more like a slow grind through the gears to get to his destination. Interestingly, Paul and Geoff have both ended up in the same place: financial success through property investment.

When it comes to investing in property Geoff believes he's made just about every mistake in the book. However, he has learned from his mistakes, preferring to describe them as life's lessons. In face he's learned so much that from his first ill-fated investment property in 1971 (trashed by his bikie tenants), he's now built a property portfolio nudging $11 million.

Geoff had no idea what he wanted to do when he left school. At his parent's urging to get a safe job, he joined the public service as a draftsman and studied civil engineering at night. In the late 1960s he speculated heavily in oil and mining companies on the stockmarket, and made thousands. He reckoned he was making more money than his boss, and told him so. ("Don't do that. It doesn't do anything for your career prospects.") Geoff was always on the lookout for money-making ideas, but, as life would have it …

A market crash saw him lose the lot in a very short time. "I lost my shirt and almost my shorts. One moment I was a guru and the next a broken fool." Barely 24 years old and he was in serious financial trouble, another way of saying "broke". Next he failed his engineering exams, and to top it all off he was called up for National Service for the war in Vietnam ("the only lottery I've ever won"). They say trouble comes in threes.

But Geoff's first property purchase was to come, a rental property he bought using two personal loans for the deposit.

Meet Geoff and Miriam Doidge

I had just got out of the army and was still looking for "get rich quick" schemes. I picked up a book in the library, *How I Turned $1000 into $5,000,000 from Real Estate in My Spare Time*, by US author Bill Nickerson. It was a real eye-opener and I went out looking for property.

Property #1: Raising the deposit

A friend told me about a house for sale in a rundown inner suburb. I offered $7000 and couldn't believe it when they took it.

I asked a bank for a loan to buy the house and was refused. So I went to a building society and they also said no, but they *would* give me a $3000 unsecured loan for furniture. My credit union said no but would loan me $4000 for a car.

I explained that I didn't want furniture and a car. Then I had a think: "Hang on, $4k + $3k = … well maybe I do need them." So that's how I bought my first house. It was 1971. The house was rented at $30 per week, giving 21% return, and no money down.

The bikies, the sheep and the Hill's hoist

Nickerson's book had a lot of detail about investment but not a lot about management. I thought, "How hard is management? You go around and collect the rent … too easy!" I went around to collect the rent and this bikie figure peered out.

This is roughly how the scenario went:

"Yeah … wot duh youse want?"

"I'm the new owner," I said nervously.

"Aww … youse wanna beer?"

Relieved to be accepted, I said, "Yeah, thanks mate, I'll have a beer."

Well one thing led to another and when I woke up next morning I realised I'd forgotten to collect the rent!

So back I went. *Knock knock.*

"I'm here to collect the rent."

"Youse want a beer?"

"Yes, thank you, don't mind if I do." Dumb.

"Well it's your shout. We shouted you last night."

And they sent me off to the pub to buy for the gang … yep, it went downhill from there.

The bikies weren't too bad, but they had one major flaw, they didn't mow lawns. They rode Harleys, not Victas. It wasn't right for a leather-clad road warrior to be a slave to the old two-stroke mower. The grass was getting longer and longer. The neighbour was worried about snakes and rats. I told the bikies something must be done. And then ...

They said they had a mower and took me around the back.

"It's got legs," I managed to blurt out.

There was a sheep, happily chewing on the long grass. Naively I thought, well this might just work, and it did, for a while. The sheep was happy, the neighbour was less unhappy, and I was happy until ...

"Come quick," the alarmed neighbour screamed into the phone. "B..b..b..b..bikies ... Shh..shh..shheeep."

I raced over there and I will never forget that sight. It was a lovely day, the wind was blowing and the neighbour's white sheets were flapping on her line. I looked over the fence to the bikies' house. And there, hanging on the Hill's hoist, was a white sheep. The bikies were having a barbecue and they had run out of ... *meat*.

"G'day ... youse wanna beer?"

It *really* went downhill from there! The bikies eventually left to be entertained at Her Majesty's Pleasure (jail) and I began my education in property management.

The lesson

Do not attempt to manage your own property unless you have been trained. You wouldn't drive a car without a licence and you need training if your financial vehicle (investment property) is to stay on the road to financial independence.

I sold that house four years later for $12,000, so I made 70% capital gain in four years and I learned about depreciation, tax deductions, tenants, management (and mismanagement).

Property #2: A rental or a home?

A friend of mine had bought a home in Sunnybank Hills, about 12 km from the CBD, and he invited me over to have a look. I was impressed, but crazily I said I'd buy one there too. And I did. So there I was, stuck in the mortgage belt, a long way from all the fun, with no tenant, no tax deductions and no depreciation.

That home taught me the massive difference between a home and an investment property (IP). One home being "paid off" on a principal and interest (P&I) loan is harder than "controlling" the debt on four or five IPs. Most homebuyers are stunned to see someone on an average income with five IPs and they just don't get it. They have never worked it out.

About this time I put my head down and passed those elusive exams. I rented out the house, took a year off overseas and spent everything I had. I met Miriam OS and couldn't bear going back to the 'burbs, so we rented a tiny one-bedroom flat in East Brisbane. The owner upgraded the flats and raised the rent. I thought, "I could do that." We went out looking for a place we could live in that also had an area we could rent out, the best of both worlds. It became our first planned investment.

Properties #3 and 4: The plan begins

I found a little house divided into two flats in Wilston, a rundown suburb, but walking distance to the train and 3 km from the city. I settled on the house in 1979 and rented out the other flat.

Little did I know that I had bought just before a boom cycle. Being a public servant I didn't even know there were cycles. I soon learned about booming prices and the dreaded rising interest rates. I had borrowed at 8% and rates went to 12% in 1982, a 50% increase in my outgoings. Scary. I learned about using fixed rates as a risk management strategy.

Properties #5 and 6: Room to move

By 1982 we were tired of living in the small flat and wanted more space, and separation from the tenant. I spotted an ad for two cute historical cottages in Albion, 3 km from the city and a walk to the railway station. Being on the same block, I was able to get a home loan rate rather than the higher investment rate. The lessons continued.

The houses had been "tarted up". In the first storm the rain poured in. I discovered that the newly painted roof was in fact rusty sheeting patched with paper and masking tape and painted over. The neighbour told me the houses had been condemned before a "bog and flog" shyster cleaned them up and sold them to me.

The market was quiet in the period between 1982 and 1985. Then the government changed the rules. Negative gearing was "quarantined", which meant any losses made on the IP couldn't be written off against your personal income to reduce your tax. Without this incentive the market basically collapsed. Investors stopped investing. Developers stopped building. Rents started to rise.

I renovated the rental cottage. I opened up the front verandah for kerb appeal, adding cast aluminium lace to make it pretty. It looked just like cast iron lacework, which was common in the area. I polished the floors myself and had my first mystical experience with that pleasure machine, the one and only airless spraygun. Two hours with the gun totally transformed this dark, dingy, multi-coloured dump into a gleaming diamond. Way to go! The house rented immediately for a positive cashflow.

From the worst in the street these houses became the best in the street. The end result was that properties we bought for $55,000 in 1982 sold for $180,000 in 1992. A 227% capital gain in 10 years. A great result.

Property #7: I liked the view

I was still an amateur investor in 1984, when I bought a block of land at Mount Tambourine, a picturesque mountain village. I liked the view. But there was no rent: all money out and none in. That meant the interest was not tax deductible. This was not an investment but an emotional liability.

Mid-life, mid-career: What crisis?

In 1985 I was passed over for a promotion, the same as happened to my dad. First I was sad, then I got mad! I vowed I wouldn't finish up as "old Doidgey" in the corner. I made a decision to leave work. I just had to find a way. I went to financial seminars; I read books; I looked and I learned. At a money workshop I discovered a device called the Moneyfinder. It literally changed my life.

The first time I used a Moneyfinder I found we were spending $13,500 a year more than it predicted. It was just vanishing. I couldn't believe it. So we divided $13,500 by 52 weeks. I opened an account and called it the Mortgage Redemption Fund and put in $260 per week. It was a struggle at first. There were always expenses I hadn't allowed for, but we stuck at it. We postponed buying non-essential items, bought takeaway meals instead of visiting restaurants and poured the savings into the fund.

At the end of the year, sure enough, there was $13,500 in the account. For the first time in my life, I took control of my finances. I sold the land at Mount Tambourine, realising it was a liability.

Properties #8–13: Turning it all around

I now had $13,500 per annum coming in, thanks to the Moneyfinder. We chose to invest in property rather than reducing the mortgage. Paying off our home loan would still take many years and that alone would not allow me to leave work. I saw the bigger picture. I could use the cashflow to build a major property portfolio, which would be my passport out of the public service. We figured that if we could do it for one year we could count on that cashflow coming in every year. We planned the next five years, on the basis of borrowing to buy.

A few years later, when I wrote my book, *The Ten Golden Rules of Creating Wealth through Property*, I totally redesigned the Moneyfinder. Use it properly and you'll find money you never had before. I can't emphasise too strongly that if you have cashflow problems complete the Moneyfinder. Find out where you spend your money. More importantly, find the amount you have for investment.

Anyway, back to the story. In a quiet market, I negotiated for six months to buy a rundown six-pack block of flats. It had a negative cashflow of $3000 per annum. No trouble, the Moneyfinder would look after that.

The bloke wanted $175k and I wouldn't go above $160k. Then he offered me vendor finance at a reduced interest. I worked out he was giving me a $15k saving so if I paid $175k I was actually only paying $160k. It was a good lesson in creative financing. It gets better.

It was 1987. On the very day I settled the government, God bless 'em, brought back negative gearing. That block went up 30% that day. The stockmarket crashed and the property market boomed. A year later we removed the drunken and non-paying tenants, painted, recarpeted, put doors on garages, raised rents and, voila, it was cash positive! So now I still had the $13,500 annual income stream from my Moneyfinder *and* a six-pack bringing in $30k per annum cash. Talk about turning your life around.

Property #14: Cutting loose

I had ideas of being a developer so I went looking for suitable land. I found a block at Thornside, a southern suburb, but my civil engineering background soon alerted me to problems with expensive foundations. The suburb wasn't ready and the margin was too skinny. I put it on the market and cut it loose for no gain.

Properties #15 and 16: Opportunity knocks

There are no problems, only opportunities. Free of Thornside I spotted an ad for two houses on a large block in what was then seedy New Farm. This suburb is really inner city, only 2 km from the CBD. It was the pits at the time, full of pimps and prostitutes. But I knew, having seen cities around Europe, that it had to change.

I turned up too late for the Sunday open house and it was going to auction the next day. I didn't have time to check on finance but I knew I was okay, being a secure public servant, and with the flats paying for themselves, and my good Moneyfinder savings record. The auction was another learning experience.

I had set my price based on how many units I could get on the block, with the current land cost per unit giving the site price. At that time it was 8 units by $15k per unit to equal $120k. That's how I set my limit. I was bidding against somebody, probably a dummy bidder, so when I stopped, of course the bidding stopped. So I was the highest bidder at $118k. Then the agent whisperer said, "If you go up another $2000 you'll probably get it."

These days, being a veteran of hundreds of auctions, I wonder why someone who is already holding the bid would go up. But back then it somehow seemed reasonable, so I said yes. They got their $2000 and I got the property. As expected, finance was no problem.

I went in and did a quick reno and rented the houses out for a 13% yield. In those days money was so tight that I only painted the front of the house for street appeal and left the rest for later. I had my development block and my cashflow. A ripper deal. And I still had my Moneyfinder money, plus six flats and another two houses, all cash positive. New Farm gentrified, as predicted. The artists started making some money and the cafe society moved in. Today the flats and the houses are worth almost $2 million and return over 25% on their original cost.

> ### ─ Reno Kings Tip ═
> *Its not what you earn; it's what you do with what you earn. This is so important. Take control of your finances. Use the Moneyfinder to find our where it is going. Sometimes the cash for a couple of pizzas or a night out on the town mean the difference between buying investment property for your future and you ending up on the pension.*

Property #17: The PPOR (home)

It was 1992 and we'd been through some challenges, including the highest interest rates in memory. I got a 15.4% loan and was told that was a very good rate. The recession had hit in 1990 and there were deals everywhere but very few people who had any spare cash.

I had just left paid work forever! Interest rates were going through the roof. People were going bust. I remember thinking, "Man, this sure beats the boring old public service." With a two-year-old son and another planned, we needed more space. I knew my next PPOR had to be in a high-growth area to milk the equity to buy more IPs. I identified the top three highest-growth northside suburbs as Ascot, Hamilton and Clayfield. We found a post-war house on a double block in Clayfield, great for future development, and sold sufficient assets, including the two houses in Albion, to pay cash for the house.

> ### Reno Kings Tip
>
> *With no non-tax-deductible debt on the home, all the interest on future borrowings against the PPOR to buy IPs would be tax deductible. This made the portfolio extremely tax effective.*

Properties #18–22: Cashing in the super

By then I had organised my affairs so I could leave work forever. I had $1.25 million in property and took a redundancy and superannuation payout of $300k. I immediately went out hunting for property to replace my income. My strategy was to offer 30% below the asking price, just to be careful. Well, I should have made it 50% below, because I soon ran out of super, and used loans to buy properties #18 to #27.

Property #18, in up-market Clayfield cost $135k. It was a low-set, brick three-bedder. Next, property #19, was also in Clayfield. The purchase price was $102k for this high-set, timber three-bedder. The agent had laughed at my original offer of $105k and came back three months later to ask if I still wanted it. I reduced my offer, and got it.

Then I took a look at nearby Hendra. Property #20 was a new display home, a low-set, brick three-bedder plus ensuite. I bought for $154k. Also in Hendra I found a similar property, #21, and paid $155k. Back to Clayfield I found property #22, a deceased estate I bought for $158k. It was a four-bedroom, high-set Queenslander.

Property #23: The "no-reno" reno

Property #23, in Hendra again, was what I also call the "double whammy" story. Hendra is fringed by the blue-ribbon suburbs of Clayfield, Ascot and Hamilton, and Hendra itself was once a haven for horse trainers and stables. It is now rapidly gentrifying and has experienced good capital gain over the past five years. There are a number of big blocks and double blocks in the area.

I was driving by and saw an "open house" sign. A quick inspection showed a two-bedroom plus, high-set house of timber and stucco and AC sheeting. Every room was painted a different colour. I estimated it might rent for $160–$165 per week. The roof was corrugated AC. The block was 809 sq m on two lots, low lying at the rear, with some slight flood problem possible. It appeared to have sewer lines down the side from the position of manholes on the road.

It's a deceased estate, and the agent suggests bids from $140k. About 10 people attend the auction. Checking the rates notice, the unimproved value of the land is $104k. I estimate the lowest price of a 405 sq m block in Hendra at that time to be $90k, so two blocks by $90k = $180k. So that's the land value. I decide that if I get it for $130k–$135k it would be good value.

Bidding starts … $80k … $85k … $90k … $100k … $102k … $103k … and then it stops. Have I missed something? The adrenalin starts flowing. I move the bidding to $111k by $500 bids on the third and final bids, until I give it a $2k jump and knock out the opposition at $113k. We retire to the kitchen with the vendor and sign up at $117k.

I had planned to paint the blue room and the pink room and the yellow room but before settlement a tenant says they love it so I rent the house at $180 per week for six months with no vacancy period. I did pay $200 to clean up the yard and $500 to make some wiring safe.

This was very good cashflow. Then the valuation on the property came in at $136k. I told the valuer he was wrong and to find me a similar block for that $136k and I would buy it, and I was proved to be right.

At this stage I had no intention of selling, but then an agent attending one of my workshops heard me talk about it and the next day approached me to see if I wanted to sell. He said he could get $220k for it. I thought,

"You're dreaming. It's worth about $180k to $190k," and said if he could get $220k for it he could sell it.

To cut a long story short, he did get a developer to pay $180k after I found a major stormwater line down the middle of one of the blocks. Otherwise I would have got $190k–$195k. At the end of six months the tenants left and I had a contract for $180k and a $62,000 gross profit! In retrospect I should have held this one as the land keeps rocketing in value.

Properties #24: What's that smell?

This property was a post-war, low-set, two-bedroom stucco house on a corner next to a block of flats. It had little street appeal, and emitted a strange smell, which no doubt deterred many potential buyers. One advantage was a highly motivated vendor. Two previous contracts had already fallen over. It was 1999 and I was entering this deal with a mate of mine. My now Reno Kings partner Paul Eslick, who I'd met the previous year when he did one of my workshops, did the project management.

We were very hard-nosed and made our written offer at $120,000. We put lots of conditions on the contract: long settlement, termite and building inspections, finance, as well as the main one, the right to carry out improvements during the contract period. As a negotiating tactic we eventually dropped some of the less important conditions, but kept the "right of entry for improvements" clause.

The contract was signed at $121,000. The unimproved value of the property was $108,000, so we were looking at $13,000 for the house, which made it not bad value.

Practically everything about the house was wrong. The master bedroom had double glass doors opening onto a front wrought iron enclosed porch. There was old carpet in most rooms hiding beautiful brushbox flooring and internal 1 mm VJ lining board leading off a rough, homemade kitchen.

The construction of the kitchen was satisfactory, but the kitchen was painted yellow, had timber knobs and was, well, hideous. We sat down and worked out a new floor plan, including adding a new bedroom, repositioning the front stairs and extending the deck, and removing the French doors from the original master bedroom, replacing the space with a wall, and using the French doors in the lounge. Then we took the loungeroom window to the new bedroom.

All the materials we used were there but were in the wrong positions. We saved thousands by reusing what was already there. The existing worn-out carpet hid a beautiful floor. The old kitchen was transformed by painting the front drawers and doors with enamel paint.

For the external work, instead of trying to match the stucco, we used stucco sheet with a similar pattern. New stairs were constructed from steel stringers already prefabricated with timber treads.

Because of the capital gains implications we decided to rent the property out for 12 months to halve the tax. The house was tenanted within one day at $260 per week. This gave a 9.7% return, effectively revaluing the house to $193,000 to yield a 7% return on resale. Total cost of the renovation was $19,000.

Oh, and we did find out where the smell was coming from. The kitchen plumbing was not connected! All the waste water and scraps were going down the sink and under the house. A hundred bucks and a plumber quickly solved the problem. It was truly a case of turning muck into money.

Properties #25–27: It's like a cookie store out there!

Maybe it should be "what you can earn by going to an auction, not what you can learn". It's June 2000.

This particular week I was too busy to look at the advertised three flats returning $16,380 per annum on a 935 sq m Res A block in a blue-ribbon suburb 7 km out from the CBD, so I asked my mate to have a look. He said they looked promising. They were on three lots (a bonus twist) and were 100 m from the train station (a major advantage), but they were asking too much, $210k.

We turn up anyway, arriving at 9.55 am for the auction at 10 am. (I don't recommend this by the way. I've been doing it so long that I don't need acres of research, and so will you after 10 years, if you last.) I assess the potential and the rents ($315 per week … we could increase it to $350 easily). I assess the land value (my secret method), and decide to buy if I can get the property at land value and a minimum of 10% return, ie, less than $163,800. I don't expect to buy, and I don't care … I have another auction at 11 am.

The auction starts. I don't want the auctioneer to pull a high bid, so I call $80k and the auctioneer accepts (to my surprise). He calls a bid of

$90k. I question the auctioneer, as I didn't see anyone bid. He points out the bidder and we exchange bids to $145k, where the bidding stops. Interesting? Is that a real bidder or a plant? The auctioneer sees the vendor and says he will sell for $150k. The other bidder goes to $147.5k. Why did he do that? He had the highest bid anyway. Is he stupid or a plant? We don't know so we don't bid.

The auctioneer passes in the property, which is what we wanted (and expected). The agent appears to negotiate with the highest bidder at $150k, can't get agreement, then comes to us. We say 14 days finance. He says no and we say okay but we want a 40-day settlement, and they agree. At $150k that's 11% return from day one … with no money down, 105% finance, and cash positive before tax deductions.

We offer 3% deposit, just enough to cover the agent's commission, and we have a deal. The agent phones me a couple of hours later. They have someone interested at $195k. We are back on the market, in two hours. Is this fun or what? I used to work all year for $40k, and you can make that in two hours! Work smart not hard (if you know how). A day in the life of an investor.

Properties #28–31: The star pupil

After seeing how Paul could add so much value to property #24, I was ready to do my first Eslick-style makeover. I like to call property #28 "the crooked house".

I had no trouble finding the property. It was on the Public Trustee's list for $150k, an old and extremely rundown cottage. The termites had feasted there, as the back bearers of the house were buried 300 mm into the ground. I offered $135k and it was accepted.

More lessons. Paul came over to see how his star pupil was going. It was a lovely, sunny day and I was painting inside.

"Why are you painting inside?" he asked. Perhaps more importantly he then asked, "Why aren't you painting outside?"

"Because it needs to be done. Duh," I said, and thought, "Dumb question."

"It's a lovely day. I think you should be painting outside."

"Yeah, well I bloody will when I finish painting bloody inside," I said abruptly. He shrugged his shoulders and left. I finished the inside painting and set up to paint outside, and then it rained for three weeks straight. Oh too late I realised what Paul meant.

> **Reno Kings Tip**
>
> *If the weather is fine, paint outside. If it showers, you can always go inside. This one tip could save you weeks of lost time.*

I had a "failed" auction on that house so I bit the bullet and rented it out two days before I was due to fly to the USA. I held it for 12 months, which reduced my capital gains tax, and sold it a year later for $189k. One of the attractions was a cafe precinct just down the road, which guaranteed good tenants and capital gain. I don't regret selling it, as it did have some major future problems with almost certain termite attack to the buried rear section and it was just so damn "crooked". Nothing was straight in the building.

Property #29, the "Pink Lady", came on the market. It had never been properly painted, but someone had got as far as putting on the pink primer. On the way to an auction I stopped to peek in the back broken window and what I saw was a perfect renovator. I went straight down to the agent and made an offer. By that afternoon it was mine at $168k.

By this time I knew what to do and had trained up some tradesmen by insisting they do our workshop to understand our strategies. This allowed Paul and I to run an advanced investors' workshop on Fraser Island while the reno was completed. All I did was put the rubbish in the bin and reap the capital gain. The property rented fast as it looked picture perfect.

> **Reno Kings Tip**
>
> *You have to know "what to do" so you can tell tradespeople what to do and what not to do. Don't expect them to instinctively know that you want a Holden cosmetic makeover, not a BMW restoration.*

I was having serious fun now. Every Friday since I left work in 1992 I celebrated by having a long leisurely breakfast, starting after my former workmates were in their "cages", sorry, offices. This memorable day my research had shown that the market was about to start a powerful up-trend. After breakfast I went for a two-hour massage and walked over the road to an agent I knew.

By 5 pm that afternoon I'd identified two properties, both "double twisters" with huge potential. Property #30 was another post-war house on a double block in Hendra. A quick reno soon turned two bedrooms into four. The value was in the land, as the area was simply booming. The house gave me holding income while the land value has since doubled.

Back to Clayfield for the second double twister, #31, again on two lots. The reno turned three bedrooms into four. We were having a problem agreeing on the contract terms. I had wanted a short settlement for tax purposes, but I eventually found out the elderly owner wanted a long contract so she could go straight to a new home. I immediately said no problem. I held that property on a 3% deposit in a fast-rising market. The property went up 15%, or more than $40k, during the contract period. A great strategy and a "win, win" for all.

Reno Kings Tip

Price is not the only issue. Find out what the seller wants and, if you can, give them what they want by negotiating on the conditions.

Properties #32–37 and 38

These properties are the Newstead flats and house development we did using our JV (joint venture) strategy. They show that you don't have to have a lot of money to get into the property market. You just have to think outside the square. (Check out the JV story next.)

Properties #39–40: JVs with Paul

Following on the success of the JV in Newstead, Paul kept his eyes peeled for more of the same. When you are on a good thing, stick to it. He came across a three-storey, contemporary, near-new house 1.5 km from the city in Kangaroo Point. I went to have a look at it. It was spectacular: four-car garage with wine cellar; the middle floor accommodated a three-bedroom plus ensuite apartment; the top floor was a fully fitted-out office. Best of all was the block of land on the sidestreet, perfect for subdivision, if we could get approval.

We made a low offer before auction, which they rejected. At auction it was passed in below our offer. We were still a serious chance here. After quite involved negotiations we increased our offer to $510k and it was ours. We signed up a tenant who pays his rent a year in advance, almost $30k. I always turn up to collect that rent.

We have recently completed property #40, a four-bedroom, two-bathroom house built for just under $248k and rented for $550 per week.

That's a gross yield of 11.5% just 1.5 km from the city. Who says you can't get capital gain and cashflow in the city?

Property #41 A quadruple twister!

I was preparing for a major workshop when I saw an ad for an open house. I turned off the computer for one hour to take a look. That's all it needed. It was a rare breed: a quadruple twister, capable of producing tornado-strength capital gains.

First twist: location. This one's just 9 km from the city, with major infrastructure spending planned, a future cafe society next to blue-ribbon suburbs, a walk to bus and rail, plenty of shopping, close to the airport, and that's just the start. Twist number two: it's on a double block. As the land goes up 100% this land goes up 200%. Twist number three: it's zoned for townhouses and is not in a demolition-control zone. Twist number four: it's currently a two-bedroom house, which Paul has shown me how to turn into a four-bedroom for less than $1000. That will kick up my rental returns while I wait for the land to increase.

I asked for a contract and I did something very rare. I paid the full price of $298k with no conditions. That property has gone up $200,000 in one year. That's equal to about 20 years of public service super.

It rented very easily for $248 per week. Some people would say that's negatively geared. Yeah right. A rental yield of 4.3% and a capital gain of $200k/$298k (or 67%) gives me a total of 71.3 % in one year. There ain't nuthin' negative about that, and I haven't started milking it's potential.

> ## Reno Kings Tip
>
> *Always look at the total return. Return = cashflow + capital gain. Cashflow pays the bills. Capital gain makes you wealthy.*

Properties #42 –51: Reducing the tax bill, and how!

I call this story "How I turned a BIG tax bill into $500,000 capital gain and created annual rental income of $111k using TBM (the bank's money)".

Hey, I had a problem. I had just done a forecast of my finances and there was a large looming tax bill. A good problem to have, as it means you actually made some money in the last year! I have an investor's philosophy that says, "You pay tax or you pay interest." I prefer to pay interest. I pay enough local council tax and land tax and stamp duty to feed a small army of bureaucrats but income tax can be minimised (not avoided) with intelligent purchase of the right properties.

This is what happened. It was my investor mate Paul Eslick who pointed out the "For Auction" sign, just 200 m from where I live. "You would have to go to that," he said.

Here is Geoff's property-buying history.

	Description	Year	Purchase price	Rent per annum	Current value	Sale price	Date sold	Capital gain	Yield (rent/cost)
#1	Hawthorne	1971	$7,000			$12,000	1975	$5,000	
#2	Sunnybank Hills	1976	$18,000			$62,000	1983	$44,000	
#3-4	Wilston flats x 2	1979	$29,000			$69,000	1983	$40,000	
#5-6	Albion duplex	1982	$55,000			$180,000	1992	$125,000	
#7	Tambourine land	1984	$13,000			$14,000	1987	$1,000	
#8-13	Wooloowin flats x 6	1987	$175,000	$48,776	$886,836			$711,836	27.9%
#14	Thornside	1988	$40,000			$45,000	1989	$5,000	
#15-16	New Farm houses x 2	1988	$120,000	$34,060	$1,135,333			$1,015,333	28.4%
#17	Clayfield PPOR	1992	$220,000	n/a	$800,000			$580,000	0.0%
#18	Clayfield house 1	1992	$135,000	$14,300	$397,222			$262,222	10.6%
#19	Clayfield house 2	1992	$102,000	$10,764	$316,588			$214,588	10.6%
#20	Hendra house 1	1993	$154,000			$212,000	2003	$58,000	
#21	Hendra house 2	1993	$100,000	$12,740	$364,000			$264,000	12.7%
#22	Clayfield house 3	1998	$158,000	$13,936	$455,000			$297,000	8.8%
#23	Hendra house 3	1998	$117,000			$180,000	1999	$63,000	
#24	Clayfield house 4	1999	$121,000	$13,936	$375,000			$254,000	11.5%
#25-27	Clayfield flats x 3	2000	$150,000	$20,436	$510,900			$360,900	13.6%
#28	Paddington	1998	$135,000			$189,500	1999	$63,000	
#29	Wooloowin	2000	$168,000	$12,376	$353,600			$185,600	7.4%
#30	Hendra house 4	2001	$290,000	$14,300	$570,000			$280,000	4.9%
#31	Clayfield house 5	2001	$268,000	$14,300	$530,000			$262,000	5.3%
#32-37*	Newstead JV flats x 6	2001	$460,000	$34,060	$681,200			$221,200	7.4%
#38*	Newstead JV house**	2003	$273,000	$26,000	$866,666			$593,666	9.5%
#39*	Kangaroo Pt JV 1	1998	$510,000	$29,768	$775,000			$265,000	5.8%
#40*	Kangaroo Pt JV 2**	1998	$247,700	$28,600	$893,750			$646,050	11.5%
#41	Nundah	1998	$298,000	$12,740	$495,000			$197,000	4.3%
#42-51	Clayfield flats x 9, gym	2003	$1,500,000	$111,030	$2,018,545			$518,545	7.4%
	Total		**$5,863,700**	**$452,122**	**$12,424,640**	**$963,500**		**$7,532,940**	
	less cost / gain properties sold		$568,000					$404,000	
	equals cost / gain properties held		$5,295,700					$7,128,940	
	LVR=original loans/ current values				**40%**				
*JVs	less 50% JV share		$745,350	$59,214	$1,608,308				
	Geoff's total		$4,550,350	$392,908	$10,816,332				
	Geoff's average yield			**8.6%**					

**Purchase price listed for #38 and 40 are development costs (rounded).

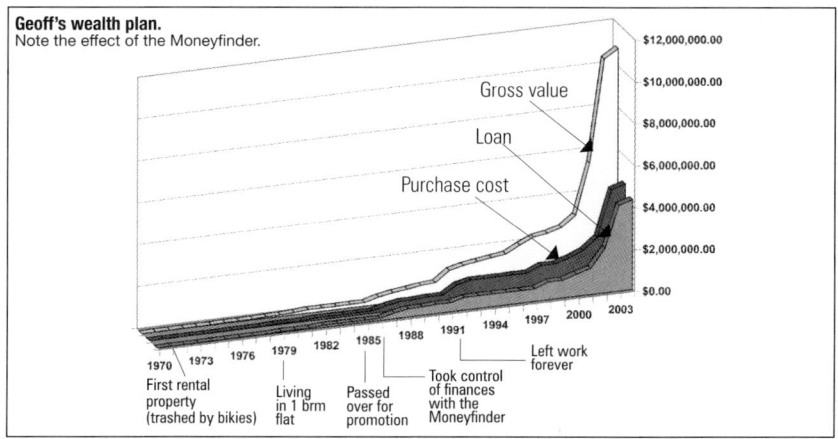

Geoff's wealth plan.
Note the effect of the Moneyfinder.

"Yeah, you're right," I thought. "I'll check it out," and check it out I did. It was a beauty! Nine fully furnished apartments in one block, and I mean fully furnished. They had TVs, air-cons, microwaves, fans, beds, washing machines, dryers, right down to tea-towels and eggcups. I just saw depreciation, depreciation write-off, everywhere. What's more, the building was only six years old, which meant I would get 2.5% of the whole building cost as a legitimate tax write-off for 40 – 6 = 34 years! The quantity surveyor will love that!

Time to get to work. The auction was in just over a week. I rang my mortgage broker. There was no way I would be able to have the finance to buy unconditionally in the time available. So I sought and got tentative approval (from my mortgage broker) for finance up to $1.2 million subject to valuation etc.

I already had my line of credit in place for the deposit, fees, stamp duty and so on. I checked with my solicitor and wrote a number of clauses to give to the auctioneer to indicate that I would be bidding on a "subject to finance" basis and the conditions of payment. I was set to bid.

┌─Reno Kings Offer─
See page 235 for Contract Clauses You Simply Must Know.

It's auction day. They have a registration book for bidders, though it's not compulsory in Queensland to register. I am going to try to "steal" it for $1.2 million unconditional, but can go to a "good deal" price of $1.5 million subject to finance. We will see. It all depends on the seller.

Hey, I know the auctioneer! He used to teach auction tactics at my workshops. I walk over to introduce myself. I give him my list of conditions and ask for approval to bid on those conditions, and I make a pointed remark like, "There won't be any dummy bidding at this auction, will there?" He appears taken aback that I would suggest such a thing. He obviously knows I will be watching carefully.

The auction begins with the usual showy preamble by the auctioneer and then it was away. Well, it goes past my $1.2 million before I can even get a bid in. The auctioneer is a delight to watch. The arms are moving this way and that, the words endlessly streaming. He is taking bids seamlessly. It's obvious why he won the Auctioneer of the Year. Better than theatre.

After some ferocious and fast action, it is passed in to the highest bidder. I forget the figure; I think about $1,420,000. I say to my friend, "It's a done deal. I think it'll sell for $1.5 mil for sure. No one is going to worry about $80k in a $1.5 mil deal … but, just in case, let's wait until the deal is signed and sealed."

We wait …

Well, we wait … and watch … and wait … and watch as the hot and sweaty suited agent runs from the highest bidder upstairs to the vendor, then back to the bidder. People drift away until there is just … the agent, the vendor, the highest bidder and me!

After about an hour I say to the agent, "I realise the highest bidder has the first right to negotiate at the reserve price, but for how long? He's had a fair go. Here are my conditions; I want to negotiate too."

"Hang on, hang on," says the red-faced agent. "We're almost there." I look over and see the bidder shaking his head sideways and I know the wait might have been worthwhile. I intercept the agent and say those magic words, "What would buy it?" He says the owner wants $1.5 million and the other bidder is about $40k short.

I think to myself, "$40k is less than 3% of $1.5 mil. The way the market is moving that's about one month's capital gain." Then I make my offer: I will pay $1.5 million, subject to the five conditions I mentioned before. Ten minutes later we're drawing up the contract.

This is when the real fun began. Getting $1.2 million (80% of $1.5 mil) of the bank's money will not be easy. I had the choice of two mortgage brokers and an existing bank. I had to get a valuation. That is always critical. They are notoriously conservative, especially on big deals. I called in our quantity surveyor. Just as I thought, he found $1 million worth of building allowance and depreciation. That's a $58,900 per year tax deduction right there. Rental appraisals were sought from local agents; they varied enormously. It is critical to get the highest appraisal possible, as the rent return is a major factor in valuing the building.

It was a battle to get the right valuation. The building was currently used for short-term rentals with no leases. This meant I would have vacant possession as I switched to medium- and long-term rentals. I researched the rentals on previous sales in the area, did forecasts of value based on different rentals, used the carrot of the QS report to add more value.

I even went to a "mortgagee in possession" auction of a block of flats nearby to see what a worst-case yield was. All of this seemed to be discarded because when the valuer looked at my block he used a severely reduced rent (25% reduced), then applied a 10-week vacancy period to every unit, even though my longest vacancy over 32 years was just six weeks. He then based his valuation on the "net rent" figure. I had never seen that done on a residential building before. It was absolutely the worst, worst-case scenario. And would you believe the value still came in at $1.5 million. I knew then I was on a winner!

Oh, by the way, there was an area in the building set up as a gym and used by the personal fitness trainer of the current owner. I approached her and asked what she wanted to do after the sale. She said she'd lease the area at a rent equivalent to a rental unit, so I now had the equivalent rental of 10 units.

Duly diligent

Then I had to do my due diligence. There were visits to the council to check that the building was built in accordance with the council requirements. I did searches on easements and drainage. I even did some research on corporate rentals but it was the wrong time of the year.

The property settled on time. It was time to rent, fast. I had interviewed three property managers to spread it around and I decided to use my tried and tested "rent fast" strategies as well. It was critical to rent fast as the negative cashflow from an empty building was over $1000 per week!

The difference between agents and adverts. I decided to advertise at the "high" rental appraisals. I could always go down. I placed my "killer" For Rent advertisement in the weekend paper and on Monday I called one agent to see how they went. Apparently it was "very quiet" over the weekend. They didn't get a call. "That's strange," I said. "My phone ran hot and I already have some applications." I've always found that the right advert at the right time with the right response gets the right result.

> **┌─Reno Kings Offer─────────────────────────────┐**
> *The "killer ad" is in Secrets of Property Investment, see page 235.*

And what a result. Within four weeks it was fully rented at or above the selling agent's appraisals, the rent that was scoffed at by the valuer. Not only had I rented the spare area to the fitness trainer, but also the storeroom to one of the tenants. Cash was pouring in. In just four weeks I had effectively revalued the building by about $500,000, generated annual rent of more than $111,000 and, the best part, by using the $58,900 write-off and prepaying a year's interest I wiped out our income tax bill.

The strategy

A year later the property is just humming along. Vacancies are almost nil. New tenants apply as soon as people leave. I would have to rate this deal as my best ever. Can anyone do this? Yes. It is a big deal by any standards, but I have applied the strategies that I have shared for the last 10 years, the strategies that anyone can apply.

1. Research values so you can spot the deal when it turns up.

2. Get out in the market. You won't find the deal watching Big Brother.

3. Organise your finance.

4. Organise your contract clauses with your solicitor.

5. Learn how to make offers. Then go out and make them!

6. Buy well. The key is making money when you buy.

7. Consult with your accountant to get the property in the right names and the right ownership structure.

8. Know how to deal with valuers.

9. Commission your quantity surveyor to maximise your non-cash deductions to minimise your income tax.

10. Learn all you can about property management so you can manage the managers.

11. Rent fast to protect your cashflow.

12. Make sure your property-wise accountant claims everything you are legally entitled to.

Knowledge, when applied, truly is power! I worked as a public servant for 28 years for $300k super – that's not super. A $500,000 capital gain and a yearly rent of $111,000, in just four weeks (and 31 years experience), while wiping out my tax bill – that's super!

Are those deals still out there? Yes, but you have to look hard and negotiate hard. There are so many people paying too much for too little. Recently I was talking to one of our workshop participants. She'd found a deal and made $100k just because no other bidders turned up at the auction, and it was just around the corner from me. How did I miss that one?

You don't know what you don't know

By the time I began to realise my ability to make money through property investment I'd already made plenty of blunders, and learned at least one lesson from each one. I was also starting to talk with people who were starting out, some who'd had some success, others who were trying and failing.

I thought long and hard each time I made an error to work out the best way of handling that particular scenario, in preparation for it cropping up again, which invariably it did. I wrote copious notes, worked on systems. Then I struck on the idea of sharing my experiences, my blunders, my lessons with others.

I presented my first workshop to a small group in Brisbane in 1993. It was free; I just wanted to spread the good news on property. By 1998 I was doing introductory seminars for about 100 people and workshops for small groups of 25 people once every three months. They shared their experiences also and it was a real eye-opener.

I started compiling my workshop notes into a workbook, and, voila, *The Ten Golden Rules of Property* was born. That was in 1995. This wonderful little book gives a structure, an organised system for buying investment property. It also includes that magical device, the Moneyfinder, Doidge style. And it takes new players and old through all the "Ls", looking, location, loans, legals and ledgers. Then there's the long term, landlords and leasing, and the beauty of leverage. Most importantly it talks about the lifestyle you can achieve with financial freedom.

It's funny you know, from the thousands of people who have bought *The Ten Golden Rules* over the years I've got heaps of emails and letters of appreciation, a lot from new players, grateful to have a reliable guide. But it's the letters from the old dogs, the ones who've been there and done that, including making the mistakes, that I really get a kick out of. They're still learning too. Sometimes it sparks them to remember how they did it in the first place and go out and do it again, and do it better.

The Reno Kings: When I teamed up with Paul

It was at a workshop in 1998. I was asking each person around the room how many investment properties they had ... three, yep, that's good in five years ... one, giving it a go. Then this bloke at the front pipes up, "I've got six."

"That's terrific," I say. "And how long did it take to accumulate six properties?" expecting him to say five to ten years.

"Eleven months," he replied and looked at me like I was a loser! You could have knocked me over with a feather (that was before I met Brenda and Les Irwin, of course). I ended up giving his money back, in return for finding out his strategies, and a few months later I invited him to take the stage at a first-ever fully booked renovation workshop.

You wouldn't believe it now, but Paul, the confident renovator, had a massive attack of stagefright. He went to jelly, couldn't move to the lectern to get to his notes. Well that was a long time ago. We did a fair bit of work together over the next few years, joint ventures and so on. Then in 2002 the Reno Kings went national.

Reno Kings Property Masters

Now of course the Reno Kings workshops get heaps of response. We offer one-day and two-day workshops just four times a year. We usually get a hundred-plus people in a workshop, and about half of the participants come from interstate, flying in to Brisbane especially for us!

The workshops really give the tools and tactics, all the fine detail, to hone investors' skills in buying property. What really sets us apart from a lot of other seminars (there are some others that are legit as well) is that we are not about selling property or marketing. We are solely there to inform and educate, to give unbiased info based on our experience with no sales pitch.

We had a bloke from Tasmania at a property workshop recently. His wife had done a Reno Kings workshop previously and they'd both done workshops in the US. It's always a good idea for both partners to do the workshop if possible. It can save a lot of arguments! He was obviously serious about the business. He and his wife have seven properties in Tasmania and they were trying to work out a way around the push from the mainland, interstate buyers sending land values up and causing a rental glut, with returns dropping. We concentrated on finding him "hotspots" for part of that workshop, so hopefully that will help him to pick up a bargain before the mainland competition.

What a lot of people get out of the workshops is the ability to talk to other investors and hear what their experience has been. They also get to ask specific questions about their own circumstances and work on real-life scenarios. Oh, and they walk away with a 400-page workbook as well. Lots of homework!

The Reno Kings website (www.renos.com.au) has heaps of testimonials from people who've done the workshops. One guy recently wrote to us about his experience of being forced out of his 15-year-old business by a multinational, almost losing everything. After doing the workshop he says that he's again, after a long while, feeling the "fire in the belly", the excitement and hope for a wonderful life ahead.

We also get our share of sceptics of course, but they're generally people who've checked the website and *not* done a workshop or, usually, not even owned property. They write in to our on-line discussion forum. We post their emails on the website too – we've got nothing to hide – and we answer them all. Check out this exchange:

Eslick & Doidge charge a fortune for seminars? What a Joke!

Of course Paul and yourself are multi-millionaires, with strategies such as charging an absolute fortune for a seminar that only millionaires can afford – what a joke! Add this to your testimonials on your website.
Good Luck
Craig

And the response?

Thanks Craig. We get very few millionaires *to* the seminars, but I do mix with the people from the seminars who have taken action, many of them with very little funds, some who have lost their whole fortune and are getting back on their feet, people who see information as an investment in their future. They can't just talk about it; they *have* to take action.

I've seen those people, most of them very ordinary people, become millionaires *from* the seminars, and I love what they have dared to do.

If you think $1000+ or - is an absolute fortune then I say raise your sights; $1000 is a ridiculous amount to earn from investing. If you didn't earn $30k in your first reno, or save say 10% on a property purchase price (that's maybe $15k–$20k) then I would say you weren't listening.

Go to the library and read some more books if you can't afford seminars. For $1000 you could read maybe 30 books. Then you would have a great background of information to move on. But watch out for analysis paralysis.

I have spent many many thousands of dollars on my own education via seminars and books and tapes and I have always got at least one good idea that I can apply for the rest of my life. Often this investment in my financial education returns my money many times over. What is the lifetime value of one good idea or the cost of one major mistake?

If I can add anything to further answer your concerns please feel free to ask. You have certainly made me think about how people on low incomes could afford to attend.

I hate to admit it but in the past I, like you, have said similar things about other seminar presenters. But of course that's different, isn't it?

Thanks for making me think about this issue.

One last thing. If anyone thinks running seminars has made Paul and I multi-millions think again! We can make more money from one good property deal than from four years of seminars. We are a very rare species: property investors who speak, not "speakers" who (sometimes) invest. We don't sell property, we buy it! And we do like to see people take action and get ahead.

Regards

Geoff

The website's got all sorts of other goodies too, a free e-zine, information about the workshops, a Learning Centre for all the resources and links. What did we do before the internet?

The upshot: Keep learning!

We're always learning. It seems we learn, we learn, we learn, and as soon as we master something another change begins. In fact, you're learning right now. There is no end to learning. As long as you continue to grow, you'll face new challenges. These will require new skills if you're to fulfil your potential.

Life is definitely a learning process. Learning is essential for success in any sphere. I don't mean learning to pass exams or learning acceptable manners, I mean on-the-street, hands-on learning.

Rental property is only a vehicle to get you where you want to go in life. It's just like driving. We all need training to get started. You get behind the wheel of your financial vehicle. You decide when you turn the key. We can help you with a strategy, a direction, a road map. We suggest you go slowly initially. As you learn from us to dodge the potholes and the dead ends, you speed up. You may occasionally take the wrong turn but you can get back on the track again. Eventually it will seem almost second nature as you set the cruise control.

Property slowly becomes fun as the early challenges to learn about selection, offers, negotiation, finance, contract clauses, renos and developments are conquered, and you accumulate IP after IP. Your portfolio then allows you choices to do what you want, when you want and how you want to. It doesn't get much better than this. You are financially free.

Geoff's tips on property selection

Look at your clients. Property investment is a business, and your clients are your tenants. And in business it pays to know what your clients want. Are they young, middle-aged or old? Low, middle or high income? Singles or couples? Will they want single, double or multiple carparks? Will they want an ensuite?

Look at the suburb. Are there lots of units and few houses? When buying recently I carefully studied the suburb. It had heaps of units and plenty of houses. Gradually the houses were being knocked down to build more units and townhouses. I figured that with fewer houses available in what was a desirable suburb then houses would be in demand.

Look at the property. Many people in the suburb were aging and living in two- or three-storey "walkups". I thought in time they would want to be closer to the ground with good security, but in a nice property with low maintenance. Throw in a bit of ground for a vegie patch to potter around in and you have a very attractive package for a long-term tenant. I bought a brand new low-set three-bedroom brick home with ensuite and lock-up garage, and added security screens and curtains. It rented before settlement day. The vacancy factor in that suburb is now about 1% for houses and 4% for units. If you know what your future tenants want you'll rent that house fast. This helps to prevent vacancy problems.

Location. This means a number of things in investment property. It's not necessarily the best house, or the best suburb, or the top of the hill. For investment property, it's a blend of price and convenience. A well-priced property can provide more "bang for your buck", ie, a good yield.

Capital gain. This is essential when you buy investment property. If you don't get capital gain your investment is not worth a damn. The yield will run your property, but capital gain gives you leverage and makes you wealthy. Avoid the top of the market unless you get it as a steal, but also be wary of the bottom of the market. If the property is located in a very poor socioeconomic suburb, yield could be high but your prospects for good capital gain may be limited. Aim for a medium-priced property, one that most people would be happy to rent.

Old versus new. Older houses on good blocks can provide high yields, especially if you can add bedrooms, although newer houses will most likely have lower maintenance costs. New houses also offer a 2.5% capital allowance on the structure, which can provide a tax-deductible edge over the higher yield and higher maintenance of a cheaper, older building.

Adding value. These days it's all about adding value. Buy a property with a twist. It might be reno potential. It might be subdivison potential or it might be niche markets. The really good deals have a combination of a number of twists.

Tenants. When you're looking at a property think the way a tenant would think. What's the distance from the train station? If it's in walking distance you'll get more tenants. Look for properties close to bus and train, ie, walking distance. How far is it from shops? And some tenants don't like noisy positions, although some tenants will tolerate noise in exchange for the increased convenience.

The 'ways. I'm not a strong 'ways man like Paul. There are areas in the 'ways you buy only if you can buy at a discount. They are on highways, railway lines, airport flightpaths, busways. Other potential negatives are next to factories, church halls, major shopping centres, large restaurants, dance halls, sports centres, schools, childcare centres, large blocks of units, public toilets, hospitals, hostels, hotels, public phone boxes. I've found these properties may rent okay initially on a quiet weekend at a lower rent, but tenants tell me they aren't renewing the lease because of the disruption and inconvenience. They actually complain to you when they can't get a park in the street or someone parks across their driveway.

When you sell you will find it is best to sell on a quiet day, a weekend, school holiday or non-work day. Tenants like to be near those conveniences but not necessarily directly opposite or adjacent. If you're looking at property with any of the above nearby, check it out at different times of the day and night. See if parking is a problem. Schools may be quiet after 4 pm but a parking nightmare at 9 am and 3 pm.

Distant suburbs. Most new houses are located in newly developing distant suburbs. While these are good for homebuyers, they can present challenges for investment property. Some tenants will love the new houses and amenities, but there will be lots of new properties in the area competing for tenants. If infrastructure like transport and shopping facilities is limited tenants may be deterred. New distant suburbs often have few industries in the area to supply jobs for potential tenants. Tenants may gravitate toward developed suburbs with more established infrastructure. Transport and cafes are probably the most powerful attractions.

Vacancy factors. Check the vacancy factor and tenant demand with local agents. Anything above 3% (ie, three houses in a hundred vacant) means a slow market. Above 10% is a disaster; stay away.

Geoff's tips on using debt

How to source an investment loan is another of the lessons I've learned along the way. Borrowed money can work for you and against you. Understand good debt (where interest is deductible, IPs) and bad debt (where interest is non-deductible, your home) and super bad debt (where interest is very high and non-deductible, credit cards, etc). In *The Ten Golden Rules* I outline 50 questions that need to be answered when comparing loan products. These cover such areas as interest rates, special rates, government charges, flexibility and penalties, right down to guarantees and third-party mortgages.

These days I recommend you find a good mortgage broker. They have access to many financial institutions, and they can ask these questions for you and save you a lot of time. Their fees are normally paid by the banks.

If you plan on doing it yourself, then, once you've gathered sufficient information to make a comparison, it's time to negotiate, but you need to negotiate with someone who has the authority to make a decision. It's no use negotiating with the teller to decrease your loan fees. Find the decision maker in the organisation. Get a personal banker.

I was once negotiating on an investment loan that was due to roll over. I was getting nowhere. I asked to speak to Head Office and was connected to the State Manager. He couldn't have been more helpful. He told me to compare the rates and fees of other banks and to ring him back. Within a week I rang back. The manager matched – and bettered – the best deal I could get from other banks. He had the authority to do so.

I've also found that if you ask at different branches of the bank, you may be presented with different fees. This gives you the leverage to request the lowest fee stated. I recently rang Sydney on their toll-free number and was quoted a $250 roll-over fee. The Brisbane branch said $550. I pointed out the lower quote and was subsequently offered the loan at a fee of $200. One phone call saved $350.

You've also got to help the financial institution lend you money. You need to prepare a professional-looking statement of your financial position. This shows you're organised and sets out your assets and liabilities cashflow clearly. It gives the bank officer a clear idea of who you are, your history, what you do and what you want.

Geoff's tips on professional advice

I can't stress enough the need to find a good accountant. Search out very carefully a "property-wise" accountant who knows and is interested in residential property, especially one who owns property. You can be sure such an accountant will know the ropes. Even if their fees are higher than your tax agent they can save you thousands of dollars above their fees.

There are also lots of simple tips for fast, efficient record keeping and for managing the details involved in rental property. For example, use one credit card solely for business purposes and another for non-tax or personal purchases, and keep a separate cheque book for each property. This works well for three to six properties but may be cumbersome for more than this. And keep all your receipts and mark them with the property, the date and detail of service or product. Write up your expenses at the end of each month, weekly if there's enough of them. It saves a lot of time in the long run.

Get a business card printed and open a trade account with a hardware store. This keeps all the little purchases recorded through the month. It gives you credit and means just one payment a month. You should also get at least 10% discount. If your local hardware store can't do it, ask another. And spend the money on a quantity surveyor to get your depreciation schedule complete, especially for the first tax return.

Unless you're on a high income and really need the tax breaks, negative gearing may not be the way to go. Concentrate instead on positive gearing. Any investment property will provide tax benefits; that doesn't mean it's a good investment. Concentrate on finding properties that will offer the potential for *strong capital growth*! That way you'll steer clear of financial troubles in the future.

Reno Kings insights

What's your background?

I was born in Queensland, in the first wave of the baby boomers. I was average at school and sport, a bit of a loner, but I liked reading; bit of a daydreamer, or so my reports said. I joined the public service as a cadet draftsperson and eventually became a civil engineer after many years failing when I got distracted by things like the stockmarket and the war in Vietnam.

Why did you get started?

Good question. My parents were always arguing about money or the lack of it. I suppose I didn't want to finish up like that. I used to sit at work and try to think of GRQs (get rich quick schemes). I had over a hundred of them, and then I discovered property.

What was your greatest fear?

I was a public servant with no other experience, so I wasn't a big risk taker. I was terrified of having to get a "real job" because I felt inadequate skill-wise. So I had to find a way to make money other than work!

Did your parents show you how to get ahead?

My parents were all about saving money, not making money: get a qualification and get a safe job. My dad was a school champion sprinter and never finished high school. He was a lowly paid clerk in the public service. Being constantly passed over for promotion killed his spirit and he died middle-aged and sad. It made a big impression on me. My mother said, "Never a borrower or lender be." I suppose I just didn't listen. She had a few shares. One of those companies she invested in 44 years ago just went broke this year. There is a lesson there.

What was your greatest mistake?

Going too slowly. Staying in the public service for 28 years. There has never been one day that I have regretted leaving. Oh, and control. A very senior financial planner told me I needed to "diversify" in the early 1990s. I had a million-dollar property portfolio, so for a substantial fee he put me into unlisted property trusts, which lost about $80,000 in six months. That cost me a block of flats I was about to buy and caused a lot of stress, but it taught me a lesson about taking control of your investment.

What do you want to achieve?

I left work 11 years ago to buy more property, write books and give seminars to show others. So I suppose I am living my dreams. Property is so much fun, and rewarding. In so many ways it will test you, try you out, but when you work out how to make it work for you, you will never look back. At a recent seminar I went to, I reset those early goals and set some very big new targets. You constantly need to challenge yourself. You are either going ahead or slowly going backwards.

How would you describe your strategy?

Buy well, add value, manage intensively, look for properties with a "twist". These days I want properties with triple twists, three ways to make money. For example, renovation, a niche market and development. Capital gain properties were my focus in the early days, but I'm a bit greedy. I want cashflow and capital gain in the same property these days. That test weeds out a lot of deals.

Where do you find your deals?

Deals are everywhere. I bought my last deal at the end of my street. That's called "gold in your back yard". I think of the property market as a giant "cookie store" where the properties are lined up and you go by saying, "No I won't have that one, I'll have this one." I have bought some great deals at auction, where the sellers mostly want to sell that day.

Any memorable experiences along the way?

The bikies and the Hill's hoist were unforgettable. Also, a giant storm in 1987 when I lost my roof sheeting. When I climbed up I found a great clear roof space. I looked through the gap and saw … the city. I built a bedroom in the roof space and got a city view all because of a storm.

What's your best renovating or money-making tips?

Strategy: buy the right property, one with a twist or two. Add value. Hold for the long term. Equipment: paint and the airless spraygun. I totally transformed a house in two hours with one. Paint is powerful. Polished floors look so great. Kerb appeal: picket fences, front yard, the front of the house.

What would you do differently?

Buy more earlier. Get a "money" education earlier. Buy more interstate properties (reduces land tax).

How has your life changed since you began your property investment?

In so many ways. Financially it's been outstanding; personally its been liberating; relationship-wise its made Miriam and I a team; education-wise it's taught me so much about the economy and assets and cashflow and business. Community-wise it's allowed me to write books, give workshops, meet and share with other investors. It's demonstrated what is possible for my kids and in a lot of ways it's a big part of my life. I shiver to think that without it I could still be a public servant!

How do you picture yourself five years down the track?

Lifestyle increasing, more travel, more toys, more fun and, yes, even more property. I've created a portfolio that will double and triple without me doing too much more. So now it's all about staying fit and healthy to enjoy the wealth and the rest of the journey.

Reno Kings Reports

Five Reno Kings Reports and Products I would recommend as essentials for anyone getting started are: The Moneyfinder; my first book, *Secrets of Property Investment*, and the second book, *The Ten Golden Rules of Property* ; The Property Rating Guide; and Forty-three Steps to Unlimited Success in Property.

See page 235 for more information and details on how to order, or go to our website: www.renos.com.au

All together now

A group of mates, a few bottles of wine, and out come the ideas.
They don't have to be pipedreams. A joint venture can be born.

One subject we've found to be of huge interest to investors is joint ventures, JVs, where investors pool their resources, their talents and their skills for the group reward.

What are the tips? What are the tricks? What are the traps of the JV structure? How can you escape the "herd" of homebuyers out there fighting and scrambling for a share of the residential market at the base entry level?

Consider the power of a joint venture between a very busy cash-rich, time-poor person (most professionals and businesspeople) and an informed real estate investor (plenty of time and knowledge, but perhaps a bit short of cash).

All of a sudden, 1+1=3. You break out of the $400,000 market and soar toward the "blue sky" of the $1 million+ market, a much less crowded playing field! There are exciting possibilities and great rewards, but there are risks as well.

In this story we'll take you on a "warts and all" journey, step by step, through a recent development with a group of "joint venturers". But I'll let Paul tell you the first bit.

Meet the venturers

It was during a Reno Kings Advanced Investor workshop on Fraser Island, making good use of Orchid House, the pole house I'd built as a fishing shack (and it's one helluva shack) with a group of mates in 1998, a few years earlier. Our group late one night and after too many bottles of red decided to do a hypothetical of a development we could do as a joint venture (JV), the now infamous "hypothetical".

"Suppose, just suppose, we all pooled our finances and made offers on properties in the $1 million+ range. We put in $20,000 each (10 people) so we'll have a deposit of $200,000 to buy (steal) a property worth $1.3 million for $1 million."

The requests and yields were outrageous: 10% yield, minimum 10% capital gain per annum, 3 km from the city, and the ability to add some savage capital gain with a worthy development. On reflection the next day it was obvious the alcohol had taken effect, because there was just nothing like this, or ever to be. It was like buying a big parcel of inner-city land for a few beads.

How wrong I was! The group kept alive our vision, much to my annoyance. These ideas only seem good in theory. That's why they're called hypotheticals, not reality.

The reality

Back to the voice of reason. We put the idea to the group again (sober, this time). After talking over the idea with their professional advisors (accountants, solicitors, etc) they were ready for our first meeting.

Ten people turned up at an inner-city coffee shop for the first meeting of the "Fraser Investment Group". We developed our core document.

The 12 Keys to Great JVs

1. Who is in the group?

2. What is the structure of the purchasing and holding entity? How will it accommodate the tax system?

3. What are the parameters for investment criteria, ie, cash-on-cash return, gross yield, required percentage for adding value, required rental increase, desired leverage on venture capital?

4. Schedule for individuals to seek their own professional advice on the structure and their personal liabilities.

5. Individual responsibilities: What has to be done, who does it and when. What happens when things go wrong, or it doesn't get done?

6. Expenditure limits and responsibilities: Who pays for what? How much is allowable without group approval? Acquisition forecast.

7. What monetary or other compensation applies to time and effort by members? Is there a need to set guidelines before the project begins? (Because it becomes an issue after the case!)

8. Exit strategies: How is the entire venture to be wound-up in the case of profit ... or loss?

9. Replacement of members strategy: What happens if a member wishes to leave the joint venture?

10. Selection of professional consultants, architect, accountant, surveyors, townplanners, etc.

11. Risk management strategy: Assessment of risk for the project, individual exposure issues, structures to minimise or contain risk, assessment of individual members' risk profiles, SWOT analysis – focus on strategies to maximise strengths and opportunities and handle weaknesses and threats.

12. Further research: What research has to be done? Who will do it? In what timeframe? How to find potential properties, such as subscribing to property valuation databases, conducting local government searches, and so on.

This led to the development of a statement of Investors' Objectives and a Management Plan. It also raised questions about the individuals' wealth goals and whether they were congruent with each other. Another issue was how the group was to be managed. Democratically? A benevolent dictatorship? Anarchistically? It's important to discuss this in the planning stage. Later it may become an issue! And keep minutes of your meetings.

Then there were questions of whether there was more planning required, such as marketing, finance and operating. There is always more to do, but it's important not to submit to "paralysis by analysis". Decide when enough planning is enough, and then make it happen! Remember, goodwill and open communication are *essential* components of a successful joint venture.

If you're setting up your own JV take this structure and work at it. Do not omit any of the components, because the one you leave out is sure to be the one that will rear up and bite you when you least expect it! And share all of it with your JV team, encourage and accept all contributions, even the wacky and way-out. Often they will *lead* a train of thought to that which is valuable.

The key, I'd say, is likemindedness. One of the group talked to me later about our "initial teething problems", and he was proud of the fact that we persisted and got through them. "That's what it's all about," he said, "persisting and working together as a group."

Due diligence

All members approached their professional advisors with a series of questions, and to discuss the proposal in general. I can't over-emphasise the importance of this step. Every individual's circumstances are different and, while getting professional advice is a good idea before any investment decision, it's absolutely critical with a JV, given the added layer of structural and operational complexity of a group investment.

After the venturers held further discussions with their professional advisors, we ended up with seven committed investors who agreed to contribute seed capital of $20,000 each, for a total of $140,000. A number of the group declined to participate for various reasons, such as commitment to other projects, though they are rumoured to be regretting their decision in hindsight.

The group decided to go with a company structure, which, while not ideal tax-wise, did optimise most of the requirements of the JV. We began formulating a business plan to use for a finance application. Then we were ready to search for a deal. The group members all came up with prospective properties and for the next month we investigated existing flats for conversion, boarding houses, subdivision blocks, and so on.

Actually, a strange thing happened during the search. We were to inspect a boarding house in South Brisbane and the night before inspection we had the "mother of all thunderstorms". Next morning there was a front-page photo of a kayaker paddling past the boarding house, which had literally "gone under" that night. (We didn't buy that one!)

Paul started pestering the agencies and found one who specialised in blocks of units. He's added his two cents worth on this:

"I cannot stress enough the importance of 'pestering the agent'. If you want the call you've got to be on the top of the list, and to do that a weekly call and fax can annoy the agent sufficiently that he will find something for you just to get rid of you. And that's exactly what happened.

"One fateful Friday morning I got the call to ask if we were interested in a 1012 sq m subdividable block in Newstead with a block of six flatettes for $460k. It was the same value as the UCV, which equates to you getting the structure for free. Are we interested? Are you insane?"

The phone call at breakfast!

I'll tell this bit, because I love the fact that every Friday I celebrate having left my public service job in 1993 with a long leisurely breakfast, starting after 9 am, when everyone else is rushing off to work. I was halfway through my bacon and eggs when I got a call from Paul. Nope, over to Paul again.

"On the dog and bone to Geoff, who's having his Friday morning ritual breakfast, and instruct him to get going. He's mumbling about being halfway through a fried egg. I'm about to blow a fuse and I reach down the phone to scramble his eggs."

Newstead's 1.5 km from the city and near the emerging James Street cafe precinct and the centre of the Urban Renewal of the Valley.

"I'm off!" I said with the last mouthful of egg.

The negotiation

I arrived at the flats and saw the agent. I recognised him as one of the very few real estate agents ever to do one of my workshops. The house was a faded, former grand colonial divided into six flatettes (own kitchen but common bathroom). At the back there was a fantastic development site. I was excited.

"The vendor's asking $460,000, and that's the UCV," Keith tells me (that's the unimproved capital value, land only).

I said, "I'll give you $415,000, with 30 days for finance."

He laughed. "Nice try, Geoff, $460,000 is unimproved land value, valued by the Valuer General's Department. So how much are you paying for the block of flats returning $32,000 per annum?"

"Aahhh, not much," I muttered.

"Not much? Not much! You're getting them free!"

"Yeah … well … ahh … could be, Keith." (I'd already decided to buy.) "I'll have to check with Paul," I said.

Paul backed my decision: "That afternoon, after Geoff went in and had a good lookover, we offered five grand more to $420k. We always like to get that extra bargain, but the vendor is not budging. Sometimes the full price is the correct price and you can miss out by being too stubborn. The deal's done at the full asking price."

This is an important point – if you know the true market value of the property, you don't have to hesitate or risk missing out by making an unrealistically low offer. Sometimes the asking price is good enough for you to make a profit when you buy. You don't always have to knock an amount off the asking price if you're satisfied it represents good value.

The contract conditions
We signed it up there and then, subject to the following conditions:

- 5 days for building inspection
- 45 days for finance (when we would carry out our due diligence)
- $16,000 deposit, sufficient to cover the agent's fee
- deposit due when the contract became unconditional
- the seller to provide a Vendor's Certificate (a council requirement)
- the seller to carry insurance until contract was unconditional

How to make water run uphill
During the contract "conditional period" we commissioned development consultants to undertake a feasibility study to establish if our subdivision and new house could be approved without any "over the top" costs. We arranged a pre-lodgement meeting with the council (at a cost of $250) and discussed our submission in depth with the council planners.

This meeting proved to be invaluable, as most criteria and problems were discussed and solutions found. The council forwarded minutes of this meeting and incorporated them into our DA (development application). We knew most of the hurdles before we'd even begun. We spent $250 to get a return of more than $300,000. That's a good rate of return!

A problem did rear its head not too much later though. New council regulations coming into force discouraged rubble pits being used as a disposal point for stormwater. We could develop on reasonable guidelines but we had to get the stormwater to run "uphill", no mean feat considering the block had an 8 m fall to the rear!

We had a problem, the same one as the seller would have encountered. The block sloped down away from the road. We found we couldn't get access to the stormwater line in the rear neighbour's yard. The owner said the unoccupied house was a "shrine" for her late husband and digging a 3 m trench to lay the pipe would desecrate her shrine.

She refused to let us enter. Without access we were in major trouble. If we couldn't get the stormwater off we couldn't develop. What do we do?

The solution

The next step demonstrates the importance of having an expert team of professionals working for you. Spending money to solve the problem saved (and made) us a substantial amount of money. Paul engaged an expert hydraulics engineer who said he may have the solution for us.

The engineer said, "The name Fraser Group sounds 'green'. Are you guys greenies? I reckon I can get the stormwater through if you are."

We all agree that we are.

"It's a roof-water recycling system. We may be able to discharge the roof water into a large water tank, and any overflow into an underground infiltration pit."

Eureka! We had the solution. Negotiations with the council were successful. The development could proceed. We had done our due diligence. We could go unconditional on the contract, secure in the knowledge that, barring any major change in circumstances, we were assured the project was a "goer".

As a group we finalised our business plan under a company name and made a formal application for finance through a mortgage broker. This was approved based on the original contract price of $460,000, and then our DA was approved. Paul's got something to add here.

"There is no substitute for being professional when it comes to finance. A well-written business plan can do you wonders. You just have to be smarter than the lender."

The valuation fiasco

By getting the DA and the BA (building application) for the new house in the pipeline, we had "added" major value to this site. We requested that the bank revalue it. Why use our own money when we can use the bank to get the finance to pay ourselves back our deposits?

They sent their "retired bank manager" on a "drive-by" appraisal. We met him on-site armed with stacks of supporting evidence of increased values, growth in the area, recent sales and estimates of values of the extra land we had "created". All this appeared to be ignored. We'd expected a new valuation of, say, $650k–$700k, way up from $460k. However, despite the supporting evidence we'd provided, it came in at $530k.

We were not prepared to accept this appraisal and negotiated with the bank to commission our own valuer. We obtained a list of the bank's panel of valuers. I interviewed the panel and found that some were twice the price of others (too busy, so charge double), some were very offhanded and some had no appreciation of an investor's position.

We commissioned a valuer who was an investor himself and so understood the development process. Where other valuers charged a fixed (high) fee, this valuer's fee was proportional to the valuation. The higher the valuation the higher the fee. We felt we had a good chance of getting a reasonable valuation. He accepted the comprehensive data we provided, took the time to understand the project, did his research and due diligence and established a site value of $678,000. We were happy – we had sufficient finance to complete without putting hands into pockets.

The bank "queried" the validity of the valuation even though it was supported by 60 pages of research (I believe the valuation was absolutely correct, maybe even low). They subsequently reduced it to $668,000, still okay for the development finance, and a $208,000 increase in value in less than a year. We were further satisfied when, at about the same time, the new Valuer General's UCV (land value) came in at $610,000, confirming that we were onto a winner. The BA approval followed shortly after.

Construction

Paul called for quotes and tenders, commissioned a builder and licensed subcontractors to build the new house. The whole construction process took 12 weeks. Paul wants to add another word here.

"I cannot say the whole process went smoothly, with a change of directors not long after taking ownership, but with JVs a lot of decisions and understandings need to be clarified up-front. Just to name a couple: entry and exit strategies, divorce or even death. We have identified some major areas you should consider if you're thinking about a JV. Read on."

Development costs of the new colonial house.

Preliminary costs	
Insurances	$2,143
Council fees	$8,599
Development consultant	$2,039
Surveyor	$4,285
Certifier	$1,169
Subtotal	$18,235

Building works	
Tree removal	$930
Earthworks	$6,122
Engineering	$3,165
Hire of equipment	$2,141
Scaffold	$1,342
Compact fill	$1,369
Welding	$361
Steel reinforcing	$3,428
Termimesh	$521
All timber, trusses, cladding, fixout, decking	$35,329
Carpentry, labour	$39,349
Plumbing – prime cost items	$9,500
Metal posts and beams	$6,179
Concrete	$10,406
Concrete, labour	$7,782
Concrete pumping	$1,065
Block supply	$851
Bricklayer	$1,506
Aluminium windows	$7,163
Subtotal	$138,509

Lock-up	
Gutter and roofing labour and materials	$8,340
Waterproofing	$1,760
Plasterer	$10,059
Garage door, auto	$1,360
Cabinetmaker	$7,260
Painting	$10,849
Tiles, materials	$3,751
Tiles, labour	$6,105
Plumber, sewerage connection	$6,749
Electrician	$7,243
Subtotal	$63,476

Fitout	
Screens, mirrors, robe doors, supply and fit	$2,099
Carpets	$3,632
Electrical whitegoods	$3,037
Internal stairs & balustrade	$3,982
Lights	$1,642
Plumber	$15,459
Floor sanding	$1,650
Insulation	$995
Timber doors	$9,308
Rubbish removal	$660
Subtotal	$42,464

Final	
Fencing	$3,760
Landscaping, materials	$3,200
Landscaping, labour	$2,668
Cleaners	$450
Plan lodgement	$445
Solicitor	$354
Subtotal	$10,877

Summary	
Preliminary costs	$18,235
Building works	$138,509
Lock-up	$63,476
Fitout	$42,464
Final	$10,877
Grand total*	$273,561

*(not including Paul's supervision costs)

Here are the overall project numbers.

Purchase price	$460,000
Purchase costs	$27,600
Subdivision, new house	$273,000
Project management	$27,000
Total costs	$787,600
Current value	$1,547,866
Net EBIT*, approx	$760,266

*earnings before interest and tax

A few questions

Here are a few common questions about JVs, answered with reference to our own experience in this JV.

What is a joint venture? Where two or more individuals join skills, expertise, capital or equity to form a mutually profitable association.

Why consider a JV? Joint ventures add leverage for the average investor. They can play in the bigger leagues.

What advantages does a JV hold for you? There are many advantages.

- It can bring those individuals with "time and no cash" together with those who have "cash but no time".

  Paul and I were experienced investors with time and expertise and that helped those participants with little time and little experience. Those who are "asset rich and cash poor" can join those who are the reverse, "few assets but high cashflow". Some members had high equity and low cashflow. They were helped across the line by the reliable salary earners with steady cashflow.

- A JV enables the partners to access far bigger projects than they could as individuals, therefore reducing the need to compete with homebuyers and small-time (individual) investors for smaller, more traditional projects.

  This was a $700k+ project and easily handled by this group. JVs spread the risk. All outgoings are shared, but so are the profits.

- A number of partners bring different skills to the corporate table. For example, we had a member with bookkeeping skills who became our treasurer.

- And of course, there's the "brains trust" effect, where a number of skilled entrepreneurs come together in an atmosphere of mutual respect and trust, to devise, design and implement their ideal property investment.

  This can work for you ... and against you. You don't want two drivers. They'll drive you apart. You need a mix of "ideas people", drivers, workers, planners, and you absolutely must have a "finisher".

What about the potential downside? Every tool this powerful has to have a double cutting edge. And JVs can multiply the challenges!

- Joint ventures are made up of *people*, so communication is crucial to success. They say the key to success in property investment is "Location, location, location". Well, with JVs, it's "Communication, communication, communication".

- The financing is tricky. Guarantees may be required. You may have "joint and several" responsibility for the loan, so a solid understanding of your potential liabilities (from your professional advisors) is critical.

  You need to know what your position and obligations will be if things don't go according to plan. Also, be aware that the loan-to-value ratio (LVR) is likely to be less than the 80% you can easily get with a single house, but that's just part of being up there with the "big players".

- Exit strategies. What plans do you put in place to handle JV members who want out? This is essential if you don't want major friction because a member can't withdraw when their circumstances change. Careful planning can go a long way toward handling contingencies if things go wrong. We did have our problems. Two members wanted to pull out due to commitment on another project.

  Paul and I bought their shares at cost, as agreed with the investors. All was very amicable and we were happy to increase our share in this promising project. Beware: It would be a different story if it was a "loser". No one would want the shares.

The sale

Agent appraisals were called and a marketing plan developed. The properties were listed at $690,000 for the original colonial, and $650,000 for the new. They didn't sell quickly enough so we took them off the market.

The settlement

All other directors went their own ways for work-related reasons or changes of circumstance, so Paul and I negotiated with them to buy their shares. This took quite some time but eventually we all agreed to a settlement.

As a result Paul and I are now left as the sole owners of the flatettes and of a swish Queenslander to the rear, on separate titles. The value of the two properties is a conservative $1.5 million, loans outstanding are $777k. We rented out the rear house for $530 per week, a 10.6% return, and both properties are running cashflow positive.

Regulatory issues

In this story we are referring to small groups of people with complementary skills and, between them, access to enough cash to tackle projects around the $1 million mark. These projects are too large for many individual investors, but too small to attract major developers and property syndicates.

Larger, organised property syndicates and limited partnerships, sold through financial advisors and publicly advertised, are heavily regulated by ASIC under the Managed Investments Act, with strict requirements as to disclosure, prospectuses, financial stability of the promoter, and so on.

Most small joint ventures and private syndicates are not regulated by the Act, provided they satisfy a few criteria, such as keeping to the maximum number of investors set out by the Act, not advertising syndicate units to the public, and not having a promoter charging fees. There are several other conditions that normally aren't a problem for small, private JVs.

Anyone setting up even the smallest joint venture or general or limited partnership should seek expert advice to establish a structure that ensures their project is not considered a regulated syndicate.

The 11 commandments for property investment structures

Supplied by one of our financial advisors, chartered accountant Richard Clarke of Horwath (Brisbane) Pty Ltd, these commandments may not be biblical or enshrined in legislation, but stick with them just the same.

1. Thou shalt protect assets and have a good management track record.
2. Thou shalt know the activity.
3. Thou shalt love thy partners as thy family.
4. Thou shalt consider how much money is involved.
5. Thou shalt examine financial projection and what-ifs.
6. Thou shalt consider financing and future capital needs and resources.
7. Thou shalt know thy neighbour.
8. Thou shalt determine in advance your dividend and its distribution.
9. Thou shalt know your investor needs intimately.
10. Thou shalt structure to the tax profile of your investor and state clearly the duration of the likely investment.
11. Thou shalt have a crystal ball.

Reno Kings Report

For an outline of the Management Plan used in the "hypotheticals" JV, go to page 235 for details, or go to our website: www.renos.com.au

Now we've got this far together ...

There is nothing more exciting than seeing those "faces" from our workshops achieving results beyond what we thought possible. How rewarding for them, and inspiring for others, when they read the stories, and how rewarding for us as part-time mentors!

These are real people, just like you. They all have life's day-to-day problems; they are not gurus. And they have something else in common. At some stage they "hit the wall". Hey, Paul and I did that too. When you look back, there was a problem, a setback, something that led to an awakening – a realisation that, for things to change, *they* had to change. For me, it was being demoted; for Paul it was being made redundant. There were similar turning points for each of our contributors.

It is astounding how people can do the same (our) workshop and go so many different directions, using so many strategies. For some it was positive cashflow; for others niche markets. Renovation was used by most as part of their strategy, while subdivision and development rewarded others. They all learned the value of research and negotiation, buying well and adding value. They discovered the inside info on loans, how to handle tenants and a thousand other things that added to the puzzle that is investment property.

To those of you who have read this book, my congratulations. It is a first step. Just like the book that started me on my own journey. We welcome you to be part of the Reno Kings community. We encourage you to use our information, to get our free ezine and our reports. Paul and I would love to meet you at our workshops and (if you take action) maybe we can write your story in our next book. Till then ...

Geoff Doidge (and Paul Eslick)
The Reno Kings

Glossary

Acronyms

ASIC	Australian Securities and Investments Commission	LOC	line of credit loan
ATO	Australian Taxation Office	LVR	loan to value ratio, as a percentage $\frac{loan}{value} \times 100$
BA	building application/approval	P&I loan	principal and interest loan
CGT	capital gains tax	PM	property manager
CPI	Consumer Price Index	POA	Property Owners Association
DA	development application/approval	PPOR	principal place of residence
DNR	Department of Natural Resources (Qld)	QS	quantity surveyor
EBIT	earnings before interest and tax	RTA	Residential Tenancies Authority (Qld)
F&F	fixtures and fittings	SWOT	strengths, weaknesses, opportunities, threats
FR	fixed interest rate	TA	trade assistant
GST	goods and services tax	TRADAC	Timber Research and Development Advisory Council (Qld)
IO loan	interest-only loan		
IP	investment property	UCV	unimproved capital value (land only)
JV	joint venture	UV	unimproved value
LMI	lender's mortgage insurance	VR	variable interest rate
LMR	low to medium residential		

Terms

annuity	An investment, typically purchased with a lump sum, which provides a monthly sum over the term of the annuity period.
building allowance	A type of depreciation on a structure claimable against tax, also known as capital allowance.
cashflow-neutral return	When all inflows are equal to all outflows, with neither surplus nor deficit; between positive cashflow and negative cashflow.
construction loan	A staged loan against end, or "built", value.
cross-leasing	Method of subdivision where whole title is shared but each landowner has exclusive rights to their portion of property, similar to strata titling. Available only in New Zealand.
current yield	Rental income as a proportion of purchase price plus costs, as a percentage. $\frac{weekly\ rent \times 52 \times 100}{purchase\ price + costs}$
debt service ratio	The ratio of loan commitments to monthly income.
due diligence	A process of review designed to ensure that the important factors driving the success of a project are as the purchaser requires them to be. For example, that the local council will approve a change of use application or that soil tests are satisfactory, or that flood levels are acceptable.
equity	That amount equal to the value of a property less the amount borrowed against the property.

flatette	Flat with own kitchen, shared bathroom.
full documentation	Required for a standard housing loan, evidential documentation such as payslips and/or income statements (including full tax returns), current bank statements for savings and loan accounts, rates notices.
gross yield	Rental income as a proportion of purchase price only, as a percentage. $\dfrac{\text{weekly rent} \times 52 \times 100}{\text{purchase price}}$
honeymoon rate	A cheap interest rate usually for a limited time, and only on initial loans. Used by lenders to attract borrowers. Gives the borrower the ability to take advantage of the cheap interest rate to make extra payments into the loan.
interest rate averaging	A risk management technique used by Geoff Doidge to manage interest rate rises. It ensures all "fixed rate, interest only" loans don't fall due at the same time.
leveraging	That process whereby an investor uses borrowed funds to gear the returns on his or her own invested funds. To leverage into an investment is to borrow at least part of the funds to invest in the project.
line of credit	A loan created with a credit limit against the value of your home/investment properties giving access to the equity in the properties. Interest is paid only on the amount of funds drawn upon within that limit.
low-doc loan	A loan primarily introduced for self-employed borrowers who do not have complete current taxation details to support borrowing capacity.
negative gearing	When a property's income is less than the property's expenses, producing a negative cashflow (a loss), used to offset other taxable income.
primary cost items	Fixtures, fittings, appliances and whitegoods. The term is generally used in building contracts and relates to finished items chosen by the purchaser.
RP data	A website providing statistical and other information about real estate, including sales history, advertising history, UCV, title details, etc.
strata title	A system of registering ownership of different accommodation units within a building. Applies to residential and non-residential buildings.
Torrens title	Freehold title, the system by which title to land is shown by one document issued by a government department (introduced by Sir Robert Richard Torrens in South Australia 1858).
two-tiered marketing	The use of "investment" seminars to sell properties at different prices: one price for locals and higher price for interstate buyers (especially common in holiday areas), often packaging financial, legal and other services. Buyer beware.
unconditional contract	A contract not subject to finance or any other conditions, whereby the failure to satisfy those conditions would result in the contract not proceeding.
unimproved capital value	Land value only, as valued by the Valuer General (also known as unimproved value).
Valuer General	The government officer responsible for valuing land in a State for the purpose of rating for land tax, and other purposes.

Recommended reading

These are some of the books in our library. We like books that are written by investors for investors, not by people who just speak about it or who earn a living by selling property. We don't sell property. We buy it! Some of these books have been written by developers and naturally enough they are out to swing you to their product and to build credibility in your eyes so that you will seek their advice. So look at the person who has written the book. Have they done what you want to do? Have they been successful? Is what they have done able to be duplicated by you? Ask yourself: What are their vested interests? Remember, at the end of the day, it is … buyer beware!

The Reno Kings

Geoff Doidge and Paul Eslick

Graham J. Airey, *The Property Investor's Handbook*, 3rd ed, Wrightbooks/John Wiley & Sons Aust, Brisbane, 2003

Robert G. Allen, *Creating Wealth, Simon & Schuster*, Sydney, 1983

Robert Balanda, *Clauses Made Simple*, 2nd ed, Balanda Holdings Pty Ltd, Surfers Paradise, 2001

Robert Balanda, *Joint Ventures Made Simple (CD and booklet)*, Balanda Holdings Pty Ltd, Surfers Paradise, 2004

Robert Balanda, *Options Made Simple (CD and booklet)*, Balanda Holdings Pty Ltd, Surfers Paradise, 2004

Leonard Barnes, *Property Power*, Wrightbooks/John Wiley & Sons Aust, Brisbane, 2000

George S. Clason, *The Richest Man in Babylon*, Signet/Penguin Group, Camberwell, 1988

Tony Compton, *Rental Property and Taxation*, 2nd ed, Wrightbooks/John Wiley & Sons Aust, Brisbane, 2001

Dennis J. Cook, *Playing the Real Estate Game to Win*, Resolution Press, Melbourne, 1991

Bruce Davies, *How to Build Riches*, Signature Books Pty Ltd, Newtown, 1998

Dolf de Roos, *Extraordinary Profits from Ordinary Properties*, de Roos Associates Ltd, New Zealand, 1997

Dolf de Roos, *Real Estate Riches*, Rich Dad Australia/TechPress Inc, Paradise Valley, Ariz, USA, 2001

Geoff Doidge, *Secrets of Property Investment*, Financial Success Systems, Brisbane, 1994

Geoff Doidge, *The Ten Golden Rules of Property*, Financial Success Systems, Brisbane, 1995

Austin Donnelly, *Realistic Real Estate Investing*, 2nd ed, Wrightbooks/John Wiley & Sons Aust, Brisbane, 2000

Paul Eslick, *The Investor's Guide to Quick and Easy Renovations*, Eslick/Doidge Seminars (available only at Reno Kings workshops), Brisbane, 2001

Alan J. Falkson, *Investing in Real Estate on a Budget*, Elephas Books Pty Ltd, Perth, 1991

John Fitzgerald, *Seven Steps to Wealth*, Toogoolawa Publications/Herron Books, Toogoolawa, 1998

Dale Gatherum-Goss, *Tax Battles*, self-published, Melbourne, 2004

Dale Gatherum-Goss, *Trust Magic*, self-published, Melbourne, 2004

Napoleon Hill, *Think and Grow Rich* (first published 1937), Wilshire Books, Cal, USA, 1999

Nicholas Humphrey, *The Australian Home Buyer's Guide 2005*, Penguin Aust, Ringwood, 2004

Hans Jakobi, *Due Diligence Made Simple*, Wealth Dynamics Int, Portland, NSW, 2001

Fred and Brett Johnson, *The Wealth Power of Property*, Quartile Property Network, Gordon, NSW, 1997

Robert Kiyosaki, *Rich Dad, Poor Dad*, TechPress Inc, Scottsdale, Ariz, USA, 1997

Margaret Lomas, *A Pocket Guide to Investing in Positive Cash Flow Property*, Wrightbooks/John Wiley & Sons Aust, Brisbane, 2004

Margaret Lomas, *How to Create an Income for Life*, Wrightbooks/John Wiley & Sons Aust, Brisbane, 2002

Margaret Lomas, *How to Make Your Money Last as Long as You Do*, Wrightbooks/John Wiley & Sons Aust, Brisbane, 2001

Margaret Lomas, *How to Maximise Your Property Portfolio*, Wrightbooks/John Wiley & Sons Aust, Brisbane, 2003

Steve McKnight, *$1,000,000 in Property in One Year*, Wrightbooks/John Wiley & Sons Aust, Brisbane, 2004

Steve McKnight, *From 0 to 130 Properties in 3.5 Years*, Wrightbooks/John Wiley & Sons Aust, Brisbane, 2003

N.E. Renton, *Understanding Investment Property*, 4th ed, BAS Publishing, Melbourne, 2004

Terry Ryder, *Buyer Beware*, Wrightbooks/John Wiley & Sons Aust, Brisbane, 2001

Terry Ryder, *Confessions of a Real Estate Agent*, Wrightbooks/John Wiley & Sons Aust, Brisbane, 2001

Terry Ryder, *Property Smart*, Wrightbooks/John Wiley & Sons Aust, Brisbane, 2002

Terry Ryder, Real Estate without Agents, Wrightbooks/John Wiley & Sons Aust, Brisbane, 2004

Jan Somers, *Building Wealth Story by Story*, Somerset Financial Services Pty Ltd, Brisbane, 1998

Jan Somers, *More Wealth from Residential Property*, Somerset Financial Services Pty Ltd, Brisbane, 2001

Peter Spann, *How You Could Build a $10 Million Property Portfolio in Just 10 Years*, HarperCollins Aust, Sydney, 2004

Peter Spann, *Wealth Magic*, HarperCollins Aust, Sydney, 2001

Carol Staines, *A Practical Guide to Interior Decorating*, Pinedale Press, Caloundra, 2003

Allan Staines, *The Australian Decks and Pergolas Construction Manual*, 3rd ed, Pinedale Press, Caloundra, 2003

Allan Staines, *The Australian House Building Manual*, Pinedale Press, Caloundra, 2003

Allan Staines, *The Australian Renovator's Manual*, new edition, Pinedale Press, Caloundra, 2003

Monique and Richard Wakelin, *Streets Ahead*, Hodder Headline Aust, Sydney, 2002

P. Waxman and D. Lenard, *Investing in Residential Property*, 6th ed, Wrightbooks/John Wiley & Sons Aust, Brisbane, 2004

"I wish I'd bought there five years ago!"

➤ What do other property investors know that you don't?

➤ Where are they getting their information?

➤ Are you buying the right type of property in the right area — or are you about to make an expensive mistake?

Australian Property Investor magazine is a vital resource for people who are serious about making money through property investment.

It's full of inspiring and educational case studies of successful property investors and specific projects like renovations, * subdivisions etc. plus market commentary from some of Australia's leading property experts.

And you'll find a wide range of useful statistics such as capital gains and rental yields to help you identify the next boom suburbs.

Don't miss the current issue of...

OUT NOW AT YOUR LOCAL NEWSAGENT!

Australian PropertyInvestor

APIO17

www.apimagazine.com.au

* Geoff Doidge of the Reno Kings is a regular contributor to *Australian Property Investor* magazine.

Reno Kings Free Reports

The following free* reports can be requested from the Reno Kings website. Simply go to www.renos.com.au/bookreports and follow the instructions.

Tips and Traps of Commercial Property Mel shares her hard-earned tips and traps on commercial property.	*The Moneyfinder* Take control of your finances. "It changed my life." – Geoff Doidge
Buying in the 'Ways How Paul buys "don't wanters" and transforms them into cash cows.	*How to Buy a House that's Not for Sale* Unconventional strategies to find that gem before it hits the market.
How to Fast-track Your Approvals Any hiccups during a subdivision or development project can cost you big dollars.	*JV Management Plan* Used in the "hypotheticals" joint venture. Step-by-step procedures for great JVs.
Contract Clauses You Simply Must Know The wrong clause can cost you your whole contract and maybe your deposit. Essential reading.	*Duplex Strategies* Duplex strategies can double your return. Paul and Jenny can give you the inside story on their strategies.
Thirty-three Ways to Add Value Cosmetic makeovers are the key to adding value quickly. Use this report to accelerate your equity and rental returns.	*How to find a property-wise accountant* Use this accountant's quiz to find a property-savvy accountant to save you tax and make you money.
Forty-three Steps to Unlimited Success in Property Details the step-by-step process to follow when you buy a property. It doesn't exist anywhere else in this simple format.	*Brenda's Q&A* Brenda has answered many questions on our website. If you would like a further insight into Les and Brenda's story or if you have a property question request this fact sheet.
The Gutter Money Report Your equity – money that's just lying in the gutter ready to pick up. Paul shows you how to leapfrog from that first property to build a property portfolio.	*The Property Rating Guide* This detailed checklist will take the emotion out of property selection. It makes you focus on just the investment criteria to rate a property for investment success.
Niche Market Opportunities There are all sorts of ideas for niche markets that can supercharge your yield and capital gain, eg, student accommodation and share housing.	*The Gant Chart* Time is money. Planning and organisation are the keys to finishing a project on time and on budget. The Reno Kings use the Gant Chart to get in, get it done and get out in record time.
Seventeen Ways to Get Finance when the Bank Says No Once you learn about research, property selection and negotiation, you will find that finance is the key to the next step. It is a must for anyone having trouble getting finance.	*Cash Cow Case Study* How an investor was bitten by a two-tier marketer and turned this problem into an opportunity to create a 21% yield and great capital gain in New South Wales.

* Conditions and limits apply

Reno Kings Products

Visit the Reno Kings website and order on-line.

Secrets of Property Investment Secrets on insurance, advertising, finding tenants fast and buying 20–25% below the market. $19.95 (ebook)	*The Ten Golden Rules of Property* "My book takes you through the whole property invetment process. It's based on facts, facts learned by me over decades of investing." – Geoff Doidge. $32.95 (incl P&H)

Great capital gain and cashflow from creative property strategies

Your next step in building a property portfolio is a Reno Kings Workshop

Let Geoff, Paul and their team of experts answer key questions

- How to increase cashflow and capital gain when the market is not moving.
- How to Joint Venture with friends or family to reduce risk and increase serviceability.
- What entity to purchase with.
- How to build a sizeable portfolio and protect it from loss.
- How to reduce non-deductible debts faster.
- How to control property for long periods with little money or risk.
- What development options are available to you and how to find them.
- How to get finance when the bank says no.
- How to get Australian market predictions from leading researchers.
- What is holding you back?
- Is your accountant costing you money?
- How to turn capital gain into low-taxed income. You don't have to sell!

Plus detailed, step-by-step case studies including:

- How Geoff spent $600 and increased his rents by $3500 per annum
- How Paul created $125,000 equity in a three-week renovation.
- How Geoff and Paul subdivided to create a $328,000 equity gain and positive cashflow only 2 km from the CBD.
- How Geoff turned a looming tax bill into $500,000 equity gain plus $110,000 rent pa in just four weeks – you must see it to believe it!
- How an astute investor earns 21% return from student accommodation in NSW.
- How a young Victorian couple made $100,000 plus on their first renovation after attending our workshop.
- How other workshop students have made significant profits from property.

And so many other strategies, tactics, techniques and tips, including research, negotiation, contracts clauses, subdivision, developments, renovations, making offers, positive gearing, strata titling, duplexes, adding rooms, niche markets, regional properties, student accommodation, affordable housing, property management, tax minimisation, asset protection, depreciation, and much more!

Comments from previous workshop students

"We were deadly serious about property investing and knew there would have to be sacrifices to achieve our dreams. We saved for two years before our home budget gave us enough money to both attend the course. We were a single-income family at the time and only on about $40k per year. The course was way more than we were expecting. We thought it was a "how to bang in a nail" type of thing. We were so wrong. After we attended the workshop, it took us around six months to get going and buy into the property market with our newfound knowledge. From the end of 2001 to the end of 2003 (18 months) we bought something like 20 properties. Our portfolio is now worth $3 million. I think our few thousand dollars for the seminar was well worth the money."
Brenda and Les Irwin, Qld

"It was in July of 2002 that I attended a Reno Kings workshop. My friends were in shock that I would spend over $1000 to attend an investment seminar. Why not just buy the book! This seminar provided a major turning point in my views on what was possible, where to go for help, what questions to ask and who to ask them of … and gave me a new burst of ambition and enthusiasm!" **Elin Power, Qld**

"My wife and I were only commenting this morning how the workshop has changed our lives and left friends wondering just how we are doing it all." **Craig C.**

"It's been more than 12 months since I attended your excellent workshop and I am now buying properties using your tips, and my equity is building. I love getting your newsletter and email updates. So thank you Geoff and Paul – although I had to borrow the money to go to your workshop it was certainly the best real estate investment I have made." **SB, NSW**

The Reno Kings Workshop is different, life changing, designed for the experienced investor and for well-read beginners

Ask for special Earlybird rate.
web: http://www.renos.com.au
email: info@renos.com.au
Phone: 1300 550 656
Fax: 1300 137 073
Post: PO Box 3141, Norman Park, QLD 4170

Limited Seats BOOK NOW!

Index
Other references to acronyms and terms are contained in the glossary, pages 230–31.